Contradiction and Dilemma

Contradiction and Dilemma

Orestes Brownson and the American Idea

Leonard Gilhooley

New York
Fordham University Press
1972

ACKNOWLEDGMENTS: to the late Thomas McAvoy, formerly archivist at the University of Notre Dame, for permission to use and cite the Brownson Papers held at the university; to Vincent F. Holden, archivist for the Congregation of Saint Paul, for like use of material contained in the Paulist Fathers Archives.

to the memory of my father and of Bob
for my mother
and for Jack

Contents

Abbreviations used in the sources.

APF   Archives of the Paulist Fathers, New York
AUND   Archives of the University of Notre Dame
BQR   *Boston Quarterly Review*
BrQR   *Brownson's Quarterly Review*
Works   *The Works of Orestes Brownson*

The notes will be found at the end of their respective chapters.

Preface

American life in the eighth decade of this century reflects an amount of confusion remarkable even for a country seldom free of turbulence. Its society appears profoundly disturbed not only by disagreement but by a failure of continuity which at best tends to temporary explosions of civic disorder—apparently acceptable disjunctions; the deeper reaches of the problem indicate a terrible, a deadly and corrosive separation. A great variety of topical events provides patent, even numbing, evidence of a social *Sturm und Drang*; what is more hidden are those elemental faults which could lead to seismic disaster.

It may be too narrow to isolate America as sole possible victim of a cultural earthquake; there are those who see the deeply flawed sub-surfaces of all Western society as being dangerously aggravated by advances long held to be beneficial to mankind. Romano Guardini is one of these; Jacques Ellul, another. Guardini, for instance, in a notably lucid and apparently neglected little gem of a book,[1] finds that modern man, convicted, in a sense, by his own technological progress, has been jailed by his inability to find adequate power to control power—he is, in short, a prisoner of his own impotence. So deeply do the chains bite, Guardini argues, so constricting are the cell conditions, that in his pain modern man has perforce been separated from his past. His lineaments severely contorted, man, as we have known him, can never again appear the same. A new, raw power, its wildness exacerbated by man's inability in our time to understand and control the works of his own mind and imagination, could destroy not only those works but man himself.

ix

Whether the thesis is true, symptoms of unease are everywhere apparent; certainly they are repeatedly evident in America. There is little question that America is the leading nation-state, and is, or at least once thought itself to be, a child—however unruly, untoward, or revolutionary—of the developing Western civilization. Physicians of the social *malaise* appear on all sides: in the serious and the popular journals, in the arts, in the sciences, half-sciences, and pseudo-sciences; their legions are complicated, their prescriptions range bewilderingly from placebo to amphetamine, from solipsism to *kibbutz*, from alliterative vacuities to napalm, from sequestered orgasm to a new Caesarism. Some are optimistic, with a curiously involuted idealist dialectic: Charles Reich, for example, finds America approaching a condition he denotes as "Consciousness III," as opposed to "Consciousness I" (chiefly the attitudes of the American nineteenth century) and "Consciousness II" (America as organized, corporate state). The movement upward to III seems, in the argument, to be a processive drive (an idea not totally foreign to nineteenth-century thought or before) and a phenomenon to be aided again by a necessary suspicion of reason (Emerson's "understanding") and defined principles.[2] Youth and the bright Marcuse may yet settle for Coué.

James Burnham, on the other hand, despairs of "liberal" failures to the point where he seems, at least to one critic, to be suggesting a "re-evaluation of fascism" and a "new Bismarck."[3]

As much to the purpose as either of these may be a recent book by Andrew Hacker.[4] The theme of Hacker's study might fairly be set thus: *l'Amérique—elle est finie.*

Tensions and frustrations are bound to arise when 200 million human beings demand rights and privileges never intended for popular distribution. It is too late in our history to restore order or re-establish authority: the American temperament has passed the point where self-interest can subordinate itself to citizenship. Calls for enlightened attitudes and concerted action will continue, but with little ultimate effect. Our history shaped our character, and that history will now run its course.[5]

America's failures—the result, it appears, primarily of American *history* rather than of its servant, *character*—are conclusions of both its strengths and those weaknesses attendant upon the results of what we shall examine as the "American Experiment." The nation today is ungovernable; its citizens represent "two hundred million egos"; some of them, in apparently sober reality, are "superfluous," victims of an illusory individuality in a state conquered by an easy acceptance of a burgeoning technology. Self-indulgence has led to apathy, apathy to desuetude. What had been so long a dream, which itself had fostered an experiment and an assumed "mission," is to end in a rather lengthy sigh of surprisingly opulent defeat:

For most Americans can no longer believe that destiny commands them to carry capitalism, Christianity, or the United States Constitution across the globe. Indeed, a growing number are persuaded that the quality of life now known in our nation is hardly an exemplary export for other lands. The all-too-evident shortcomings of the American democracy disqualify our system as an object for emulation. There is a growing suspicion that the American nation has lost its credentials as a teacher of moral lessons; that our presence abroad is evidence only of power, carrying no enlightenment in its wake. . . . A willingness to sacrifice is no longer in the American character; and the conviction that this country's beliefs and institutions merit global diffusion is in decline. What was once a nation has become simply an agglomeration of individuals. . . . Americans must acknowledge candidly that we are no longer capable of being a great power . . . , [that] our nation is in a stage of moral enervation . . . , [and that] we lack the will to carry out a worldwide mission of redemption and reform. . . . America's history as a nation has reached its end.[6] [Having] abandoned the responsibilities of citizenship [Americans] think only of comforts and pleasures.[7]

The dream is a dead wench.

These are certainly serious observations, stated, often with a serious force, by a thoughtful and perceptive observer who may finally suffer that fatal stroke of insight: he may be right. *Recht*, in Louis Bredvold's distinction, is being shut out by *Macht*, and Americans, a curious breed by any analysis, may have to relearn (if they can) what past powers, now moldering in the gray dust, lived into: an assumed justice, divorced from first principles, attacked incessantly by greed, weariness, and the starkly assumptive, quotidian demands of satisfaction *now*, passes on to deep-set human rapacity those nicely balanced, agonizing demands for decent leadership. Careful deliberation is a requirement of character; if character is to help create history rather than merely to serve the flow of events, it must have some *Grundpunkt* for its weary service to vigilance, a precision of thought, and the consequent rigorous ordering of the selfish will. That character depleted, its organizing principle gone, the body politic runs to fat; its mind, with matching obesity, sits brooding on temporary measures to ease the ineluctable end, and cares not at all for what comes after. Hacker's short comfort does seem rather small beer: relax and enjoy what one can of inevitable decline.[8] This season of discontent may be our last winter.

Perhaps Hacker is right. But, again, perhaps what should be reopened is the whole question of what America is—or should be, or what it was once thought she should be. As R. W. B. Lewis once put it:

A century ago, the challenge to debate was an expressed belief in achieved human perfection, a return to the primal perfection. Today the challenge comes rather from the expressed belief in achieved hopelessness. We stand in need of more stirring impulsions, of greater perspectives. . . . Perhaps a review of that earlier debate can help us on our way. We can hardly expect to be persuaded any longer by the historic dream of the new Adam. But it can pose anew, in the classic way of illuminating as it did in the American nineteenth century, the picture of what might be against the knowledge of what is; and become once more a stimulus to enterprise and a resource for literature.[9]

The purpose of this book is to review (i.e., to "respect") the complex of the American Idea through the eyes of a major American commentator of a century ago, Orestes Brownson. If, for example, the picture of Emerson uneasily graced the office walls of later nineteenth-century industrialists, as Van Wyck Brooks has pointed out, the irony is not so much delicious as dangerous. Perhaps a study of Orestes Brownson's work can clarify why this may be so.

Brownson's work is, if one reads the evidence aright, a significant part of American history, especially of its intellectual history. Recent commentators, widely disparate in their opinions otherwise, continue to insist upon the vitality of his thought and its deep pertinence to these times. It cannot be argued, as we shall presently see, that each or any agrees with Brownson's solution upon a particular point; their honest observation, however, pays fee to his considerable stature. Allen Guttmann writes of Brownson as one "whose importance has been increasingly recognized";[10] to Russell Kirk, the nineteenth-century writer is "one of those dead who gives us life."[11] Arthur Schlesinger, Jr., fresh from his significant, practical contributions to the Kennedy and Johnson administrations, has reissued his biography of Brownson, still the best available. In 1966, Schlesinger wrote:

The age of Jackson was a time of the breaking-up of the religious and political creeds of the early republic, and Brownson was a product of the resultant intellectual mobility and confusion. His special talent was in expressing his view of the moment with exceptional clarity and power, and his writings thus open an astonishing variety of windows on his age. At the same time, one feels the pathos of modernity in this stormy pilgrim. . . . His life still touches contemporary nerves—from the antagonisms of capital and labor to the place of the Catholics in American society, from the nature of American culture to the death of God . . . Orestes Brownson remains . . . vigorously alive as a figure in American intellectual history.[12]

In part, at least, Brownson thus may help a reader to the *status quaestionis*. If R. W. B. Lewis (echoed by Daniel Boorstin, among others) feels the need for an informed "debate" upon the basic assumptions of the American Idea, Brownson as well as any man can pose with clarity and sureness so many of the apposite questions. What, indeed, is the current idea of justice, and whence come its life-giving waters? Can *any* theory of progress have modern intellectual purchase? One must seriously consider today the true meaning of a democratic government, the need for any society at all, and of any government in that society. Implicit in these considerable questions is the danger of centralization of governmental power as opposed to the weakening of a feasible social organization through the denial of support to or the undercutting of "legitimate" central power. What is the hard meaning of a "civil" right (or a "natural" right, for that matter—or, indeed, a "right" itself)?

The possibility of a philosophy of history is in point as is the need for the interaction (and the quality of that interaction) of a nation-state with other nation-states when the beast upon arrival at Bethlehem may find only a high-mounted master with no visage at all. The continuing concern, then, over the "meaning" of America must again encompass the stark, even desperate relevancies. Guttmann writes that

Ignorance of the past is—in technical jargon—socially dysfunctional. . . . The past is *instrumentally* instructive in that it aids us in understanding the present and the future. . . . But the past is also *humanely* instructive. . . . The problem for social democracy is not only to assure everyone the material basis for a good life but also to expand, preserve, and make available for all men the diverse, priceless achievements of the past as well as the present . . . [even] in an age of advertiser-financed mass media. . . . It seems unlikely that a people uninterested in its origins—however inglorious they may be—can respond fully to its present, or worry intelligently about its future.[13]

To expect solutions—to expect agreement—from and with Brownson is to ask for much more than this book intends. Much of his mastery was in the isolation and sharply etched presentation of the *question,* given his own lights which were considerable. Clarity and depth of thought, not yet totally unwashed attributes, are everywhere reflected in his work. Whither that thought leads, and whether one can accept its destination, is clearly the work of ultimate judgment by the reader. At all events, one hopes that it may be agreed of this man that he understood with admirable perception the burden of a modern poet's lapidary comment: "History at all times draws / the strangest consequence from remotest cause."

For reasons explained below, every reasonable effort has been made herein to allow Brownson to speak for himself. Critical comment by the author has been restricted chiefly to footnotes which, he hopes, have a close and necessary, if irritating, relation to the text.

Two recent works on Brownson have come to the writer's attention while this book was deeply into the publishing process. For that reason, and regrettably, their possible contributions could not have been acknowledged here.[14]

As is true so often in these matters, recognition of one's indebtedness to colleagues is merely a matter of justice. I am particularly grateful to the late Professor Francis X. Connolly of Fordham University who originally suggested a study of Brownson; to Professors Joseph E. Grennen, William Ross Stott, John D. Boyd, Gabriel M. Liegey, Charles Hodges, Andrew Breen Myers, and Vincent F. Blehl for their encouragement and advice; and to Thomas R. Ryan, that most generous and able Brownsonian.

I am also indebted to the extraordinary aural patience of Lawrence Gordon Meegan and, in especial, of Eleanor Federell Nanni. My gratitude to the late Harold C. Gardiner is deep—and for many courtesies, indeed.

None of these friends and associates in any way contributed to what weaknesses this book contains. I am father to those orphans.

Montvale, New Jersey   LEONARD GILHOOLEY
April 1971

NOTES

1. *The End of the Modern World* (New York, 1956).
2. *The Greening of America* (New York, 1970). For another theoretical "phasing" of history and the future, see William J. Thompson, *At the Edge of History* (New York, 1971).
3. James Burnham, "Notes on Authority, Morality, Power," *National Review*, 22, No. 47 (December 1, 1970), 1283–1289; Murray Rothbard, "The New Libertarian Creed," *The New York Times*, Feb. 9, 1971, p. 39. Charles Frankel, a "liberal" philosopher, who "would not confuse Edmund Burke with a leader of the John Birch Society," predicts that "if liberalism goes . . . , what follows is a radicalism turned wholly doctrinaire, a conservatism turned irretrievably callous, and an illiberal society" (*National Review*, 22, No. 47 [December 1, 1970], 1274–1277). See also James Burnham, *Suicide of the West* (New York, 1965).
4. *The End of the American Era* (New York, 1970).
5. *Ibid.,* p. 8.
6. *Ibid.,* pp. 220–230.
7. *Ibid.,* p. 228.
8. *Ibid.,* pp. 230–231.
9. *The American Adam* (Chicago, 1955), pp. 9–10.
10. Allen Guttmann, *The Conservative Tradition in America* (New York, 1967), p. 82. See also Guttman's "From Brownson to Eliot: The Conservative Theory of Church and State," *American Quarterly,* 17 (1965), 483–500.
11. Russell Kirk, "Catholic Yankee: Resuscitating Orestes Brownson," *Triumph* (April 1969), p. 26.
12. Arthur M. Schlesinger, Jr., *A Pilgrim's Progress: Orestes A. Brownson* (Boston, 1966), pp. xi–xii.
13. Guttmann, *Tradition,* pp. 178–180.
14. See Per Sveino, *Orestes A. Brownson's Road to Catholicism* (Oslo, 1970; New York, n.d.); Hugh Marshall, *Orestes Brownson and the American Republic* (Washington, D.C., 1972).

1

Introduction

THE "AMERICAN IDEA" REPRESENTS A PHENOMENON common to nineteenth-century discussion and criticism: the assumption that some sort of National Idea existed which embodied the ideals and aims of a nation and which must be expressed, however implicitly, in the national literature. England, for instance, had its National Idea; Germany had its own, and America, the burgeoning giant of the Western world, had its particular National Idea. Whatever one may think today of vague nationalistic expressions as a guide to action, there is no doubt that they once existed and were, indeed, formidable influences upon national thought. Certainly this was true in America, as E. K. Brown long ago pointed out.[1]

In America, especially in nineteenth-century thinking and usage, the American Idea, which purported to symbolize the concrete purposes of the New World, actually was composed of three closely related concepts: the dream of those who founded the republic or of those whose thinking influenced the founders;[2] the experiment in the government of free men by free men;[3] and, finally, what Arthur Ekirch has called the concept of a "peculiar American mission"—that is, the ultimate yet continuing goal set by the experiment, which was itself a product of the original dream.[4] Americans would not so much wither into wisdom, as Yeats put it, as spring into it. When it is used in these pages, therefore, the phrase "American Idea" will be understood to subsume three other terms: the American Dream, the American Experiment, and the American Mission.

In its broadest sense, the American Idea meant that America was a virgin land which presented to its people an opportunity to design

1

a new nation, one which would be free from the clutch of European institutions and the influences of European history. Its positive impulse was the formation of an ideal state, reminiscent of that which Plato had envisioned, and which many after him had attempted to delineate. Its negative impulse was its denial of the past, particularly of the old concepts of government and of unjust social organization. Hence the American Idea begins in a "dream," the dream of a democratic state which, by abolishing the class-distinctions associated with the past, would allow the largest scope to the powers of the individual, and thus approximate *de fide* the ideal of the perfect state.

But the dream was not a mere fantasy. Rather it was a desirable end which could be achieved by trial and error, by experiment. It was believed that a hard-headed instinct for making things work would, in this new land, achieve the far, pure purposes of the American Dream. When the experiment was completed—when, in short, the ideal democratic state was achieved—then the third phase of the American Idea would emerge: the American Mission. Briefly put, this meant that America was to be not only model but missionary. Conceived in the dream of the Old World, America was born to be the instructress of her Mother: the New was to be the savior of the Old; American democracy would yet lead the entire world to the recognition of the rights of man and to the establishment of the universal reign of justice. The Dream, the Experiment, and the Mission—these three, then, were the concepts which made up the American Idea.

This idea taken as a whole or in the isolation of its individual parts has affected a good part of American literature and history, as comparatively recent studies have emphasized. Frederic Carpenter's examination of relevant criticism on the subject has discovered that it extends from Emerson's "The American Scholar" to F. O. Matthiessen's *American Renaissance*; indeed, the study of the matter has expanded so rapidly that in relatively recent years "at least seven authors have devoted complete books to the subject."[5] Therefore, in spite of some vagueness attached to a phrase like the "American Idea," it is a useful term in discussing a most important nineteenth-century literary and intellectual assumption—what Carl Jung might have called a "psychic fact"—in America. For even if a modern commentator were to consider the American Idea as too vague a concept, he can hardly deny that, during the nineteenth century and since, writers have used it, or some term approximating it, in their analyses of certain central threads in the fabric of American life, literature, and thought.

What is proposed here, then, is a descriptive examination of the existence and development of the American Idea in the work of Orestes Brownson, a nineteenth-century man of letters whose general importance has recently been re-established through the work of Harold Laski, Arthur Schlesinger, Jr., Perry Miller, R. W. B. Lewis, C. Carroll Hollis, and Russell Kirk.[6] These men, who range from the extreme right to the extreme left of the intellectual spectrum, have seen Brownson as one of the important figures of his time, and for different reasons. Schlesinger and Laski, for example, are great admirers of Brownson's early and radical "Laboring Classes" essays; Kirk is interested in the increasing conservatism in Brownson's thought after 1844. All these men are agreed at least upon Brownson's importance for our time; all are agreed upon his position as a potent intellectual force in his own time. Schlesinger, perhaps, speaks for them all when he writes:

Against the background of his time Orestes Brownson stands an important and expressive figure. He symbolized the intellectual restlessness and vitality of the period before specialization made it impossible for one man to work with equal facility in a dozen fields. . . . In the diversity of his interests he typified the generation. . . . There was hardly a question, large or small, that agitated the country from 1830 to 1870, on which Brownson did not make comments. To many of them he made contributions. . . . Brownson had the courage to face the life around him and the sharpness to see what the problem of the future was to be. . . . His observations on society had a profundity no other American of the time approached.[7]

Orestes Brownson, an "alert trend-spotter and . . . able cataloguer of the intellectual forces of his day," as R. W. B. Lewis puts it, made significant contributions to the examination of and the dialogue concerning the American Idea in the nineteenth century. He examined it from every angle: indeed, he was at one time its great defender, and, at another, its severest critic. As editor of the *Boston Quarterly Review* and, later, of *Brownson's Quarterly Review,* he returned again and again to this theme; in some of the most forceful and thoughtful essays written in his time he provided for his contemporaries food not only for thought but also for action. This book hopes to make available for the current reader Brownson's views of the American Idea as he thought them through during the major part of his career.

II

As we have seen, R. W. B. Lewis has emphasized the necessity of "a review of that earlier debate" of the American Idea. Daniel Boorstin has echoed Lewis' suggestion in a plea which insists that the American Idea "was one of the longest, strongest threads in our [national] thinking."[8] Russell Kirk has argued that an uncritical acceptance of the American Idea is no longer possible, and has implied that when a study of that idea in the nineteenth century is made, especially of the "innovations" which it fostered, it will be discovered that after Hawthorne Orestes Brownson was "the most important" of the opponents of the Idea. "In the latter half of the twentieth century," Kirk goes on, "more attention may be paid to Brownson than he has received in the past hundred years . . . , [for] something like a conspiracy of silence has kept his name out of histories of American thought."[9]

In a review of this important earlier debate, one in which Brownson figured so largely, Brownson should be allowed to speak as much as possible for himself.[10] "Conspiracy of silence" are strong words indeed, and a review of Brownson's part in the nineteenth-century discussion should, at this time at least, be descriptive or denotative. Thus, *what* Brownson said is central to this work. There is little doubt that Brownson's opinions were changeable—some would say inconsistent—and there exists the possibility of misrepresentation if his views at one period are not understood in the context of what he said at other times. Moreover, Brownson was a journalist whose intellectual growth and development had the disadvantage of being periodically subject to judgment by his contemporaries—the editor and practically sole writer of a quarterly review, he could be called to account four times a year. Although such periodic criticism may very well be understandable, it may also lead, quite inadvertently, to the kind of neglect which Kirk has remarked. For Brownson's contemporaries themselves were often deeply, even emotionally, involved in many of the problems with which he struggled, and they would naturally be quick to seize upon every turn of his lively mind. The danger was that they would miss the complexity of the whole in their eager attempt to isolate and disprove a part. It was then a short step to assign a motive to every seeming change, and ultimately to dismiss Brownson as one who, like Dryden's Zimri, was everything by starts and nothing long. Once this point of view is assumed, the opinions of such men as Brownson may be dismissed from importance. J. H. Allen, writing of Brownson in 1882, could say that "the lesson of his life was told for us above thirty years ago, and the strong, stormful, rude yet tender-hearted man passed away, leaving hardly a ripple in our memory to remind us of what his influence had been."[11]

Schlesinger believes that some of the topics central to Brownson's essays were "unpopular" in his day, and have only recently

become fashionable for historical treatment. . . . A generation after his conversion . . . [his contemporaries] had pretty much forgotten everything about Brownson save his vehemence, his instability and his Catholicism. . . . Orestes Brownson thus fell victim to the accidents of history and vanished from America's remembrance of her past. His extraordinary intelligence and profound honesty deserved a richer reward.[12]

Again, Leonard McCarthy's study of Brownson's rhetoric[13] has revealed that Brownson was involved in another problem of *ad hoc* journalism—the use of several rhetorical styles adapted to specific occasions and purposes. The problem of understanding the immediate emphasis given a particular point, therefore, is one which Brownson's own method makes difficult, and necessitates an exposition of his basic ideas in their immediate local context.

Therefore, this book proposes no definitive examination of Brownson's "mind"; what it hopes to achieve is a contribution toward that final and necessary study. To this end, the years 1838–1860 have been selected since they represent the critical years of Brownson's life, that is to say, those years which witnessed his major growth and development. Furthermore, these were years (with the exception of 1843) in which he edited and wrote his own *Reviews*. These *Reviews* are Brownson's chief contribution in the years prior to the Civil War, and it is in them essentially that his growth and development can be most closely studied. Consequently, what will be undertaken here is a study in context, an issue-by-issue, descriptive review of the presence, growth, and development of the American Idea from the first number of Brownson's first *Review* to the final number of its successor in the years immediately preceding the Civil War. In the course of this year-by-year examination, we shall pay attention to what Brownson actually said, and to the charge of inconsistency which has been raised against him. This will be done in order to clarify what inconsistencies we can, and to render more understandable those inconsistencies which may remain. The essay, therefore, will be more descriptive than critical. The primary concern here is what did Brownson have to say about the American Idea in his *Reviews* from 1838 to 1860?

III

America, a restless continent, was founded by men who had been shaped by the association and experience of a thousand years of developing Western civilization. These men, curious products of medieval other-worldliness, Renaissance humanism, a new theology of covenant, and the effects of a burgeoning rational philosophy, were themselves as restless of mind as of place. Not wholly conscious of the influences which were in play, they had had a dream, tenuous at times, rather vague and fleeting, but still of sufficient temper to enlist strong sympathies and brave wills of the sort which could set an ideal and expect confidently that their successors would be worthy of their own vision.

What helped prompt that great undertaking was, then, something akin to what we now call the American Dream,[14] first dreamed in Europe where the roots of American culture really lie. The frontier, after all, for all its influence in forming American institutions had to have something to shape;[15] the matter to which it helped give form was itself made up of the achievements, aspirations, and the hopes which the founders of this country brought with them as surely as they had brought their Bibles and their axes.

As the dream edged outward into reality, the accent changed somewhat and there developed what might be called the American Experiment—the working-out of the dream in a practical theater. As late, for example, as 1812 there was still doubt that the experiment would ever really take root; by the end of Andrew Jackson's term as President, however, the experiment had become truly viable, and practical men could speak and act more confidently. These Americans of the 1830s and '40s believed in the truth of a cosmic order—of either a providential, deistic, or immanent origin; the confluence of a natural law of Platonic cast and the moral law of Judaeo-Christian faith; and, finally, something called the American

Mission.[16] The Mission was the end to which the American Experiment, informed by the American Dream, was to direct its efforts. The American Mission, then, was to be the culmination, the goal. The three terms all represented separate properties of the American Idea.

None of the components is to be understood as having remained fixed in concept and strictly delimited in all phases of its being. Indeed the changes in them individually are many and varied, and even divisive: the American Civil War was fought over fundamental differences in the interpretation of all three. General definitions must suffice; what we attempt here is merely to indicate the existence of these general terms, their pervasiveness, both consciously and unconsciously in American thought generally, and then, before examining them in a more concrete way in the thought of a nineteenth-century American writer, to see something of that complex of ideas which undergirded not only all three separately, but the three taken as a whole—the American Idea.

There are many assumptions implicit in the American Idea. None exists in isolation; all can be found interpenetrating, and relying on each other for support. There is danger of distortion unless this point is understood. Nevertheless, the following seem of especial importance, and may be taken separately if it is postulated that distinctions here are logical rather than real. The ideas are these:

1. The idea of Progress;
2. The optimism, stemming from the Renaissance view of man, and, less remotely, from the confident assertions of the Enlightenment;
3. The perfectibility of man;
4. The importance of democracy and Christianity as indispensable societal forces, and of their immediate relation as absolutely necessary, each to the essential working out of the other.

The idea of Progress, it is generally agreed, is perhaps the most important of "the ideas which have held sway in public and private affairs for the last two hundred years."[17] It is, adds the same commentator in another place, "one of the most profound and germinal ideas at work in the modern age."[18] Even the great opponent of the efficacy of the idea, William Ralph Inge, testifies to its importance in the shaping of the modern Western mind.[19]

According to J. B. Bury,[20] the idea itself, considered historically, is of relatively recent origin. It was a concept more or less antithetic to the assumptions of ancient Greek civilization, for example, because of its limited historical experience, the emphases in its thought upon degeneration and the cycles of history (even if one admits the Epicurean inroads upon Greek pessimism), and its pre-occupation with the present, the here-and-now; Progress is essentially a futuristic philosophy. Nor did the establishment of the Roman rule of law, imposed by force and, therefore, leading to wide-spread slavery, prepare a seedbed for the idea of Progress.[21]

The temper of the medieval mind was also inhospitable to such an act of faith as Progress. Indeed, in contrast to the temper of much of modern Christian thinking, "the whole spirit of medieval Christianity excluded it."[22] The medieval idea of Divine Providence must be seen quite apart from any notion of a worldly utopia: it had released man from the deadening influence of Fate, and yet it foresaw the possibly sudden imminence of the end of the world. Allied with this sobering possibility was a kind of general pessimism about man's temporal condition which led to a hope framed in eternal rather than mundane terms. There was in medieval man, as Romano Guardini has put it, a lack of "any desire for exact empirical knowledge of reality. . . ."[23]

The Renaissance was "one of the conspicuously progressive periods in history, but the conditions were not favorable to the appearance of an idea of Progress, though the intellectual *milieu* was being prepared. . . ."[24] Although thinkers in this age discarded much of the medieval synthesis and set reason in a central position in the City of Man, they abdicated a considerable amount of their freedom by too closely serving as masters the ancient writers whose authority they more or less recognized.[25]

With the French historian Jean Bodin and the English philosopher Francis Bacon, the stage was prepared for the entrance of the idea of Progress, properly made up and costumed by seventeenth-century Cartesian philosophy.[26] The idea of the progress of knowledge is credited to the Cartesian Fontenelle;[27] the original explicit statement of the idea to the Abbé de Saint-Pierre, another philosopher of Cartesian stamp and a Deist,[28] who was among the first to turn the face of history to the future in time.[29] The Abbé had great influence upon such historians as Turgot and the Encyclopedists, for, as Bury notes, "his principles are theirs. The omnipotence of government and laws to mould the morals of peoples; the subordination of all knowledge to the goddess of utility; the deification of human reason; and the doctrine of Progress."[30]

With the Enlightenment the idea of Progress burst into full flower. As a theory it contributed greatly to the rise of the new industrial civilization, and itself received renewed impetus from the achievements of those who were increasing Western man's ability to bend natural forces to his needs—and, more darkly, to his appetites. What entered here, then, was something new: the idea of Progress, while remaining in the abstract what Bury calls an "act of faith," was also becoming, especially in America, a philosophy of action.[31] In other terms, the element of Progress implicit in the American Dream was transposing itself into the American Experiment.

For America was the promising land of the rational speculators. Admittedly, it was the cherished object of the dreamers, the polished planners, the heady theorists in the French *salons* or the more cloudy thinkers in the German university towns; at the same time it was the working place of the practical men, the doers, the restless men, scornful of the past and impatient of the present. Ultimately their hero was to be Andrew Jackson whose face was the face of the American 1830s. The rough frontiersman pushing into the illimitable riches of the West seldom looked back. But if Jackson heralded the Experiment, Jefferson was the pre-eminent early exponent of the Dream. And behind Jefferson were the *philosophes,* of whom only one represented all the phases of the liberal philosophical movement, the "most universal of them all," the Marquis de Condorcet.[32] His influence upon Saint-Simon was considerable, and Saint-Simonism gave rise to copious varieties of practical theories for the implementation of the Golden Age on earth.[33] Auguste Comte, for example, was a disciple of Saint-Simonian doctrine. Though Charles Fourier "regarded himself as a Newton for whom no Kepler or Galileo had prepared the way,"[34] he too is in the general tradition, and no one at all familiar with the America of the 1830s and '40s—with Brook Farm—can forget the direct influence of Fourier in American life through what seems to have been the initial agency of Albert Brisbane.[35]

The idea of Progress, then, helped inform the American Dream; the idea became a philosophy of action in America: the American Experiment. And the American '40s and '50s saw its influence upon what, as we have seen, Arthur Ekirch terms "the concept of a peculiar American mission."[36]

Carl Becker has given, perhaps, the best short definition of Progress in the sense in which this essay will use it: "Briefly defined, it implies that mankind, by making use of science and invention, can progressively emancipate itself from plagues, famines, and social disasters, and subjugate the materials and forces of the earth to the purposes of the good life—here and now."[37] It need be added only that the "here and now" treated as static in the immediate application of the fruits of the seed is also considered less pointedly but no less forcefully as in flux to the future—as becoming.

Spawned in Cartesian philosophy, given impetus and scope by the French, German, and English philosophers of the Enlightenment—but especially by the French[38]—the idea of Progress found an outlet for its fancy in the New World, and a prepared laboratory for its practical aspects on the American continent.

Generalizing from the results of . . . material and cultural advancement, the American people made the idea of progress both a law of history and the will of a benign Providence.[39] In the years 1815–1860, the period covered by this [i.e., Ekirch's] analysis, we may safely conclude that the idea of progress was the most popular American philosophy, thoroughly congenial to the ideas and interests of the age.[40]

It thus seems true to hold that the Idea of Progress was developing sufficient intellectual ambience a century ago to explain the rise of man from magic through religion to the place in which rational science would seek not only to destroy metaphysics but to replace it. If Freud, and Einstein, and Planck, those sullen Titans, were still in the shadows, the *novi homines* were as yet fairly disdainful of any dark lessons from the Cave.

For allied to the notion of Progress, at times as effect to cause, at others as cause to effect, was the idea of optimism.[41] With the renewal in the Renaissance of the central focus to man—however ultimately naked and lost man became after Copernicus—and with the added insistence of the Cartesians upon the importance of the individual human reason, there was finally, in the sphere of religion, the Protestant appeal on matters of vital truth to the individual judgment. It is true—and the paradox is of great interest—that in early Protestantism optimism was hardly the goal of either Luther or Calvin: the former was seeking in many ways to reconstitute the Middle Ages; the latter, in a curious if not complete reversion to pre-Hellenic thought, made of salvation a kind of theistic whim, a matter of magic, almost, of the caprice of God. Yet, in both systems, the seed of opposite reaction, exactly as a Newtonian might have predicted, lay in the stress both leaders placed in the individual judgment of the individual man. When the reaction did come, it came in a double channel, each seemingly antithetic to the other. For, on the one hand, the Deists spoke from the platform of eighteenth-century confidence in "nature" and reason, and, as Carl Becker has said, "to that optimistic age, . . . God was assumed to have designed the Universe in such wise that man was master of his fate: by taking thought he could always with the assistance of the 'laws of nature and of nature's God' add a cubit to his stature."[42] The deistic strain was to have a marked effect in American thought,[43] culminating, perhaps, in its influence upon Unitarianism.

On the other hand, the Romantic reaction seems to have been directed not only against Calvinistic pessimism but also against the attempted deification of human "reason." It postulated, with Kant and Coleridge, a new mode of knowledge, a Reason higher than reason, an intuitional mode which reduced deistic reason—Thomas Paine's common sense—to mere understanding. "The eighteenth century with its chain-of-being and its concept of a fixed universe had partly given way before a vision of a world whose limits were constantly expanding and whose denizens had a passion for physical progress. This vision was widely followed on an open road of intuition, optimism, and faith."[44]

A distinguishing mark of both views, however, was optimism. The idea of Providence, central to the medieval outlook, seems to have been honored in the latter day by judicious citation and written applause; but, after Copernicus and Voltaire, the medieval idea was generally devitalized, and it became a catchword in the fashionable opinions and among the fashionable philosophers and their imitators. Yet the ideal remained with changed emphasis—that is, that the perfect can be eventually attained and "that its arrival can be hastened by human agency. . . . [The Abbé de] Saint-Pierre offered men a religion without a God; a century later philosophers had discovered a teleology in *natural development*[45] and learned to regard man as the climax of a divine purpose which utilized human effort for the attainment of an ultimate perfection."[46] In the intuitional approach—the one so seminal in New England—assumptions ran from these to ones postulating a logic in matter itself (though not necessarily originating there) which pushed on to an Ideal in which, for example, the conscious stone could grow to beauty.

Optimism led man to believe that with the help of rational means—or, for the Transcendentalists, intuitional ones, sponsored by the individual religious sentiment—man could, through the additional agencies of science, of planning, and of psychology, or by losing himself in the Oversoul, ameliorate the general condition of mankind and of himself. He could, in short, not only make his own peace in his own heart, but make his God there as well.[47]

The third term, one of the four chief assumptions of the American Idea, follows as end to means the optimism of the Enlightenment. The perfectibility of man, a complicated interweaving of many ideational strands, is, perhaps, an amalgam of Renaissance humanism, the thought of the *philosophes,* and the internal revolts of latter-day Protestants which not only led to a proliferate sectarianism, but which lost the black baggage of original sin somewhere in the explosion.

The *philosophes* taught that by reason man may be master of things, that he can imagine a society in which all men enjoy freedom and happiness, and that he can deliberately create the society he has imagined. They directed their most powerful blows against the traditional and clerical view . . . that man is a creature fallen and perverse, who cannot be saved from self-destruction except through the gift of grace.[48]

With the triumph of Unitarianism in America and with its own ultimate dethronement by the Transcendentalists, this "traditional and clerical view" of original sin was overthrown. If this was man's world, and if man was to prosper in terms of his recognition of natural laws—which could include the natural law of his self-divinity—then he need obey these laws only. If he did, where, short of perfection, could man stop? This idea enclosed both progress and optimism since, first, the gradual amelioration of man's social, political, and economic ills was considered possible;[49] second, the gradual achievement of these aims—and the American Revolution was symbolic here—seemed to argue advance already made. For, even if Providence was now merely an honorific title, suitable for the perorations of Sunday ministers, ubiquitous politicians,[50] or itinerant revolutionaries,[51] there were constant acts of faith in (1) the deistic natural law; (2) the working-out of the Idea in history;

or (3) as Marx cited it later in the century, the working-out of logic implicit in matter itself.

Now all these were acts of faith really, but the appeal was to history for proof, and history seemed to deny the older cyclic theories or theories of degeneration;[52] the current of movement, of advance, was perceptible to capable men. Whither, then, was that movement directed but ultimately to perfection? Consequently, in all these ideas—progress, optimism, perfectibility—the accent was on the future,[53] the point of comparison, the past, the point of observation, the present. History seemed to link them all in a happy aspiration.[54] And in "that eighteenth century dream of perfectibility a belief in the essential goodness of human nature, a love of mankind, and a faith in reason . . . never faltered."[55]

Finally, Ralph Gabriel insists upon the supporting nexus of democracy and Christianity in nineteenth-century America:

The secular faith of democracy and the religious faith of a changing Protestantism were not only closely related but were mutually inter-dependent. They complemented each other. There was no suggestion of rivalry between them. Together they provided the American with a theory of the cosmos which gave significance and direction to human life, and with a theory of society which gave a meaning not only to the relation of the individual to the group, but of the United States to the congregation of nations.[56]

Democracy as an experiment, especially an American experiment, was forged by the processes of history, and held as arbiter, even in its experimental stage, the most judicious governance of the political needs of man for peace, justice, equity, and a competent social order. It was the political instrument as much as it was the child of Progress; it was central both to the American Dream and to the American Mission, the carrying abroad to the "congregation of nations" of the new gospel: American democracy would "save the world from the oppression of autocrats. . . . [This] was a secular version of the destiny of Christianity to save the world from the governance of Satan."[57] The latent principles of democracy—the freedom and worth of the individual, the moral law and its sovereignty—were Christian principles and were an integral part of Protestant Christianity. As Carl Becker has put it,

there is more of Christian philosophy in the writings of the *Philosophes* than has been dreamt of in our histories. . . . The underlying preconceptions of eighteenth-century thought were still, allowance made for certain important alterations in the bias, essentially the same as those of the thirteenth century. . . . The *Philosophes* demolished the Heavenly City of St. Augustine only to rebuild it with more up-to-date materials.[58]

Democracy and Christianity—whatever one seemed to mean by the latter term—were then carefully intertwined, and in the New World the coupling not only helped inform but was itself informed by the American Idea.

IV

Thus by 1815 the pattern of the American Idea, especially in the Experimental and Mission phases, had taken hold, and, as Ekirch has shown, it was carried along by that complex of ideas, that climate of opinion, that secular faith which has been called progress. As the century advanced into its second quarter, progress became, as we have seen, "the most popular American philosophy."

Clearly, there were able exponents of this popular philosophy. And these men not only used the popular forums in an age of oratory, but also the periodical press, which in those days had an enormous influence upon the public mind.[59] Among the influential magazines of these years there were two which ranked in quality and influence with such contemporaries as *The Southern Literary Messenger, The Dial,* and *The North American Review*—two quarterlies which drew from Harold Laski the adjective "astonishing": *The Boston Quarterly Review* and, later, *Brownson's Quarterly Review.*[60] The first of these, wrote Laski, has a "permanent significance in American intellectual history";[61] the other was a worthy successor. The editor of both magazines was Orestes Augustus Brownson of whom Ekirch has remarked that he was "the author who perhaps devoted the most attention to the idea of progress of all American religious writers before the Civil War."[62] Granted the intimate connection between Progress and the American Idea as it has been sketched here, we might expect that these magazines would have a relatively similar importance to the exposition of the American Dream, Experiment, and Mission. This is true and, indeed, true in several senses. For these magazines record not only some of the most well-articulated arguments for the American Idea, but also the more sober arguments *against* it, and thus provide in themselves a kind of cultural dialogue, an understanding of which R. W. B.

Lewis finds indispensable to any informed criticism of an historical period, especially of the second quarter of the nineteenth century in America.[63]

Orestes Brownson, a restless man in a restless time in a restless country, is a figure whose importance may be as easily overvalued as underrated. If, as Matthew Fitzsimmons put it, "the Protestant career of Orestes Brownson sums up a large part of the intellectual history of the nineteenth century's first forty years,"[64] his "Catholic" career after 1844 sums up many of the conclusions of the kind of modern re-evaluation of America's cultural history which forms the theme of such studies as Randall Stewart's *American Literature and Christian Doctrine*. Professor Stewart, speaking of those writers such as T. S. Eliot who in the last four or five decades have decided that a "return to Christian fundamentals . . . is the chief need of our time," describes such "thoughtful" people in these terms:

These people (I reject the name "intellectual" used substantively, as by and large an unfortunate usage) are the ones whom I mean to designate as "neo-orthodox." They were probably brought up in the Christian faith, whether Catholic or Protestant. They almost necessarily fell into various kinds of agnosticisms and infidelities. And after having suffered from spiritual famine, like the prodigal son in a far country, they have at length undertaken to arise, and return to their Father . . . to Christian fundamentals, though the position to which one returns can never be quite the position from which one fell away.[65]

In almost every particular Stewart could have been summarizing the career of Orestes Brownson.[66]

Born in grim Vermont in 1803 of Yankee parents,[67] Brownson lost his father early and found himself living from the ages of six to fourteen with foster parents, New England Congregationalists. By his own admission he had no childhood;[68] his earliest interests were in reading, especially of Scripture and in religious subjects generally.[69] His early religious leanings were deeply influential, as was, no doubt, the sober, grinding existence of life on a stone-laden New England farm, overseen by the rigid, consistent, Calvinist-tinged Protestantism quite common at the time in the rural North. Naturally bright, compulsive and intense in argument even at an early age, he lacked formal schooling until, after accompanying his mother and the rest of his family to Ballston Spa, New York, he briefly attended an academy there, in times when he was not employed in a printer's office. This school experience terminated his formal education.[70] A Presbyterian at nineteen in refuge from the authority of his own reason, he found his chosen church abdicating its responsibility, as he saw it, to be authoritative. In 1823 he left the Presbyterian Church, changing as he said "from a supernaturalist to a rationalist. . . . [This was] the commencement of my intellectual life. . . ."[71]

The following year he left to teach school in Detroit, but, while there, he fell ill and, during his convalescence, read a considerable number of Universalist tracts, books, and pamphlets, for, as he wrote in *The Convert*: "I was unwilling to be an unbeliever, and felt deeply the need of having a religion of some sort. Liberal Christianity was a vague term. . . . Its chief characteristic was the denial of what was called Orthodoxy, and taking nature and reason for the rule of faith. The only definitive form under which I was acquainted with it was that of Universalism. . . ."[72]

After some study Brownson was ordained a Universalist evangelist in Jaffrey, New Hampshire, in 1826, the year before his marriage to Sally Healy. Until 1829, he served as a Universalist minister in Litchfield, Ithaca, Geneva, and in Auburn, New York, where he edited *The Gospel Advocate and Impartial Investigator,* a semimonthly, "the most widely circulated and the most influential periodical in this country . . . devoted to Universalism."[73]

In 1829 he left Universalism because, as he put it,

My disposition was practical rather than speculative, or even meditative. . . . I sought the truth in order to know what I ought to do, and as the means of realizing some moral and practical end. I wanted the truth that I might use it. . . . Universalism had made me doubt the utility of all labors for another world, and I was forced to look for a work to be done in this world.[74]

Before he found such work when he eventually joined the group attached to Frances Wright and Robert Dale Owen, in 1829, he published in the *Gospel Advocate and Impartial Investigator* for June 27, 1829, his "creed" of five points which "would embrace all the essentials of true religion." Thus, he wrote of this creed many years later that he had "rejected heaven for earth, and God for man, eternity for time as the end for which I was bound to labor."[75] The end of man was individual happiness, and the collective happiness of mankind in this world to develop man's whole nature, and so to organize society and government as to secure all men a paradise on the earth. This view I held steadily and without wavering from 1828 till 1842. . . . The various systems I embraced or defended . . . social . . . political, ethical . . . aesthetical, philosophical, theological, were all subordinated to this end, as means by which man's earthly condition was to be ameliorated. I sought . . . to attain the means of gaining the earthly happiness of mankind. My end was man's earthly happiness, and *my creed was progress*.[76]

In his association with Fanny Wright and Owen he was the editor of the *Free Enquirer and Genesee Republican and Herald of Reform*.[77] The influence of William Godwin's *Political Justice* was great at this period,[78] as was the personal magnetism exerted by the incomparable Fanny who believed that the American mind needed rousing "to a sense of its rights and dignity . . . to withdraw it from the contemplation of an imaginary heaven after death, and fix it on the great and glorious work of promoting man's earthly well-being. The second step was, by practical action, to get adopted . . . a system of state schools. . . ."[79] These schools, as Brownson readily admitted, would follow the popular theories of Locke and Condillac, and their establishment would be the goal of a secret society, formed along the lines of the European *Carbonari*.[80] Brownson, in fact, may have become an agent for such a society, but, if so, his tenure lasted but a few months. Yet, when the "Working-men's Party" was founded in Philadelphia in 1828, and in New York in 1829, it had as its objective when Brownson joined it the control of political power in New York to the end that the school system as indicated could be established.[81] This party hoped to succeed by "linking our cause with the ultra-democratic sentiment of the country, which had had, from the time of Jefferson and Tom Paine, something of an anti-Christian character."[82]

Yet Brownson soon saw that a workingman's party could not be effective; although himself a zealous reformer, he recognized that little was to be gained merely by having schools which turned out "well-trained animals—a sort of learned pigs." Man was more than an animal, and Brownson found that he could not "carry out my reforms without love, disinterestedness, sacrifice";[83] the former evangelist soon found himself "reverting with regret to his early religious principles and affections." He quit the party and resumed the life of an independent preacher in Ithaca, New York, where, during the years 1831–1832, he became editor of *The Philanthropist*.

From 1832 to 1834, under the influence of Dr. Channing, and having labored as a Unitarian minister in New Hampshire, he applied himself to learning German and French. In 1834 he went to a Unitarian congregation in Canton, Massachusetts, where he had in the parsonage a quondam boarder and fellow-student, Henry David Thoreau.[84] While in Canton, Brownson contributed to the *Christian Examiner* and the *Christian Register*. In 1836 he moved to Chelsea, Massachusetts, joined the Transcendental Club, became an independent preacher in Boston, and, since, as he says, "I did not lose sight of the great end I proposed,—the progress of man and society,"[85] he organized the "Society for Christian Union and Progress," the end of which was "the union and progress of the race." Immediately thereafter he published *New Views of Christianity, Society and the Church,* a work explicitly influenced by the thought of Benjamin Constant, Victor Cousin, Heinrich Heine, Schleiermacher, and the Saint-Simonians.[86]

In 1836–1837 with his name becoming more and more well-known, he edited the *Boston Reformer,* and continued membership in the Transcendental Club. Through George Bancroft, a rising political figure—as was Brownson himself in the party of Jackson—he was appointed to the political post of steward at the United States Marine Hospital at Chelsea. Freed now from financial stress, Brownson could and did turn to the project which had become increasingly important to him: the founding of his own Review.

It may be well at this point to look briefly at Brownson's own statement of his views written shortly before January, 1838. An admirable compendium is given in his *New Views,* published in 1836.[87]

To Brownson in 1836, man's consciousness and the universal history of mankind sustained the view that the "religious sentiment" (as opposed to religious *institutions*) was "universal, permanent, and indestructible." The institutions, mere outgrowths of the religious sentiment, were mutable by nature, since they showed growth and development in proportion as man grew and developed. Individuals die, the race does not, and the "reproductive energy of religion survives all mutations of forms, and so do new institutions rise to gladden us . . . to carry us further onward in one progress."[88] The Christian Church, once capable of directing mankind's progress, could do so no more, since its present concept of truth was only a partial realization of the whole. The Church was out of step with the time: the fault was not humanity's (for its inevitable law was to grow), or Jesus', but the Church's itself. Never the perfect fulfillment of Jesus' thought, it had been adequate only for its time. Yet up to its inevitable downfall it was "as truly Christian as the progress made by the human race admitted." It had once been useful; it was no more.

After contrasting the "spiritualism" of Asia and the "materialism" of Greece and Rome, Brownson argued that Jesus' work had been designed to bring balance between these two extremes, to become a reconciliation of the two poles, an "atonement" in which all antithesis was destroyed by love. The Church had been intended to embody all this—the holy, that is, in the mind of the God-man;[89] its success would have meant the realization of atonement, of the reconciliation of the two forces in love. But the Church rejected Christ the Mediator for Christ the Redeemer, and, taking its stand with spirit (or "spiritualism"), it had deprecated matter (or "materialism") and, therefore, had actually rejected Christ as uniting the two. How, now, was impure, material man to unite with pure being? Man was depraved: he could not work out his own salvation; by condemning matter, the Church condemned man, or had, at least through its ascetic ideal (celibacy of the clergy, fasting, etc.), made a necessity of the renunciation of matter, of the world.

Protestantism, that "insurrection of materialism," had revived an ancient ideal when classical antiquity was reborn; its art and literature were not so much exhumed as released from bondage, and had again been given life in the sun, as the Catholic Church had itself fostered the thought of Judea, Egypt, and India. Protestantism revived, too, the use of reason (since under the reign of spiritualism all questions are submitted to authority with reason prohibited); with the revival of reason came now new life to philosophy, especially experimental philosophy. ". . . philosophical materialism, in germ or developed, has been commensurate with Protestantism."[90] The tendency, then, was toward matter and away from spirit. As the material took gradual precedence after the Reformation, Protestantism became as one-sided in its way as Catholicism had been in its own.

True Protestantism, however, had died in the French Revolution. Since that time the pendulum had swung back toward spiritualism, as man began to despair of improving his material condition, and lost the confidence, Reformation-born, of a strong faith in the material order, a faith which especially marked the eighteenth century.[91] "Our republic [the United States] sprang into being and the world leaped with joy that 'a man child was born.'[92] Social progress and the perfection of governments became the religious creed of the day. . . . A new paradise was imaged forth for man, inaccessible to the serpent, more delightful . . . more attractive than that which the pious Christian hopes to gain."[93] The voice of hope was heard from France, until its throat was cut by Napoleon. After that, wrote Brownson, optimism decreased, "democracy became an accusation, a faith in the perfectibility of mankind, a proof of disordered intellect."[94]

Among the results were the renewed influence on European thought (especially German, French, and English) of the Orient and of Plato (e.g., in Byron, Wordsworth, and the Schlegels). Materialism was almost dead; it produced no sound works, no new, "kindling" doctrines. Though "materialism" still predominated, it was rather a static tradition than a dynamic force.

It was the "mission of the present" either to dispense with all religion, or to build a new church, so designed that neither materialism nor spiritualism would ever again be given absolute reign. Both were good: the question became one of proportion. Between the two the peace of *mésure* had to be made. "This disclosed our Mission. We are to reconcile spirit and matter . . . and realize the atonement. . . . Progress is our law and our first step is Union."[95] The realization of atonement, the proper reconciliation of spirit and matter, will mark the second coming of Christ.

Brownson then conducted a review of the various sects (especially of Calvinism,[96] Universalism, and Unitarianism) and, having found them all only partial in their various truths, he opted for a new eclecticism which would resemble the attempt of the ancient Alexandrian philosophers. This new eclectic approach, which he called "the philosophy of the nineteenth century," and which followed the lead of Victor Cousin,[97] attempted to bring into one corporate rational structure the best features of all systems. The point was to meet in amity that other outcropping of the *Zeitgeist*, the tendency to association which was inspired by God. The accommodation of these two was to mirror the earlier meeting of Christian inspiration and Alexandrian eclecticism, i.e., to become a New Church.[98]

The evidence indicated, Brownson continued, that this meeting was already taking place in the United States. Americans had a philosophical bent, which "fits us above all other nations to bring out and realize great and important ideas." There were in this country both freedom and faith in ideas, and these requirements were needed for experiment, for trial of new ideas. "It is here in the United States then that must first be brought out and realized the true idea of atonement."[99]

The influence of this doctrine of atonement would be conclusive—i.e., "that spirit is real and holy, that matter is real and holy, that God is holy and that man is holy," and that spirit and matter need not be sacrificed one to the other; that both, furthermore, were elements of an harmonious whole. This doctrine would correct our estimate of man, the world, religion, God, and so renovate our institutions as to create "a new civilization as much in advance of ours as ours is in advance of . . . the Roman Empire."[100]

What follows in Brownson's *New Views* may be gathered from the lead sentences of the paragraphs which ensued: "Slavery will cease. . . . Wars will fail. . . . Education will destroy the empire of ignorance. . . . Civil freedom will become universal. . . . Industry will be holy. . . . Church and State will become one . . ." etc.[101] Further, "The Church will be on the side of progress, and materialism and spiritualism will combine to make man's earthly condition as near like the lost Eden of the eastern poets, as is compatible with the growth and perfection of man's nature."[102]

Chapter x of *New Views* was entitled "Progress." Since God has designed men with his greatest gift—that we are progressive beings—we were, so the argument ran, less perfect than we would become: the actual existence of evil, therefore, presented little difficulty. The chief glory of man's nature was this capacity for progress; it was "the brightest signature of our divine origin, and the pledge of our immortality."[103] Indeed, moral evil might even aid progress itself since it existed "by the superintending care of Providence," and its existence might aid progress by pointing out to man his duty. "Man's duty is illimitable progress; his end is everlasting growth. . . . Progress is the end for which he was made. To this end, then, it is his duty to direct all his inquiries, all his systems of religion and philosophy, all his institutions of politics and society, all the productions of genius and taste . . . all the modes of his activity. This is his duty. . . ."[104]

Humanity was just beginning to grasp this point, to get a glimpse "of its inconceivably grand and holy destiny." The time was ripe for humanity to "accept the law imposed upon it for its own good. . . . Its future religion is the religion of progress. The true priests are those who can quicken in mankind a desire for progress."[105]

Clearly, then, in Brownson's *New Views* the separate elements—progress, optimism, perfectibility, a Christian view of politics and society—were in operation, and were under the aegis of that new breed of philosophers, the American people. The American Idea raised here to a kind of Church became the Dream, the theater, and the future of mankind. His idea of progress made of it man's duty, indeed, his *end*.[106] Nor was this all. Man's capability for progress was at the very root of the entire moral order. The pessimistic note which Brownson had sounded about his own time dissolved in his bright view of the future of humanity, for man was perfectible—especially man in the United States.[107]

Again, reacting now very definitely against his denial of Christianity in the 1820s, he affirmed the need of religion as foundation to the social, educational, and political changes which were to come.[108]

Brownson's views in 1836 were partially designed, in Schlesinger's words, "to answer the contention of the Saint-Simonists . . . that Christianity could not be the social ideal of the future."[109] This group regarded Christianity (as well as the Church) as obsolete—good for its time but outmoded by the law of progress. Brownson, though a progressivist, denied that true Christianity was superannuated; it was (as later he and Theodore Parker would for a short time agree) the "permanent" part of Christianity, as the institutions to which the religious sentiment gives rise are the "transient" element. It seems that Brownson applied the same law historically to social and political institutions which the Saint-Simonians had applied to religion. Yet here is the root, perhaps, of what might be termed Brownson's early conservatism, or, at least, his early relative conservatism. For Brownson now and throughout the rest of his career there had to be some permanence in the flux of things. Lying somewhere near the source of this conservatism, then, was a Christianity which in some vague way was the creature of Providence and which gave shape both to Progress considered as necessary change, and to permanence. Further, as an "eclectic," Brownson saw good in political institutions and even in "God-patented nobles" who were the aristocrats of the mind to whom the future belonged.

He was, therefore, not the thorough-going progressivist which Heine was, for example; by comparison he was—and the term again is relative, as perhaps it always is—a kind of conservative radical even in 1836.

Two further points may be noted: first, the general vagueness of his views, especially his almost visceral enthusiasm for Progress, a term he never adequately defined; second, his lack of concrete detail about the exact form the new organization would take. What was needed, he wrote much later, was a "great man"—"a New Moses, a new Christ"—who, having realized the ideal within, would realize it externally for all men. Brownson's task, as he saw it, was merely to sketch the essentials of the idea.[110] But America was chiefly the land of the new Church, the place toward which the conscience of the world was tending; for Brownson, the wind was rising and the rivers flowed.

This essentially was Brownson's general position when late in 1837 he undertook the editorship of his own journal, *The Boston Quarterly Review,* whose first number, under date of January, 1838, was published in December, 1837.

NOTES

1. "The National Idea in American Criticism," *Dalhousie Review,* 14 (July 1934), 133–147.
2. Gilbert Chinard, "The American Dream," *Literary History of the United States,* edd. Robert E. Spiller, Willard Thorp, *et al.* (New York, 1955), p. 192. The imprecision often associated with nomenclature in this matter may be seen in the following commentary: "Our [American] margins were partly psychological, for we had an American Idea, or, as James Truslow Adams called it, an American Dream, which at most times commanded a deep if inarticulate fealty." Allan Nevins, "American Crises and American Leadership," in *Times of Trial: Great Crises in the American Past,* ed. Allan Nevins (New York, 1958), p. 19.
3. Tremaine McDowell, "The Great Experiment," *Literary History of the United States,* pp. 219–227.
4. Arthur Ekirch, *The Idea of Progress in America, 1815–1860* (New York, 1951), p. 36.
5. Frederic I. Carpenter, " 'The American Myth': Paradise (To Be) Regained," *PMLA,* 74 (December 1959), 599; see also *idem,* fn. 1. E. K. Brown pushes such American self-consciousness back to W. E. Channing in 1819 ("The National Idea," p. 133). Vague,

rather visceral celebrations had, of course, been part of the post-Revolutionary euphoria. The Connecticut—or Hartford—Wits, for example, had been part of that national adolescence.

6. Harold Laski, *American Democracy: A Commentary and Interpretation* (Cambridge, 1949); Arthur Schlesinger, Jr., *Orestes A. Brownson: A Pilgrim's Progress* (Boston, 1959); Perry Miller, *The Transcendentalists* (Cambridge, Mass., 1950); R. W. B. Lewis, *The American Adam* (Chicago, 1955); C. Carroll Hollis, "The Literary Criticism of Orestes Augustus Brownson" (1954 dissertation, University of Michigan); Russell Kirk, *The Conservative Mind* (New York, 1953).

7. Schlesinger, *Brownson*, pp. 293–294.

8. Daniel J. Boorstin, "We the People, In Quest of Ourselves," *New York Times Magazine* (April 26, 1959), p. 32. In his letter of resignation as Secretary of State, John Foster Dulles wrote that "I was brought up in the belief that this nation of ours was not merely a self-serving society, but was founded with a mission to help build a world where liberty and justice would prevail" (*Time*, April 29, 1959, p. 9).

9. Russell Kirk, "Two Facets of the New England Mind: Emerson and Brownson," *The Month*, 8, No. 4 N.S. (Oct. 1952), 212–213. Brownson's views should be of interest not only to modern conservatives such as Kirk and Dulles, but also to liberals like former Senator Eugene McCarthy who has suggested that the conservative antipathy to government activity stems from the American idea of the innocence of man and the corruption of society (see Eugene McCarthy, *Frontiers in American Democracy* [New York, 1960]).

10. Very often it is not safe to make general paraphrases of Brownson's thought. His reasoning at times is close and tightly woven, however prolix his rhetorical style; his phrasing on occasion is, in a sense, idiosyncratic. Words like "democracy" or "progress," for instance, are carefully delimited, and have the meaning assigned to them by their author, rather than a looser or more popular meaning. On this difficulty see Theodore Maynard's suggestion in his *Orestes Brownson* (New York, 1943), pp. 442–453.

11. Cited in Schlesinger, *Brownson*, p. 296.

12. *Ibid.*, pp. 296–297. See also *ibid.*, pp. 190–194, and *passim*; Maynard, *Brownson*, pp. ix–xiv.

13. See the dissertation (Fordham, 1960) by Leonard McCarthy, "Rhetoric in the Works of Orestes Brownson," pp. 92–95.

14. Chinard, "The American Dream," pp. 192–215.

15. The classical statement of the importance of the frontier to American institutions is, of course, that of Frederick Jackson Turner, *The Frontier in American Life* (New York, 1920).

16. Ralph Henry Gabriel, *The Course of American Democratic Thought* (New York, 1956), pp. 22–23.

17. Charles A. Beard, "Introduction" to John B. Bury, *The Idea of Progress: An Inquiry Into its Origin and Growth* (New York,

1932), p. xi. See also Charles A. Beard, *A Century of Progress* (New York, 1933), p. 3; Carl Becker, *Progress and Power* (Stanford, Calif., 1936), p. 2; Carl Becker, *The Heavenly City of the Eighteenth Century Philosophers* (New Haven, 1932), p. 139; Kingsley Martin, *French Liberal Thought in the Eighteenth Century*, ed. J. P. Mayer (London, 1954), p. 299; Jacob Salwyn Schapiro, *Condorcet and the Rise of Liberalism* (New York, 1934), p. 238.

18. Beard, *Century of Progress*, p. 3.

19. *The Idea of Progress* (Oxford, 1920), pp. 3–7. To say as does George Malone that the idea of Progress was practically the "Weltgeist" (*The True Church: A Study of the Apologetics of Orestes Brownson* [Mundelein, Ill., 1957], p. 62) is, of course, to overstate the case. The Orient has been singularly free of the notion of Progress until recently. This may have been in part true because the rational philosophy of Descartes and Bacon, germinal to the idea as Bury points out, was anathema to the ruling Oriental philosophies.

20. *Progress*, p. 6. Others trace the Idea back to more primitive times. See A. Ekirch, *The Idea of Progress*, p. 12 n. 3.

21. Bury, *Progress*, p. 8.

22. *Ibid.*, p. 24. Bury argues earlier that the process of progress "must not be at the mercy of any external will," i.e., external to the "psychical and social nature of man." Otherwise, "the idea of Progress would lapse into the idea of Providence" (p. 5).

23. *The End of the Modern World*, p. 33. Generally speaking, this may be true. But there is another side to the question. See Walter J. Ong, *Frontiers in American Catholicism* (New York, 1957), pp. 61–64.

24. Bury, *Progress*, p. 29.

25. *Ibid.*, p. 30.

26. For Bury, Cartesianism in short meant the "supremacy of the human reason, progressive enlightenment, the value of this life for its own sake, and the standard of utility" (*ibid.*, p. 140). See also Ekirch, *Progress*, p. 12.

27. *Ibid.*, p. 98. Fontenelle was, of course, involved in the important controversy of Ancients and Moderns. See Bury, *Progress*, pp. 119–126.

28. *Ibid.*, p. 118; p. 129.

29. *Ibid.*, p. 129; p. 137; p. 143.

30. *Ibid.*, p. 141.

31. Ekirch, *Progress*, p. 11; Martin, *French Liberal Thought*, pp. 278–279.

32. Schapiro says of Condorcet's *Esquisse d'un Tableau historique des progrès de l'esprit humain* that "no other volume, produced in eighteenth century France, presents so faithfully the views of man and of the world held by the philosophes." Elsewhere, he cites Benedetto Croce's comment that the *Esquisse* was "the last will and testament of the eighteenth century" (Schapiro, *Condorcet*, pp.

259–260; p. 306 n. 71). See also Ekirch, *Progress*, pp. 14–17; Bury, *Progress*, pp. 282 ff.; Martin, *French Liberal Thought*, pp. 286–294; Chinard, "American Dream," p. 197.

33. For Condorcet's influence upon the English Utilitarians, on Saint-Simon and Comte, see Schapiro, *Condorcet*, pp. 262–263.

34. Bury, *Progress*, p. 279.

35. Ekirch, *Progress*, pp. 139–140. Other French philosophers of importance both to the development of the idea of progress and to the American Dream are Victor Cousin (Ekirch, *Progress*, pp. 21–22), Guizot (*ibid.*, pp. 22–23), and Pierre Leroux (Bury, *Progress*, pp. 319ff.). All these men, and, of course, Saint-Simon, directly influenced Orestes Brownson.

36. See *supra*, n. 4.

37. Becker, *Century of Progress*, p. 3.

38. "It was more especially in France . . . that the doctrine of progress, of perfectibility became an essential article of faith in 'the new religion of humanity'" (Becker, *Heavenly City*, p. 139).

39. This, according to Bury, is impossible; the difficulty points up the extraordinary capacity of optimism often to recur to first principles without probing them. And, as had been said elsewhere, the American people, certainly in this respect, were optimistic.

40. Ekirch, *Progress*, p. 267.

41. This judgment is verified by Walter Ong. "In a certain sense," he writes, "this optimism is America. It is both a cause and a product of that very real state of mind which students of American literature call 'the American dream'" (*Frontiers*, p. 12).

42. *Progress and Power*, p. 2.

43. Merle Curti, *The Growth of American Thought* (New York, 1943), pp. 104–106.

44. G. Harrison Orians, "The Rise of Romanticism, 1805–1855," *Transitions in American Literary History*, ed. Harry Hayden Clark (Durham, N.C., 1953), p. 190.

45. Italics mine.

46. Martin, *French Liberal Thought*, pp. 280–281. An "ultimate perfection," according to Condorcet and others, would be achieved chiefly through education (*ibid.*, p. 291).

47. This concept of a kind of autotelic theology may seem an exaggeration. It did not seem so to a competent observer in 1844. Reviewing Frederick H. Hedge's *Conservatism and Reform*, Orestes Brownson accused Transcendentalism of attempting to spin "even God himself out of the human soul, as the spider spins its web out of its own bowels" (*Brownson's Quarterly Review*, I, 1 [1844], 136). "Germanicus" Hedge was, of course, one of the original members of the Transcendental Club. *Brownson's Quarterly Review* will be referred to in these footnotes as BrQR; the earlier *Boston Quarterly Review*, as BQR. The footnote format adopted for both journals seems to give the simplest and clearest reference to Brownson's work. Brownson's journalistic method renders clumsy and prolix

the usual type of periodical citation. The number of citations necessary in this book, the awkwardness of giving specific titles to some
material untitled in the original, and the similarity (even sameness)
of certain titles in different years, are some of the problems involved.
The method adopted in this book follows in general the lead of
George Malone, the first of Brownson's commentators to bring together in a clear fashion both a citation of the original work in
the *Reviews* and the corresponding information in *Works*. See
Malone, *The True Church*, pp. 5–6.

48. Martin, *French Liberal Thought*, p. 299.
49. Beard, *Century*, p. 4.
50. See Ekirch, *Progress*, *passim*, for such comments by ministers and
    politicians.
51. For Thomas Paine's curious attitude, see V. E. Gibbens, "Tom Paine
    and the Idea of Progress," *Pennsylvania Magazine of History and
    Biography*, 66, No. 2 (April 1842), 202.
52. Beard, *Century*, p. 36.
53. Becker, *Heavenly City*, p. 118.
54. This is especially true of the French thinkers (*ibid.*, p. 140).
55. Schapiro, *Condorcet*, p. 270.
56. Gabriel, *American Thought*, p. 39. This commentator also lists five
    parallels between the democratic faith and Protestant Christianity
    (p. 38).
57. *Ibid.*, p. 38.
58. *Heavenly City*, p. 31. Kingsley Martin agrees; he calls the French
    Revolution "a religious revival" (*French Liberal Thought*, p. 278).
    For the relation of the French Revolution to medieval thought,
    see *ibid.*, pp. 277–278.
59. James Playsted Wood, *Magazines in the United States* (New York,
    1956), pp. 44–68. Wood seems not be aware either of the *BQR*
    or, later, *BrQR*, perhaps because as he notes on page 61: "circulation
    is a primary index of a periodical's strength." Yet he properly praises
    the *North American Review* as "a publication of real power and
    influence because it was read and studied by the leading men of
    the country"; however, he says in the same place that it "never
    had a large circulation" (p. 46). These words might apply, then,
    also to the cited *Quarterly Reviews*. Ray Allen Billington says of
    BrQR that it was "widely circulated" at least in the period
    1850–1854 (*The Protestant Crusade, 1800–1860* [New York,
    1938], p. 290). Wood's history is deficient in its unhappy exemption
    of Brownson's quarterlies from importance. See also Arthur A.
    Schlesinger, Jr., *The Age of Jackson* (Boston, 1945), pp. 369–373,
    for a comparison between the excellencies of the *North American
    Review* and Brownson's quarterlies.
60. Harold Laski, *American Democracy*, p. 664. The comment is pri-
    marily directed to the *BQR*. For a publishing history of both quarter-
    lies see Frank Luther Mott, *A History of American Magazines* (New
    York, 1938) I, p. 685 n. 1.

61. Laski, *American Democracy,* p. 664. He indicates by inference the parallel importance of *BrQR* (pp. 269–270).
62. Ekirch, *Progress,* p. 172. The classification of Brownson as a "religious writer" is hardly apt in a strict sense prior to 1844. *BrQR* had that stated purpose; the earlier periodical did not.
63. Lewis, *The American Adam,* p. 2. With regard precisely to this whole area is involved what Lewis calls the "Adamic myth." For Lewis' recognition of Brownson's importance, see *ibid.,* pp. 174–193 and *passim.*
64. "Brownson's Search for the Kingdom of God: The Social Thought of an American Radical," *Review of Politics,* 16 (1954), 26.
65. Randall Stewart, *American Literature and Christian Doctrine* (Baton Rouge, 1958), pp. 128–129.
66. Since there seems little need for a greatly detailed biography here, only the most pertinent details will be given. Although there is no really definitive biography of Brownson, there are good biographical studies. Apart from the works by Schlesinger and Maynard already cited, there is the three-volume work by Henry F. Brownson, *Life of Orestes Brownson* (Detroit, 1898–1901). Short sketches can be found in the already cited works of Malone and Hollis. The latter work also contains a helpful chronological table (pp. 1–2). Brownson's autobiography, *The Convert,* can be found in *The Works of Orestes Brownson,* ed. Henry F. Brownson (Detroit, 1884), v, 1–200. (These volumes will be hereafter cited as *Works.*)
67. Theodore Maynard has a complete genealogical table (*Brownson,* pp. 23–24 n. 8). Included here is the interesting note that "Bronson Alcott and Orestes Brownson had reason to believe themselves distantly related."
68. *Works,* v, 4.
69. Some of the books at his disposal were " 'the English classics of Queene Anne's reign, . . . 50 volumes of the English poets, with another work on *Universal History* [my italics], Locke's *Essay on the Human Understanding,* and Pope's *Homer* . . . various monographs of American history. . . . I devoured them all, but no book with more intense interest than the Bible' " (Orestes Brownson, cited in H. F. Brownson, *Brownson's Early Life,* p. 6). It may not be insignificant to call attention to the number of eighteenth-century works (especially of English poetry) which are included here.
70. His humility (warranted or not) in the face of what he occasionally thought to be his inadequacy in this matter is expressed in the draft of his letter to Victor Cousin in Paris, September 6, 1839 (the draft is in the Archives of the University of Notre Dame—hereafter cited as AUND).
71. *Works,* v, 19.
72. *Ibid.,* p. 20.
73. *Ibid.,* p. 31.
74. *Ibid.,* pp. 39–40.

75. *Ibid.,* pp. 43–44. The "creed" is cited in full on page 44. Article
I cited his belief that every human being should be honest; II, that
all should be benevolent and kind; III, that men had a right to
procure and a duty to help others to procure food, clothing, and
shelter; IV, that every man should cultivate his mind in order to
aid in improving the condition of the human race, and therefore,
human happiness. The final Article asserted that, acting on these
principles, men serve God in the best possible way and are most
acceptable to God. The bias here toward the social amelioration
of the race is patent.
76. *Works,* IV, 48; italics added.
77. The best and fullest treatment (together with Henry Brownson's)
of Brownson's early periodical labors from 1828 to 1838 will be
found in Chapter One of Hollis' work. See also Clarence Gohdes,
The Periodicals of American Transcendentalism (Durham, N.C.,
1931), pp. 38–82.
78. Godwin's influence was not only in matters of thought, but perhaps
also in style. I have seen little made of Brownson's 1857 statement:
that Godwin's book is "one of the most remarkable works in our
language. . . . I think it has had more influence on my mind than
any other book except the Scriptures, I have ever read." Brownson
implies his own study of Godwin's style; he praises it highly, and
says that Godwin "is almost the only English writer, since Burke's
unhappy influence on the language, who has written truly classical
English . . ." (*Works,* V, 50–51). This opinion, it must be repeated, was given in 1857.
79. *Ibid.,* p. 67.
80. *Ibid.,* p. 62.
81. *Ibid.,* p. 63.
82. *Idem.*
83. *Ibid.,* p. 65.
84. Henry F. Brownson suggests that it was his father who "roused
Thoreau's enthusiasm for external nature" (*Early Life,* p. 204).
See Thoreau's letter to Brownson, December 30, 1837, in *Early
Life,* pp. 204–206. The original of the letter is preserved in AUND.
There is confirmation of this influence upon Thoreau in M. J.
Harson, "Orestes A. Brownson, LL.D., 'A Man of Courage and a
Great American'," *Catholic World,* 79 (April 1904). Yet Kenneth
Cameron feels that, although Brownson did exert some lasting influ-
ence upon Thoreau, Henry Brownson's claim is an "extravagant"
assumption (p. 54). Both Harson and Cameron cite Amos Perry,
a Harvard classmate of Thoreau's, in their separate arguments. See
Kenneth W. Cameron, "Thoreau and Orestes Brownson," *Emerson
Society Quarterly,* 51 (1968), 53–74.
85. *Works,* V, 74. During this period Brownson's thought had come
under the influence of Benjamin Constant whose major idea was
that, though the individual man has a moral sentiment natural to
him, the external expressions of that sentiment—as symbolized by

institutional forms—change as his intelligence advances. "This theory of the progress of religion corresponded with my theory of the progress of mankind," wrote Brownson (*Works*, v, 73). The discussion of Constant's influence will be found in *The Convert, ibid.*, pp. 71–75.

86. *Ibid.*, p. 83.
87. See *Works*, IV, 1–56. As late as 1842 Brownson felt that *New Views* was "upon the whole, the most genuine statement of our whole thought . . . that we have made" (*BQR*, v, 1 [1842], 1).
88. *Works*, IV, 4.
89. *Ibid.*, p. 10. Brownson's criticism of the Catholic Church as tending to "exclusive spiritualism" was an idea he had found, as he said, in Heinrich Heine and the Saint-Simonians. See *Works*, v, 86.
90. *Works*, IV, 21.
91. *Ibid.*, p. 25.
92. The Biblical imagery surrounding this oblique statement is significant: the "Adamic myth," the cult of the New Sion, the general relevance of Christian fundamentalism of a Calvinistic persuasion, are indivisible from the American Dream.
93. *Works*, IV, 25. See Chapter One of R. W. B. Lewis' *American Adam*.
94. Brownson's perspective led him to see a decline in optimism. If decline there was, it was momentary, partial, and minor.
95. *Works*, IV, 32.
96. *Ibid.*, pp. 33–40. Calvinism, interestingly enough, was for Brownson here merely "a continuation of Catholicism" (p. 36).
97. Cousin's dictum as interpreted by Brownson: "All systems of philosophy are true in what they affirm; false only in what they deny, or only in that they are exclusive" (*The Convert, Works*, v, 85). In the same place Brownson went on to say that he had applied this formula to religion "with Leibnitz, though I knew not then that Leibnitz had so concluded, that all sects are right in what they affirm, false in what they deny or exclude." It might be noted also that, according to Bury, Cousin's philosophy was "in the main . . . Hegelian" (*Idea of Progress*, p. 271). The form of Brownson's argument here—the accommodation of contrariety through means of a third term—has significant progenitors.
98. Brownson noted at this point that the coming-together may already have taken place in Germany "in the movement commenced by Herder, but best represented by Schleiermacher" (*Works*, IV, 44–45).
99. See H. F. Brownson's editorial note, *Works*, IV, 45. The importance of William Ellery Channing must be recognized as having provided what Brownson called the "synthesis of eclecticism and inspiration."
100. *Ibid.*, p. 47.
101. *Ibid.*, pp. 48–50.
102. *Ibid.*, p. 49.
103. "This capacity for progress though it be the occasion of error and sin, is that which makes us moral beings" (*ibid.*, pp. 51–52).

104. *Ibid.,* p. 54.
105. *Ibid.,* p. 55.
106. See George Ripley, "Brownson's Writings," *The Dial,* 1 (1840), 27–28.
107. This was still his explicit faith in 1839. See the draft of his letter to Cousin, September 6, 1839, AUND.
108. The period before Brownson's conversion (i.e., prior to 1844) is usually described as a "liberal" period. This term—like "conservative"—is a slippery one: compared to Robert Dale Owen and Frances Wright, Brownson in *New Views* was almost reactionary.
109. Schlesinger, *Brownson,* p. 55.
110. *The Convert, Works,* v, 87.

2

BOSTON QUARTERLY REVIEW, 1838-1840

THE UNRESOLVED SPIRITUAL CONFLICT of the 1830s in New England had left its mark upon Orestes Brownson quite as much as he himself had impressed indelibly his character upon it. Although one of the original members of the Transcendental Club (he had attended its second meeting), he could never quite convince its more "transcendentalist" members such as Emerson, or its more exotic members, notably Margaret Fuller or Bronson Alcott, that radicalism in religion must transpose itself successfully into practical life. Perhaps this failure came about because Brownson's weapon most often was the discursive intellect, and theirs was not. In any event, they would and did agree in principle: Fuller and Emerson made frequent appearances at the later Brook Farm, and were, successively, editors of *The Dial*. But to Emerson, Brook Farm was "the age of reason in a patty pan"; to Margaret Fuller, a forum for her "conversations." Bronson Alcott tried to achieve the practical application of the ideal, at both Brook Farm and Fruitlands, but Orphic sayings plowed no furrows, and the stubborn logic of the ledger book doomed both experiments. Even the most practical of the Transcendentalists, as Hawthorne saw, never clearly made the transition from ideal to real, and it is merely ironic that when Brook Farm went up in smoke, the immediate victim was the phalanstery, that awkward symbol of the severely logical but highly impractical theory of social planning advanced by Charles Fourier.

Brownson saw this earlier than Hawthorne, though both were for a time enthusiastic supporters of the new group. What had appealed to Brownson originally was the emphasis which Transcendentalism had placed upon the interior sentiment as opposed to logical deduction in the ascertainment of the bases of religion and morality.[1] That this view itself formed one of the bases of the revolt against Unitarianism seems beyond question. In 1836, indeed, Brownson had, according to Hollis, come "as near to taking over the New England group . . . as he ever would. . . . He was really the only leader the new group had in 1836 . . . [for] he had caught the democratic upsurge of the era, and strained zealously to idealize and christianize it."[2] Yet Brownson could not hold this position; his association with political "radicals" hardly endeared him to New England, especially to its educated upper classes, even though his accent upon the new political spirit had the support of both William Ellery Channing and George Ripley. It is clear to Hollis at least that, from this high point, Brownson gradually declined in immediate influence upon the Boston circle, since, precisely because his religious radicalism impinged upon his passion for social amelioration and political reform, he "had lost the audience he most prized, the new thinkers."[3] What might save the situation was a journal of his own which, without the understandable but irksome editorial censorship of the doctrinaire *Christian Examiner,* or the impossible guidance of the deeply conservative *North American Review,* or which, minus the uneasy ultra-Jacksonian reputation of the *Boston Reformer,* might re-establish contact between Brownson's mind, and the New England elite whose assent and influence he sought. With Bancroft's aid, he was granted the sinecure which provided the economic protection which allowed Brownson to risk the publishing of his own journal.

In an early letter of a correspondence which would later (1843) ripen into editorial association, John L. O'Sullivan, editor of the projected *United States Magazine and Democratic Review,* wrote to Brownson and, after detailing his plan for the magazine, cited approvingly the words Brownson himself had written to O'Sullivan earlier: "thinking men to write freely from their own rich minds and free hearts."[4] The words might have formed a motto for the *Boston Quarterly Review.*

Begun, as its editor wrote, "with the hope of contributing something to the moral pleasure and social progress of my countrymen,"[5] the *Boston Quarterly Review* was the product not of the urging of friends (who had argued against such a publication) but of an "inner voice" which Brownson felt he could not disobey. Seeking to solve the problem of the destiny of man and of society by thinking for himself, Brownson believed himself to be in a minority; yet his views, he decided, were worth consideration by others. His naked thoughts were, like Milton's, demanding to be out, and "hold my peace I cannot."[6] He undertook the *Review,* he averred, for himself, and for all those who had ears to hear; while he no longer felt as once he did that as a reformer, "a bold Innovator," he had had infallible solutions to the problems of mankind, yet he felt it a value for ideas to be exchanged, and his own not unworthy of consideration in the intellectual marketplace. A partisan of no organized group of any kind, he was interested in advancing the "Great Movement" of Jesus of Nazareth, "whether it be effecting a reform in the Church, giving us a purer and more rational theology; in philosophy seeking something profounder . . . than . . . heartless Sensualism . . . ; or whether in society demanding the elevation of labor with the Loco foco, or the freedom of the slave with the abolitionist,[7] I own I sympathize . . . [with] the progress of Humanity wherever I see it."[8] This was to be Brownson's review—a term he used since it "is indefinite and allows me to discourse on any thing I please";[9] it would be forthright, free, and "open to the discussion of all subjects of general and permanent interest by any one who is able to express his thoughts—providing he has any—with spirit, in good temper, and in good taste."[10] Brownson, a thinking man, would write freely from his own rich mind and full heart.

Central to his thought—indeed, serving as a theme for the early issues of the *Review*—was the American Idea, of which, unquestionably, Brownson was enamored. Whether in his own essays or in those few which he accepted for publication from such men as W. E. Channing[11] or George Bancroft,[12] the theme reappears constantly, played in the major key of progress with a crowning harmony of such instruments as democracy, liberalism, literature, and education. Even Christianity, conceived as an idea rather than as an institution, and yoked to democracy, is made to contribute to the nationalistic fugue of Brownson's vision.[13] Whether the accent be placed upon the dream, or the more practical aspects of the idea, or upon the notion of mission, the complex is seldom far from the thoughts of the editor, and is reiterated to the point of extraordinary emphasis.

One difficulty ought to be examined at this point. The extent of Brownson's "conservatism" in this his early "liberal" period has been generally hurried over, although it has called forth an occasional brief mention.[14] The result has been that the pre-1841 Brownson has been seen as "an American Marxist before Marx" in Schlesinger's unfortunate phrase,[15] chiefly because his "Laboring Classes" essays of 1840 tend to become the early paradigm of Brownson's thought. They are not. Hollis suggests that a reappraisal "is demanded by the evidence."[16] And that evidence, it seems, goes quite beyond a thin but perduring conservatism in religious philosophy, and indeed serves, though its author seems unaware of it, to strengthen R. W. B. Lewis' more or less original contention that tradition and a sense of continuity was exerting a strong influence upon Brownson in the early 1840s.[17] The point here is that his double sense did *not* originate after the "Laboring Classes" essays of 1840.

America, Brownson had said in *New Views,* was to be a nation of philosophers. The first issue of the *Boston Quarterly Review,* in an article laying the groundwork for a series of articles on metaphysics, allowed Brownson to make this early summary statement:

We Young Americans, who have the future glory of our country and of Humanity at heart, who would see our country taking the lead in modern civilization, and becoming as eminent for her literature, art, science, and philosophy, as she now is for her industrial activity and enterprise, must ever bear in mind the greatness and sanctity of our mission. We must set an example worthy of being followed by the world. We must feel the dignity and immense reach of the work to which we are called . . . in our love of truth, and in our sympathy with Humanity in all its forms. A great and glorious work is given us; may we be equal to it, and worthy of achieving it.[18]

Again, in reviewing the first issue of the *United States Magazine and Democratic Review,* Brownson insisted that a country's literature cannot be national and, therefore, of value, unless it is "*informed* with the national soul . . . the Great Idea of the nation."[19] America's national soul is "democracy, the equal rights and worth of every man, as man. This is the American Idea."[20] If any American writer rejected the Idea, whatever else his qualities, he would not be an *American* writer. "This Idea is the only element of life that American literature can possess."[21] That this democratic spirit must be united with a Christian one "is a great and kindling truth"[22]—and one which recognizes the extension of the Idea into the religious area. The American Experiment, therefore, Brownson added, is

Christian and democratic, as was the Mission. It was a serious work, and Americans must be a serious people.[23]

According to Brownson in 1838, the American nation had been founded by men who from the first moment of their dream had "fermenting in them their dominant idea . . . , freedom."[24] This liberty, as shown by the history of American institutions,[25] had grown naturally, since the growth of a nation was merely the natural unfolding of the idea with which it had begun its career. The institutions of a nation seldom if ever received a new idea: original ideas merely develop,[26] and every nation had an original idea peculiar to it. America is "the country in which the noble ideas of man and society, which French and German scholars strike out in their speculations, are to be first applied to practice, realized in institutions."[27] These works and this experimentation were precisely for "us young Americans, to quicken within us a sense of the dignity and reach of our mission . . . and to enable us to elaborate the glorious future which awaits mankind."[28] Progress was the irresistible law for Americans: "this republic shall yet prove itself the medium through which the human race shall rise to the knowledge and enjoyment of the inalienable rights of Man."[29]

In his review of Emerson's Oration before the Literary Societies of Dartmouth College,[30] Brownson saw the American mind as original, independent, creative both in the formation of its political institutions and in the general practical cast which progress had taken in this country. He looked more favorably now than heretofore upon the "business habits of our country men, and [sought] to declaim less and less against their money-getting propensities."[31] These drives, he now believed, were a blessing of God, for this material emphasis was indispensable to the progress of the American experiment. The earnest merchant—"the soul of the chivalric knight is in him"[32]—was acting out through his endeavors the spirit of the age, and giving more service to Humanity than ever the warrior-prince, so honored by the literary elite, had performed.

In this same article Brownson saw much hope for the American Idea in the general excellence of the periodical press to which he gives extravagant praise, indeed.[33] What is necessary is to have both scholars and men of practical affairs "engage heart and soul in the great American work . . . a great work, a glorious work to be done."[34]

The same issue (January, 1839) contained an attack upon Locke's philosophy, which, it is argued, disinherited the mass by its fatal and insidious attack on liberty. Men who had no inherent power to attain truth were not free. Therefore, Locke destroyed all "free actions of the mind, all independent thought, all progress." The social contract was no answer, for "its Magna Charta is preserved in the archives of the state, not engraven on the heart . . . of man." Democracy, then, became an illusion and, in fact, an "attempt against nature." A Lockian, in consequence, could never trust the people, the masses; he must "labor to concentrate all power in the hands of . . . the enlightened and respectable few." This attitude placed in jeopardy the American Experiment. And the argument closed with an indictment of Harvard for its use of Locke as a required text. Harvard had a duty to the American Idea.[35]

Before he completed his January, 1839, issue, Brownson named the party of Jackson as the party of progress marching toward the establishment of the kingdom of God on earth.[36] "Ideas are omnipotent; bring out the true idea, it will choose the leader, and organize the party. . . . Adhere to the democratic idea . . . a sacred course . . . dear to Humanity. . . . [The Democratic party] may rest assured of complete success, for the world is under the government of justice, not of iniquity."[37] By January, 1839, then, the Democratic party had become for Brownson explicitly the practical, political vehicle for the realization of the American Idea.[38]

The last important statement of the American Idea in the years prior to 1840 was given in the number of the *Quarterly Review* for October, 1839. The Democratic party, "the American party," the party of Christianity and progress,

gathers round the idea, which it is the mission of American institutions to realize. The idea, which lies at the bottom of our institutions, is the supremacy of Man. Here [in America] is to be established and developed not the sovereignty of the sacerdocy, . . . of the city or state, . . . of the king, . . . of the noble few, the high-born . . . the rich, . . . of estates, or corporations, but the sovereignty of Man. Here man is not made for the state, but the state is instituted for man. The order of civilization which it is ours to develop, is an order of civilization in which things are subordinate, and subservient to Humanity. Humanity in all its integrity is in every individual man. Then every individual man is to be raised to empire. . . . This is the American Idea. This idea in the political world is translated by universal suffrage, that is, the equal right of every man to his voice in the choice of political agents, and through them in the laws, which shall be enacted, or governmental measures which shall be adopted. . . . The Democratic party is the Christian party . . . the party of liberty . . . the American party. The idea of this country is, we have said, the supremacy of Man. This supremacy is attained only by the broadest freedom. The American idea, under another aspect then, is that of liberty. The democratic party is the Christian party.[39]

The essayist then repeated a favorite idea: a political party, like a nation, was built from one major seminal idea; it could not receive a new one. The great idea of the Democratic party had two aspects: the supremacy of man; the reign of Eternal Justice. The mission of the party was to "unfold the great idea of Justice, and reduce it to practice in all man's social and political relations. It stands, therefore, not as the representative of a fraction of the race, but of the race itself, and, therefore, like the race is immortal."[40]

To Brownson's mind this was clearly the way of Progress; the party was to be its instrument. "Progress is simply the better and fuller application of Justice to our social and political relations. All the progress, which in the very nature of things now can be, must come from the unfolding of the idea which constitutes the life and soul of the democratic party."[41]

Brownson's faith, then, was that the American Dream had formed into the practical Experiment. That Experiment would have as its concrete instrument the Democratic party, the party of Jackson. As the American nation could be healthy and thriving only by the enfolding of its own Great Idea, so, too, its instrument—the specific party which, as has been noted, stood not for the fraction but for the whole—must likewise work out its grand idea. This was the way of progress and, to use George Bancroft's phrase, of Eternal Justice ruling through the People. The components of Brownson's faith prior to 1840 were four: Progress was the law, Justice the end, Humanity (the race) the beneficiary, and the Democratic party the agent.

The specific form of governmental organization upon which the Experiment depended, however, also received much thought and treatment from Brownson in these early issues. He seemed to be hurrying toward some essential connection between the needs of Humanity, a word used in the most vague sense, the promise of democracy, and the cloak of a misty if not mystic Christianity over both.

We have already seen the interest in furtherance of the movement of Jesus of Nazareth which Brownson evinced in his Introductory Statement. And very early in his *Review*—in the fourth article to be precise—he began his examination of democracy. This was followed by a close look at the social and political aspects of Christianity, and then by a study of the links between the two.

Dismissing other possible definitions of democracy,[42] he settled upon the work "taken as the name of a great social and political doctrine . . . and of a powerful movement of the masses towards a better social condition. . . . A democrat [thus] . . . is rather a philosophical than a party democrat. He takes the word [Democracy] in a broad philosophical sense."[43] This was the sense in which the *Review* would advocate democracy, and, since the "philosophical doctrine" is as yet little more than vague sentiment, those grounds would be examined upon which democracy as a true governmental concept could be persuasively legitimated.

Brownson began with a discussion of the power of sovereignty in the democratic state by which he meant "that which is highest, ultimate, which has not only the physical force to make itself obeyed, but the moral right to command whatever it pleases. The right to command involves the corresponding duty of obedience. What the sovereign can command, it is the duty of the subject to obey."[44] If such sovereignty was to be vested in the people taken collectively, or in the majority, then the people taken collectively could demand absolute obedience of either the individual or the minority. Those who obey, then, were slaves. The freedom involved was freedom for the state only, for the individual or the minority would be disenfranchised. Further, since, logically, the interpretations of justice, truth, wisdom, and virtue would be subject to majority interpretation, then this interpretation could in the same way be forced upon the minority. A situation of this sort, the editor continued, was unconscionable because the rights of every man (including that of liberty) were not grants from a majority, but belong to the individual inasmuch as he was a man.[45]

Yet sovereignty did reside somewhere: people considered as a state or as individuals were under law and were accountable to a higher authority. That authority could not be resident in a man (e.g., a king), or in an aristocracy, since these were men, and were themselves bound by a higher Authority. Therefore, "the Sovereign of Sovereigns, the king of kings, the lord of lords, the supreme law of the people and of the individual" is Justice,[46] and the sovereignty of Justice "is what we understand by the doctrine of democracy."[47]

This judgment was made of sovereignty considered absolutely. Considered relatively, since high civil and political power is needed for order in the state, the necessary authority was delegated through Justice to the state, a grant which could not ever be stretched beyond the object of the delegation. For, if that should occur, proper resistance by the individual was "neither unjust in itself, nor inconsistent with social order."[48]

This limited or relative sovereignty, Brownson continued, was best vested in the people, rather than in a king, an aristocracy, or a theocracy, because government tended to be administered for the good of the governors. It was, however, important to remember that the people as individuals must be guarded against the people as the state.[49] But the sense of legitimacy of the limited sovereign was indispensable to social order and political stability.

True democracy, then, 1) denied absolute sovereignty to the state; 2) asserted it for Justice, which is but "the political phasis [*sic*] of God . . . identical with God."[50] Thus, in asserting Justice, the democrat must assert God, a truth which Brownson, following his current eclectic fashion, had derived from theocracy. From the aristocratic ideal, the truth was gleaned that there were "God-patented nobles," i.e., especially capable men who were "natural chiefs of the people, and these men ought to govern" for these were men in whom God dwelled "in the greatest perfection."[51]

Freedom in a democracy, therefore, was the right and duty to act in accordance with the demands of Sovereign Justice. Since the great political problem of the epoch was the determination of boundary as between the duties and rights of the state, and of the individual, the moralist's mission was to aid in this adjudication, and "it is to our country that we must look for constitutional government in the worthiest sense of that word."[52]

In conclusion, Brownson repeated the idea that individual rights *are* rights, not grants or sufferances, but rights whose root was in God. Using the Pythagorean phrase, he concluded that "MAN MEASURES MAN THE WORLD OVER."[53]

In the second number of the *Quarterly Review*, the editor began his discussion of Christianity and of its relation to the democratic movement. Jesus, he wrote, was not God but man; the "Christ" he defined as "pure disinterested *Love*."[54] Jesus' originality was that as the son of Man his love was universal, a love of Humanity, and this love was not "mere piety, nor patriotism, nor friendship, but it was PHILANTHROPY."[55] His work was to bring together all mankind in Christ (i.e., Love), and weld all members of the human family into the unity of the spirit of Love. This, Brownson argued, was a new, a unique concept, found in no prior civilization, Oriental or Occidental; it was, in fact, that "which constitutes the originality and peculiarity of the Christian movement"[56]—i.e., that Christianity sheds over piety, art, science, philosophy, and patriotism "a pure light . . . a freer, richer sentiment, to make them all harmonize with, and contribute to the freest and fullest development of human nature, man's highest possible perfection."[57] Christianity's point of departure and point of arrival was the same: the love of man as man.

Therefore, all who labored for this same end showed forth more or less the Christ dwelling in them;[58] the American mission consequently became the Christian melioration of man's lot *in this world*,[59] and, to achieve this, there was need to enlist all powers of man and all his activities in the service of the democratic ideal.

Brownson pointed out that in America it was a "pretense" that the current government was a Christian[60] one and that American commonwealths were Christian commonwealths. Such, indeed, had not been the design of the founding fathers. A sense of liberty deriving from their notion of Justice had been their dominant idea, and this gave shape to the concept of a free commonwealth. "They may not have fully possessed their idea, they may not have generalized it to the extent that it will bear, but . . . they had it from the first moment fermenting in them."[61] To the fathers Justice *was* Christianity—that is, their theology and church polity—and their mistake was that their "notions of Christian ethics" were taken "as their measure of natural right, instead of taking as we do, man's innate sense of natural right as the proper measure of Christian ethics."[62] Their disenfranchisement of others stemmed from this mistake. Yet their end, according to Brownson, was not a Christian monopoly, but a society founded upon their highest idea of Right. The history of American institutions proved that their highest concept was that of liberty, the seed of this nation.

Brownson then argued that the natural growth of a nation was merely, as we have seen, the natural unfolding of the idea with which it began. America's growth was the unfolding of that idea of liberty which was both implicit and explicit in its foundation. One type of government (e.g., theocracy) could not "grow" into another (e.g., democracy), until the old had been destroyed and the new replaced it. Had the Puritan fathers founded a theocracy, American government would have developed into a theocracy. It had not done so. The history of America "proves that freedom, not religion, is the dominant idea of our institutions."[63] And it followed, as Brownson saw it, that liberty of conscience was not only sacred in this country but the supreme law.

One may find a supporting argument in the *Boston Quarterly Review* for October, 1838. The natural association of the clergy and Christianity generally—as well as that of men of letters[64]—in America was with democracy, that is, if Christianity was considered here "merely in its social and political aspects, in its bearings upon man's earthly condition."[65]

Jesus had had a two-fold mission: 1) to make atonement for sin, and raise man to heaven; 2) to found a new order of things on earth. In this latter sense Christianity has a political and social character, and is concerned directly with this world. Then, depending heavily upon Félicité de Lamennais' *Paroles d'un croyant*,[66] Orestes Brownson accepted the tension existing between the two systems (the one supporting the doctrine of liberty; the other, the doctrine of absolutism), and felt that the destiny of man depended on the outcome. The world, he noted, still following de Lamennais, was progressive, and revolution was merely a sign of this fact.[67] Since Brownson believed that such upheavals are inevitable—Christianity itself had been the greatest of all revolutions—they must be directed to the development of a sense of justice. Christianity, which was the equality of all men before God, was the root of all Justice for Humanity. The religious equality which Christianity sponsored tended also to produce social and political equality, and to guarantee the direct object of all true society—namely, the protection of the liberty of conscience and of thought for all citizens. The cause of liberty, the people's cause, the cause of democracy, could be furthered simply by application of the logic inherent in Christian assumption. Yet the Christian clergy, ignorant and clasping feebly to outward modes, served the cause of absolutism.

In this connection, America, having achieved political equality, had gone beyond Europe, but, Brownson went on, there was not as yet social equality in the country. The Church, which was not merely a constabulary force, must aid in this work, or die. Above all, it must never defend the absolutist order. The ineluctable drive of progress was toward liberty; the people "pursue freedom as a Divinity, and freedom they will have,—with the Church if it may be, without the Church if it must be, [the Church] . . . *must preach democracy.*"[68] The clergy of all communions must associate with democracy and recall the Church to Christianity. If they did, the editor argued, they would meet the needs of Christianity, "make democracy an honor and not an accusation, give the people the powerful and hallowing support of the religious sentiment, baptize liberty in the font of holiness, and send her forth with a benediction to 'make a tour of the globe.' "[69]

Much in these views suggests what has indeed been the dominant critical opinion, that Brownson's revolutionary religious ideas were carried over into the order of political and social life. In fact, Brownson's early association with radical groups sustains the belief that even prior to July, 1840, Brownson was a radical in the denotative sense, and that "liberty" was his crutch as later it was to be his cross. While one can hardly deny the truth of much of this, it still remains true that Brownson was not just a melioristic Marat. For one thing his sense of Christianity, however amorphous his concept was, spared him that. For another, he was as complex a man, perhaps, as nineteenth-century America produced, and at any period of his life he cannot be summed up in such slippery terms as "liberal," "radical," "ultra," or even in the converse. Finally, with Brownson, there is always the problem of emphasis. A short consideration of the problems of writing a review practically single-handedly four times a year will show that time and care were two commodities which, in the nature of things, were luxuries.

For example, in the first two issues of the *Quarterly Review,* the primary accent is upon the radical changes necessary in society. Remembering that the problem of tension between order and liberty would plague him all his life,[70] one notes the secondary emphases which are, to say the least, conservative.[71] "The American people," wrote Brownson in the first issue of the *Review,* "are not revolutionists. They are conservative, and to be conservative in this country is to be a democrat."[72] Bold speculation does not necessarily live in easy wedlock with violent action; in fact, any precipitate conduct would "promote violence, bloodshed, or suffering." He argues for

"orderly and peaceful measures. . . . We must not dream of introducing change all at once."[73] Men should speculate freely and speak
boldly,

but let the men of action who have more enthusiasm than reflection,
greater hearts than minds, and stronger hands than heads, guard against
impatience. . . . Our principle is, no revolution, no destruction, but
progress. . . . Let [the truth] be uttered . . . it will [prevail]. . . . We
hold ourselves among the foremost who demand reform, and who would
live and die for progress, but we wish . . . no violence in pulling down
old institutions, or in building up new ones. . . . In action we would
cling to the old usages and keep by old lines of policy, till we are
fairly forced by the onward pressure of opinion to abandon them. We
would think with the Radical, but often act with the conservative.[74]

Here spoke no wild-eyed *sans-culotte*.

Brownson's praise of John Quincy Adams is in point,[75] as are
his arguments on the subject of slavery. For here, fearing a trend
toward a centralization of power (however "liberal" that appeared,
or appears), he felt that the North tended to submerge the individual
in the state, since the unreflecting masses were being directed by
power in a few hands. He feared that "the individual from an
integer may become a mere fraction of the body politic."[76] Therefore,
it seemed to him that the South provided "a salutary check, which
arose from the insistence there upon "the individual importance
which each man possesses in consequence of being himself a sort
of petty sovereign."[77] The South, in consequence, was the defender
of individual freedom; the North, of social freedom. Though both
were necessary, the latter demanded a strong government, the
former, a strong people. To destroy this national poise would be
to endanger not only the Union, but liberty itself. And the individuality of the South "is the effect of the institution of slavery."[78]
The northern demand for associations, corporations, societies, part-
nerships, was demanded by commercial and manufacturing pursuits.[79] But their proliferation constituted a danger to individual
liberty, for, as Brownson wrote in his essay on James Fenimore
Cooper's *American Democrat,* "Power has a perpetual tendency to
extend itself."[80]

Brownson warned against rash speculation, and voiced his regret
about departing from the "faith of our fathers";[81] he rebuked those
who in the name of liberty made attacks upon the "cherished sentiments of the community";[82] and, speaking of those "who can see

nothing to venerate in [their] forefathers, and who [bow] not before the wisdom of antiquity," he continued

Progress there may be, and there is; but no man can advance far on his predecessors,—never so far that they shall sensibly diminish in the distance. These arrogant reformers with the tithe of an idea, who speak to us as if they had outgrown all the past, and grasped and made present the whole future. . . . The more we do really advance, the more shall we be struck with the greatness of those who went before us, and the more sincere and deep will be our reverence for antiquity. The darkness we ascribe to remote ages is often the darkness of our own minds, and the ignorance we complain of . . . may be only the reflex of our own. Progress we should labor for, progress we should delight in, but we should beware of underrating those who have placed us in the world. "There were giants in those days."[83]

Edmund Burke may never have put the case more cogently than this "pre-Marxian Marx."

The accent upon Orestes Brownson's "conservative" strain which has been placed here is not intended to deny the radical cast of by far the greater proportion of his views in the years 1838–1840.[84] Further, much of his conservative comment was designed to protect *American* institutions[85] which themselves were radical enough compared to the organization of European governments as a whole. Yet the conservative element, tenuous, perhaps, but always tough, which pervades the *Boston Quarterly Review* through these early years is even more impressive when one remembers that it was sustained during the period when Americans were still suffering the effects of the depression of 1837. This fact may not be ignored if one is to understand, first, the "Laboring Classes" essays in proper perspective; second, the gradual change (as it has been assumed) in his attitudes after 1840; third, the essays in the *United States Magazine and Democratic Review* during 1843, pieces which so alienated what passed for thoughtful radicals in America. It is significant that during the period of the *Boston Quarterly Review* Brownson's political thought came at least partially under the influence of the brooding, clean-cutting intelligence of John Caldwell Calhoun.[86]

By 1840 the American Idea was firmly fixed in Brownson's angle of vision. For America to him was already at the apex of man's advancing course: it was the spearhead which would pierce the future. The course was forward, always forward; qualitative advance was the destiny of man. Under the guidance of Justice, the God of the American Christian democrats,[87] progress was not alone an act of faith, but, upon the whole, a creed susceptible of historical proof. Moreover, the inevitable working-out of the democratic state-church, or church-state, the American experiment, guaranteed a coming social felicity which would make living flesh of the American Dream. Yet a *caveat* is never far from Brownson's lips. For part of his eclecticism was the great conviction of the value of tradition—however emotional his attachment at this time—and a stubborn *pietas* toward the "giants in those days." This, too, therefore, was a sober part of Brownson's vision, of his conception of the American Idea. Indeed, it may be that this seemingly minor element prior to 1840 may have served as a significant bridge to those essays after 1840 which ultimately helped shape the pilgrim's progress to the Catholic Church.

Brownson had indicated that his *Review* would close with the October, 1839, number; but his mind was changed, and the issue for January, 1840, appeared on schedule. In his introduction to that number he rededicated himself to the great idea of freedom, or liberty under the sovereignty of justice; that included his own freedom to investigate everything on the basis of pure reason, and, what is most interesting, of experience. By experience he meant not personal experience alone, or immediate empiricism in the positivistic sense, but also the accumulated experience of the race.[88] The appearance of these comments in that important year of his life, 1840, seems to reinforce the remarks made here in regard to the strong temper of his bent toward the wisdom of the past.

Brownson reasserted his desire to serve the party of the American Idea, the Democratic party, and in other ways extended his preoccupation with the American Experiment. Literature, for instance, was to subserve the Experiment totally; it was to spring forth born of the seed of the great "work to be done for the human race,"[89] following from the "law of Providence,"[90] and from America's status as divorced from Europe.[91] The coming struggle between the "movement" and "stationary" parties (between man and money, labor and capital) would be resolved in favor of the former who were attuned to the rhythms of God's Providence.[92] The contributor to a living American literature must be one who would "live and labor," who would give himself freely to the work of social regeneration.[93] He must sing not only for America, but ultimately for the human race,[94] since America was the nucleus of the new world to come. And, prior to his first "Laboring Classes" essay, Brownson introduced two ideas which would have great weight with him during the years immediately following.

The first of these, published in April, 1840, was written in agreement with Saint-Simonian doctrine. Brownson herein argued that, although the right of ownership of property is recognized, the right of hereditary descent of that property is denied.[95]

And again in the July issue he repeated his distinction between the Movement party (in religion, the Transcendentalists; in politics, the Democratic party), and the Stationary party (the followers of Andrews Norton, the Unitarian leader, and the relics of the Federalist party), and he spoke of the Transcendentalists as being not of foreign but of "American" origin.[96] "[Transcendentalism] claims for man the power of knowing, and especially of knowing the truth of that religion which God has revealed to us by his Son, and on which depend the hopes of the race for Progress here, and of the soul for a heaven hereafter."[97] Further, he argued in this pre-"Laboring Classes" essay, philosophy now was no longer dependent upon theology, and was superior to it. Atheism was an untenable position since "it sinks God in nature," while pantheism is unacceptable since "it sinks nature in God." Three causes are at work in history: man, nature, and Providence, and all are to accomplish Progress which is the Mission of Humanity.[98]

Brownson's essays on the "Laboring Classes"[99] are perhaps his best-known pieces, and need but a comparatively brief review here. Indeed so familiar have these essays become, and so typical of his thought are they assumed to be, that Harold Laski can write that "it is important to realize that all Brownson's work of serious stature was done before this conversion [to the Catholic Church in 1844]." This is merely ignorant.[100] These essays are of great importance, of course; they do, in several ways, bear the fruit of an earlier seed; however, in their emphasis especially against "conservatism" they contradict things he had said prior to their composition, and much that he wrote after they were published, and even before his conversion, or the termination of the *Boston Quarterly Review* in 1842. Briefly put, they seem typical of one deeply important aspect only of his many-sided mind.

Essentially, Brownson predicted a bloody crisis between the forces of capital and labor. After reviewing the appalling conditions of the laborer all over the world, and after indicting the wage system—that industrial buffer of the conservative middle classes—as inferior to the southern system of slavery, he decided that the great work of his time and of the future was to realize for the working man the social equality "which God has established,"[101] either by throwing over the wage system, or by providing the laborer with a fiscal independence, so that he could be an "independent laborer on his own capital—on his own farm or in his own shop."[102]

The usual reformer's answer, the usual "religious" answer—i.e., reform the individual, and thus reform society—simply would not work. The present system operated to the advantage of the priestly class as well as that of the bourgeois and upper classes; thus, the evil was inherent in all social arrangements.[103] The system, in short, was at fault, and, proper Christianity, not that of the churchly or priestly caste, but the Christianity of Jesus demanded its overthrow by the masses.

The cause of the trouble, Brownson made clear, was rooted in "religion . . . charge it to the priesthood."[104] This "sacerdotal corps" which, through control of individual freedom by laws of morals, and by assertion of the supremacy of moral power over physical force "can only enslave the mass of the people" in bondage to the priests. The remedy was to destroy the priestly caste, for Jesus came to do precisely that;[105] he instituted no priesthood, but tried to break its power and summon the human race to freedom, to call every man to be his own priest.[106] Therefore, three things must be done: first, the priestly order must be destroyed; second, there must be a restoration of the reign of Justice, the Christianity of Christ wherein no man could get to heaven who did not labor to establish the Kingdom of God on earth.[107] And, third, the government, which was the agent rather than the master of society, must limit itself by circumscribing its own powers; thus, it must repeal the laws oppressive to the laboring class, and enact legislation to enable those classes to attain equality. The power and force of government was indispensable here to destroy all privileged monopoly.[108]

Brownson then suggested as an example of the evils requiring governmental action the "greatest [inequity] of them all"—the "hereditary descent of property, an anomaly in our American system."[109] Americans had abolished hereditary monarchy and hereditary nobility, and need only be consistent with a theory of property.

Briefly put, the suggestion was made that a man may keep honestly acquired property until his death, whereupon it should revert to the state "to be disposed of by some equitable law for the use of the generation which takes his place."[110]

Brownson recognized that the United States was not yet prepared for such a change; however, he felt that the people here were prepared for its *discussion*. Furthermore, he was convinced that this change would not and could not be peaceably effected: physical force would at some point be necessary.[111] A bloody and terrible class-war would precede such a radical change, a struggle from which, "however inevitable it may seem to the eye of philosophy, the heart of Humanity recoils with horror."[112]

The second article on the "Laboring Classes" appeared in the October, 1840, number of the *Review*. In essence it was a defense of the first,[113] organized under five heads: Responsibility to Party, Opposition to Christianity, Opposition to Priesthood, Proletaries, and Descent of Property. A conclusion was appended.

Brownson denied that he had been a traitor to his political party; but, as a thinking man, he refused to be a slave to any party.[114] He had become a Christian in 1830, he maintained, and remained one on the terms of his own reason.[115] It is precisely on those terms that he had criticized the priesthood, and, though admitting that the Catholic idea of the priesthood was the most advanced and sensible, he insisted that the law of Progress had rendered even that priesthood anachronistic. He restated and defended again an idea which could so easily be misinterpreted: if both systems were to be permanent ones, the slave was better off than the wage operative. His proposition for the abolition of the entailment of property he again urged and this time more clearly in terms of the American Idea, for his proposition was, as he saw it, a "logical conclusion from the admitted premises of the American people, and *a fortiori,* of the democratic party. . . . What in a word is this American system? Is it not the abolition of all artificial distinctions, all social advantages founded on birth or any other accident. . . ?"[116] This to Brownson represented the equality of Justice; else, American protestations were mere "Fourth of July Oratory."

The origin of the right of property, the editor contended, was not so much a creature of political and civil institutions, nor was it founded on "first and original occupancy"; but it was rooted securely in "creation, production."[117] Basing his argument upon the will of God as evidenced by the Bible, and upon the indispensability of the possession of the earth to man's sustenance, he argued that man was not created to hold property in common, but as an individual. The real question became: how much property to each? And the answer came in two parts: 1. discover the relation men bear to one another (and Christianity has the truth); 2. discover the relation men bear to one another before society (and Democracy is the solution here). Brownson saw his own theory as virtually the same as Jefferson's.[118]

The essay concluded with an attack upon the "conservative spirit" which, the writer held, would be responsible for the bloody and imminent class-war. This spirit "fights against all reforms; it would hold the human race back to the past, and never suffer it to take a single step forward. . . . It has only been in mortal encounters that the Future has as yet ever been able to force its entrance."[119]

With the possible exception of the clarification of his views on property, it is difficult to see anything new in what Brownson here contributed to general ideas. One might, of course, argue that his synthesis itself was new, and that may very well be true. Beyond that—and obviously, it is important—there appear here both logical extension of known general ideas to their logical conclusions and stronger emphases which had been muted to some degree before. Upon the whole, taking the individual arguments one by one, he had said little that his readers had not already gagged upon or swallowed, if not digested. His views, for instance, upon the priesthood had been his, although with less pointed emphasis, as far back as 1836 and the *New Views,* if not earlier; he had given his argument on property in the April issue of 1840 without stirring up any hue and cry.[120] His accent upon social equality was the logical development of his own peculiar democratic-christian nexus[121] which he had probed several times, and which he had developed in part, as has been pointed out here, from the Abbé de Lamennais. His attack upon the "conservative spirit" may present a problem, but one must remember that Brownson's version of Christianity was not that of a religion born in the nineteenth century without forebears of any kind; it was, on the contrary, a religion which was traditional in the extreme: he wanted to return to the pristine religion of Jesus, which the Churches, in his view, had destroyed.

Furthermore, there is reason to believe that his target was the middle class in both England and America;[122] there is no overwhelming evidence of any desperate Jacobinical intent in the essays. The prediction of bloody class-war was a prediction, not an expressed wish or political aim. The argument for his lack of febrile radicalism can be maintained even when one considers the almost ruthless review of *France, Its King, Court and Government*, a book assumed by Brownson to have been written by Lewis Cass. This review has an interest of its own, especially for its defense of the French radicals.[123]

Brownson's sometime master, Victor Cousin, also based his historical thinking upon the overarching importance of an idea—e.g., the idea of the infinite (the Orient); the finite (the Occident); and the juncture of the two (the modern world).[124] An Hegelian, he had been interested in the action and reaction of the countering forces in the working-out of the master idea. While it seems true, as René Wellek has pointed out,[125] that German influences upon Brownson were, perhaps, slight, it is also true that a diluted Hegelianism infiltrating Brownson's mind with Cousin's thought may account in some measure for the recurring emphasis in the *Boston Quarterly Review*, 1838–1840, upon the master idea of progress, the high design of Providence, the American Idea. Indeed, at one point, Brownson seems to argue that the amelioration of man's lot, the union of the good of society and of the individual, which would bring proper liberty to man, can result only through the operation of two opposing powers (liberty and necessity, fate and free will, human drives and divine grace, strength of will and force of circumstance), a seemingly necessary contrariety, a kind of systole and diastole implicit in being which, through interacting forces, subserve the progress of the idea—in Brownson's case, the American Idea. An understanding of this principle allowed for "bold speculation" carried out on the level of the discursive intellect, and the "Laboring Classes" essays certainly represented that. The end of this sort of thinking was to anticipate the future and prepare for it. That all this had overtones of the American nationalism of the 1830s cannot be denied. Nor can one ignore the increasing vacuum left in religious, cultural, and intellectual life which had been caused by the increasing debility of American Protestantism. That curious secular syndrome of later Americana—the religion of Democracy—does not perhaps have its origin here, for its beginnings go back to the New Covenant if not beyond; but the impetus which was given to the American Idea by such as Brownson who, quite

laudably, were attempting to rescue religious dynamism from devitalized forms, could take two roads only: Brownson was to take one,
and Walt Whitman the other. In between, in varying postures were
to be placed ultimately such men as Mark Twain, Henry James,
and, more recently, T. S. Eliot[126] and Hart Crane.

Preoccupation with the American Idea was never far from Brownson's mind in the early years of his first review. Under the influence
of his democratic, liberal views, he argued that American literature,
for example, could never be independent and virile until it reflected
the national idea of America and her institutions. The Democratic
party, the party of social as well as political democracy, was the
"Christian party"; it existed to protect individual and minority rights
as well as those of the individual. Freedom, not religion as such,
was the dominant idea of American institutions. Yet the "new
church" of his 1836 pamphlet *New Views* still seemed to be some
kind of church-state. The "Laboring Classes" essays drove home
his radical points which denied the right of the hereditary descent
of property. And these arguments were made especially as sugges-
tions to further the goal of a social democracy.

However, part of Brownson's early view of the American Idea
was his sturdy defense of individualism, and of the necessity of
a strong sense of tradition. What support he gave Transcendentalism
stemmed in part from the importance it assigned to the interior
religious sentiment of the individual. He rejected Locke on the
grounds that Locke's philosophy undercut individual freedom, since
it had denied the inherent powers of individual men to attain to
truth. Thus it represented a threat to the American experiment.

Again, Brownson was no majoritarian democrat. When "man
measures man the world over," this meant, for Brownson, individual
man, not man in the mass. His theory of sovereignty was designed
to uphold the dignity and value of the individual man as against
the encroachments of the mass mind. He was no radical innovator,
but a man who abhorred violent change. And even in those radical
"Laboring Classes" essays, Brownson does recognize the right of
individual ownership of property.

These famous essays, thrown out by Brownson's own admission
as outlines for discussion, were emphatically not designed as Brownson's blueprints for the American state. Even Brownson's severe
attack upon the conservative spirit was an extreme assault upon
an extremist position. A careful review of his own writing in the

years 1838–1840 must suggest a balance which is not sharply evident in these well-known essays. Thus it may very well be that, however brilliant and prescient they are, they may not be so emblematic of his thought as their popularity might suggest. He did not counsel revolution so much as he feared at this time its inevitability, and his fear of violent change may curiously have been transmuted into a rage against contemporary threats to the viability of the American Idea. It must be added, too, that as far as the American Experiment was concerned Brownson was a minor prophet. The bloody class-war which he envisioned did indeed occur elsewhere; it did not occur, we might remember, in the country nearest his own heart. Nor did he hope that it would.

The passion of these essays, therefore, must indeed be noted and evaluated; but they must not be permitted to obscure entirely the more conservative elements at work in Orestes Brownson. The American Dream was still liberty for the individual; the Experiment was the gaining of that liberty under political conditions which recognized ultimate sovereignty in God, and proximate sovereignty vested in the people as individuals, not in the mass. This had been his position before the "Laboring Classes" essays; it would be his position thereafter. It does seem an extraordinary point of view for a "pre-Marxian Marx."

November of 1840 saw the election of William Henry Harrison; the Democratic party had been defeated, and with it had gone down the concrete agent of the American Idea.

This act struck to the heart of Brownson's belief in [the people]. He could no longer ascribe the defects of society to the fact that the democratic principle had been obstructed: they came from democracy itself. . . . The flood of Whig votes washed away Brownson's faith in the people. . . . Orestes Brownson had put his soul into the people's cause; and in the people's defeat he lost a shining faith that did not return. The people had sold their birthright for a barrel of cider, and Brownson never forgave them.[127]

The rich mind and free heart of this man would hesitate hardly at all to tell them so.

NOTES

1. See Alexander Kern, "The Rise of Transcendentalism, 1815–1860," *Transitions,* p. 259. Brownson held this view, derived from Constant,

before his Transcendentalist period, but the Transcendentalists' emphasis upon something akin hastened his acceptance of membership in the Club.

2. Hollis, "Literary Criticism," pp. 26–27. After appearance of Emerson's *Nature,* leadership passed to that curious half-Yankee of Concord.

3. *Ibid.,* p. 33.

4. O'Sullivan to Brownson, August 13, 1837, AUND.

5. *BQR,* I, 1 (1838), 1.

6. *Ibid.,* p. 3.

7. The combination of religious and social "radicalism" is clearly set forth here. The former was intellectually acceptable in New England; the latter had not so universally the same credentials. Again, Brownson's insistence upon freedom of the slave with the "abolitionist" is an example of the unfortunate *ad hoc* emphasis which plagued his career. The truth is, as we shall see, that he had little use for the Abolition movement considered in itself, though he was—when his argument is carefully considered—set against the *idea* of slavery. See n. 49 of this chapter.

8. *BQR,* I, 1 (1838), 6.

9. *Ibid.,* p. 7.

10. *Ibid.,* p. 8.

11. See *Ibid.,* pp. 106–120; Gohdes, *Periodicals,* p. 49.

12. See *BQR,* I, 4 (1838), 389–407; Gohdes, *Periodicals,* p. 48. It might be noted also that the article on Whittier's poems (*BQR,* I, 1 [1838], 21–32) is also taken up most explicitly with this theme. Hollis, "Literary Criticism," Chapter 2, suggests, though Gohdes does not, that this article is not by Brownson, but by either Elizabeth Peabody or George Bancroft.

13. This nationalistic aspect also impressed a critical reader and penetrating observer. Wrote Henry David Thoreau to Brownson (Dec. 30, 1837): "I have perused with pleasure the first number of the Boston Review. I like the spirit of independence which distinguishes it. It is high time that we knew where to look for the expression of *American* thoughts. . . . We can depend upon having the genuine conclusions of a single reflecting man" (italics are Thoreau's). See H. F. Brownson, *Early Life,* p. 206.

14. Hollis, "Literary Criticism," p. 98; p. 136. Hollis sees Brownson as "essentially conservative in his religious philosophy" (p. 98). It is that and more.

15. Arthur M. Schlesinger, Jr., "Orestes Brownson, An American Marxist Before Marx," *Sewanee Review,* 47 (July 1939), 317–323; Schlesinger, *Brownson,* p. 100.

16. Hollis, "Literary Criticism," p. 98.

17. *Adam,* pp. 178–187. Lewis feels that Brownson's "sense of the profound value of continuity . . . found its first serious expression in a long article of October, 1842, when he was part way toward Rome . . ." (p. 187). The full fact seems to me to be that Brown-

son's sense of continuity, stability, tradition, and order is present from the beginning in the *BQR*.

18. *BQR*, I, 1 (1838), 85.
19. *BQR*, I, 1 (1838), 125.
20. *Idem.*
21. *Idem.* Later in 1838 (*BQR*, I, 4), Brownson, speaking of the American preoccupation with practical matters up to now, reminded his readers that the forthcoming American literature would obliterate by its excellence the literature of the Old World (p. 435). America was destined for world leadership: to lead in science, art, morals, and in matters of intellect. America, in short, was the land of the future (pp. 435–436). Its ruling Idea would one day rule all Humanity. For Brownson's views upon the superfluity of a "literary class" in America, see *BQR*, II, 1 (1830), 9–10. Such a class, said Brownson, "would have been at war with the mission of this country" (p. 10).
22. *BQR*, I, 1 (1838), 125–126.
23. *BQR*, I, 2 (1838), 170.
24. *BQR*, I, 3 (1838), 315.
25. Brownson regarded the American political system "as the most brilliant achievement of Humanity, a system which centres all past progress, and which combines the last results of all past civilization. . . . Humanity has been laboring with it since . . . *the birth of the new world*. . . . We take our stand on the Idea of our institutions and labor with all our soul to realize and develop it" (*BQR*, I, 4 [1838], 494–495; italics mine).
26. *BQR*, I, 3 (1838), 315.
27. *BQR*, I, 4 (1838), 440. Brownson may mean Hegel and Cousin especially. See his important explanation of Cousin's "Rationalistic Theory," *Works*, IV, 381. Especially note his central discussion of a nation representing an idea, an explanation seminal to Brownson's whole approach at this time.
28. *Ibid.*, p. 444.
29. *BQR*, I, 4 (1838), 498.
30. *BQR*, II, 1 (1839), 1–26.
31. *Ibid.*, p. 10.
32. *Ibid.*, p. 12. Here is Brownson on Burke's *Reflections on the Revolution in France*: "The glowing language of Burke is literally true, and in a far higher sense than that in which he used it. 'The age of chivalry *is* gone.' That of economists and calculators *has* succeeded; but the glory of Europe is not, as he deemed it, 'extinguished forever.' No. The glory of Europe and of the world never blazed forth as now . . ." (*BQR*, I, 2 [1838], 161; italics are Brownson's).
33. *BQR*, II, 1 (1839), 17–18. For other optimistic comments upon the magnificent future of American literature—of what he called "our wood-notes wild"—see *BQR*, II, 2 (1839), 259–260.
34. *BQR*, II, 1 (1839), 25.
35. *Ibid.*, pp. 110–112.

36. *Ibid.*, p. 132.
37. *Ibid.*, p. 135.
38. For the importance of education and schools to the American Idea, see *BQR*, II, 4 (1839), 411–416.
39. *Ibid.*, pp. 506–517.
40. *Ibid.*, pp. 512–513.
41. *Ibid.*, p. 513. See *BQR*, I, 1 (1838), 48–49; I, 2, 149–154; *ibid.*, pp. 200–237; I, 3, 382–383; I, 4, 449; II, 1 (1839), 7–16; II, 4, 510–513. These are merely selected references. For other pertinent material, see Ekirch, *Progress*, p. 52; p. 78; pp. 137–139, especially n. 18; p. 172.
42. *BQR*, I, 1 (1838), 33–35.
43. *Ibid.*, p. 36.
44. *Ibid.*, p. 37. This is an important point, especially as it is made so early in Brownson's thought. See, for example, the article by Carl Krummel who emphasizes Brownson's attachment to "obedience" in Brownson's "Catholic Years." One cannot miss the implication. Yet it can be seen here that the idea was logical to Brownson even *before* his most radical essays on the "Laboring Classes" in 1840. Carl Krummel, "Catholicism, Americanism, Democracy and Orestes Brownson," *American Quarterly*, 6 (Spring 1954), 19–31. Cf. Guttmann, *Tradition*, pp. 81–86.
45. *BQR*, I, 1 (1838), 40.
46. *Ibid.*, pp. 42–43.
47. *Ibid.*, p. 44.
48. *Ibid.*, p. 45.
49. *Ibid.*, p. 48. The logical extension of this argument formed the basis of Brownson's early attitude toward slavery and the Abolitionists. In sum, Brownson, holding no sympathy for slavery as an institution, still insisted that since the Federal Union was made of the independent sovereignties of the several states, one state or one section of the Union had neither moral nor legal right to enforce its will in these matters upon another. Neither had the majority the right to act thus to the detriment of vested rights of the minority, any more, for example, than the United States might wreak its sovereign will upon England or France. Brownson, a foe of governmental caprice, or of anything which led to it, opposed the Abolitionists because he saw them as a pressure group, tending to a mob whose passion could be swayed by specious argument, or wild and vicious rhetoric. See especially *BQR*, I, 2 (1838), 238–260 (incorrectly printed as "160"), especially 242; *BQR*, I, 4 (1838), 473–499 for Brownson's early views.
50. *BQR*, I, 1 (1838), 53–54.
51. Again, an important point. There is a reminiscence of this idea in the concept of the "providential man" which, some years later, Brownson was to derive from Pierre Leroux (with an assist from Carlyle and his "Heroes"), and a solid base for an even later idea, derived at least partially, perhaps, from Balmes and Donoso

Cortés—of the "optimates." It does seem surprising that an idea such as this should be introduced in Brownson's "liberal" period: it seems "conservative," even Federalist. The reader will note, a few pages on, that Brownson may have been more "conservative" at this period than is generally supposed. See also *BQR*, I, 3 (1838), 372–374.

52. *BQR*, I, 1 (1838), 63.
53. *Ibid.*, p. 67; the emphasis is Brownson's.
54. *BQR*, I, 2 (1838), 131.
55. *Ibid.*, p. 133.
56. *Ibid.*, p. 140.
57. *Ibid.*, p. 146. This statement, examined closely, is what we have defined here as the American Dream.
58. *Ibid.*, p. 151.
59. See *BQR*, II, 3 (1839), 326ff. This 1839 essay is as nearly "Jacobin" as anything Brownson wrote prior to the "Laboring Classes" essays. Its tone seems much more emotionally radical than his more temperate previous utterances (e.g., see pp. 348–349). Yet there appears here, too, the following: ". . . every man, who loves his neighbor as himself, seeks earnestly for the truth, and obeys the truth so far as he sees it, is a Christian, in the only worthy sense of the term, whether he be called [Atheist], Jew, or Pagan, Mahometan or Infidel. . . . Let [this] doctrine . . . be brought out and firmly established, and the Church, really universal, will be built up . . . [not through a special society called the Church] but by diffusing truth and love through all hearts and making them the basis of the State, and of all social institutions. The State will then be holy, religious, because it will be organized and administered in accordance with the inimitable truth of things, the will of God, and the nature and wants of man. This is the grand result contemplated in the mission of Jesus . . ." (p. 350).
60. In the discussion which follows, Brownson means the reader to understand by Christianity a positive system of religion, a positive institution. For he says that if one means by Christianity the "great principles of justice, meekness, love which constitute the essence of Christianity," then there is no question, no problem (*BQR*, I, 3 [1838], 325).
61. *Ibid.*, p. 315.
62. *Idem.*
63. *Ibid.*, p. 316.
64. An article written by George Bancroft ("On the Progress of Civilization, or Reasons why the Natural Association of Men of Letters is with Democracy," *BQR*, I, 4 [1838], 389–407) develops this idea.
65. *BQR*, I, 3 (1838), 445.
66. *Ibid.*, pp. 445ff. For an indication of Brownson's debt to de Lamennais, see Schlesinger, *Brownson*, p. 206. For Brownson's own comment, especially upon his early admiration for de Lamennais' "great

Idea"—i.e., the "connection of liberty and religion"—see *BQR*, III, 1 (1840), 117–119; *BQR*, III, 4 (1840), 516.

67. *Vox populi, vox Dei*, it will be noted, was a slogan supported by Brownson at this time. Years later, it became a constant irritant to him. See *BQR*, II, 1 (1839), 136.

68. *BQR*, I, 3 (1838), 467; italics Brownson's. Brownson's comment on Voltaire is interesting here, especially in light of Carl Becker's thesis previously mentioned: "Voltaire was a poet, and some may allege, also, an infidel; but he is a devout believer whenever he sings, and his loftiest and truest poetry is found in those passages in which he approaches nearest the Christian faith, and utters the religious sentiment" (*BQR*, II, 2 [1839], 145–146). Cf. Becker, *Heavenly City*, pp. 30–31. For a continuing Brownsonian emphasis upon this theme after the "Laboring Classes" essays see *BQR*, III, 4 (1840), 516.

69. *BQR*, I, 3 (1838), 473.

70. In the October, 1838, issue of the *Review*, Brownson criticized English literature on the ground that "the element of order and its adherents are separated from the element of liberty and its adherents" (p. 439). On the contrary, in French and German literatures the two are united, working in harmony. "Progress, the perfectibility of man and society is admitted and contended for, at the same time peaceable and orderly means by which to effect it are pointed out. . . . [The tree] is not made higher by being plucked by the roots, and held up by artificial means" (p. 440).

71. One can argue, of course, that the arguments which follow were attempts to win over the more religiously inclined conservative Bostonians. Accepted, this proposition would argue a sense of caution, even of dishonesty, in Brownson which would, it seems to me, have to stand on this evidence alone. It may be by far the best and most fair procedure to take the statements at face value.

72. *BQR*, I, 1 (1838), 34. For what may be an even stronger statement, see *BQR*, I, 4 (1838), 495.

73. *BQR*, I, 1 (1838), 72.

74. *Ibid.*, pp. 72–74.

75. *BQR*, I, 2 (1838), 253 (incorrectly printed as "153").

76. *Ibid.*, p. 257 (incorrectly printed as "157").

77. *Idem.*

78. *Ibid.*, pp. 258–259 ("158–159").

79. Here is Brownson on the nineteenth-century "mass man": "The individual finds the government so far from him, and his own share in it comparatively so insignificant, that he soon comes to feel himself individually of little or no importance, and when he so feels, he ceases from all manly defence of his rights and loses himself in the mass" (*ibid.*, p. 259 ["159"]). In another place (*BQR*, I, 3 [1838]) he calls this tendency to merge the individual in the mass "The only dangerous tendency in the country" (p. 376).

80. *BQR*, I, 3 (1838), 375. Cf. Brownson's statement that "The possession of power almost always corrupts" (*BQR*, III, 2 [1840], 222). Lord Acton's famous dictum is brought to mind. Brownson's influence upon Acton generally is noted by all the biographers. Correspondence between Brownson and Acton is available in AUND. For further background material see Abbot Gasquet, O.S.B., *Lord Acton and His Circle* (New York, 1906); Hugh A. MacDougall, *The Acton–Newman Relations* (New York, 1962).

81. *BQR*, I, 4 (1838), 510.

82. *Ibid.*, pp. 515–516.

83. *BQR*, II, 2 (1839), 228. This was a powerful case for tradition. In connection with this it might be mentioned that Brownson's early warm praise of Bishop Cheverus and of the Catholic Church has generally gone unnoticed. See his review of Huen's *Life of Cardinal Cheverus* in *BQR*, II, 3 (1839), 387–389.

84. See Schlesinger, *Brownson*, p. 81.

85. See *BQR*, I, 4 (1838), 494–495.

86. See Schlesinger, *Brownson*, p. 77. H. F. Brownson prints the correspondence between the two men in *Early Life*, pp. 302–305; 320–322 (part of this letter is missing in AUND); 323–325; 361–362. There is in AUND Brownson's draft of a letter to Calhoun, Febr. 5, 1844. For a Brownson admission of his intellectual indebtedness to the Southerner, see *BQR*, IV, 2 (1841), 256.

87. "The belief that justice was essential to the state was not new. It had come to America with the *Mayflower*; but few Americans in 1838 thought systematically about government, and Brownson's statement of principles was a novelty" (Schlesinger, *Brownson*, p. 76).

88. *BQR*, III, 1 (1840), 4–19; III, 2, 258.

89. *BQR*, III, 1 (1840), 72.

90. *Ibid.*, p. 73.

91. *Ibid.*, pp. 72–73. See also *BQR*, III, 2 (1840), 212 for the differences between Europe and America. The great American error is the ignorance of these differences.

92. *BQR*, III, 1 (1840), 74–77. The struggle will shake "society to its centre." See also *BQR*, III, 2 (1840), 258; 213–214. Says Brownson, "Now as it is the mission of this country to make every man free and independent, the true American party is constantly laboring to amalgamate the operative [the worker] with the employer, to abolish the whole class of proletaries . . ." (p. 214).

93. *BQR*, III, 1 (1840), 78.

94. *Ibid.*, pp. 78–79. Note the statement of purpose of the American mission.

95. *BQR*, III, 2 (1840), 221. Here is the doctrine presented in April, which, when restated in the "Laboring Classes" essays, caused such furor. Brownson's bewilderment may be partially understandable.

96. *BQR*, III, 3 (1840), 272.

97. *Ibid.*, pp. 282–283. Brownson agreed with the Transcendentalist recognition that in man exists the capacity for knowing truth intuitively, of obtaining a scientific knowledge of an order of existence transcending the reach of the senses; he disagreed when they seemed to argue that feeling replaces reason, dreaming, reflection, fancy, understanding. The words here are used in Brownson's sense, not that of Emerson, for instance (p. 323). In short, he opposed with growing spirit the subjectivist tendency in Transcendentalism. See, e.g., *BQR*, III, 1 (1840), 11.
98. *BQR*, III, 3 (1840), 317–319.
99. *BQR*, III, 3 (1840), 358–395; *BQR*, III, 4 (1840), 420–512. See H. F. Brownson, *Early Life*, pp. 240ff.; Schlesinger, *Brownson*, pp. 89–100; Maynard, *Brownson*, pp. 92ff. For a Marxian interpretation, see Helen S. Mims, "Early American Democratic Theory and Orestes Brownson," *Science and Society*, 3 (Spring 1939), 166–198.
100. See Laski, *American Democracy*, p. 310, for the relation of the statement to the "Laboring Classes" essays. See, also *ibid.*, p. 744. To make the argument clear-cut, one need only cite in simple rebuttal Brownson's *The American Republic: Its Constitution, Tendencies, and Destiny* (1865).
101. *BQR*, III, 3 (1840), 373.
102. *Idem.*
103. *Ibid.*, p. 375.
104. *Ibid.*, p. 378. His reasons follow (pp. 378–383). The lack of essential difference between Catholic and Protestant priesthoods in this matter is discussed on pages 385–386.
105. *Ibid.*, p. 384.
106. *Ibid.*, p. 385.
107. The moral and intellectual energy in the United States would, properly directed, "transform this wilderness world into a blooming paradise of God . . ." (*ibid.*, p. 390).
108. *Ibid.*, p. 393. Note that earlier in this chapter attention was called to the fact that Brownson had opted for the control of governmental power, which power he felt as itself tending toward a monopoly, since power tends to perpetuate itself. He guarded his recommendation here by the prior characterization of government as the *agent* of society, rather than its master. He does not answer the question what is to be done if, to break monopoly, the government must itself become a monopoly. See n. 80 of this chapter.
109. *BQR*, III, 3 (1840), 393.
110. *Ibid.*, p. 394. In a footnote (pp. 393–394), Brownson makes it abundantly clear that this doctrine, while not novel, is his own and not that of his friends, who are probably opposed to it; nor is it his political party's. Therefore, if readers abominate the idea, Brownson alone is to be blamed. He has meditated his suggestion on property for "many years"; he expects it to be "Condemned almost unanimously." For a parallel modern suggestion—and one

interestingly, if somewhat vaguely, rooted in Biblical theory—see T. Harry Williams, *Huey Long* (New York, 1970), pp. 660–663, and *passim*.

111. *BQR*, III, 3 (1840), 394.

112. *Ibid.*, p. 395.

113. The entire issue of October, 1840, was written by Brownson with the exception of one minor review. Its whole tenor is defense; its theme, progress. For example, the issue opens with a discourse entitled "Progress, Our Law" which Brownson had delivered to his Society for Christian Union and Progress over two years before. There can be little doubt, then, of the importance of this concept to Brownson's thought at this time. And the influence which most pervaded his thought generally, according to René Wellek, was French rather than German (see "The Minor Transcendentalists and German Philosophy," *New England Quarterly*, 4, No. 4 [December 1842], 672). Brownson himself says that he got little help from German philosophers (*BrQR*, I, 1 [1844], 8).

114. In an "End of Volume" note (*BQR*, III, 4 [1840]), Brownson explained that since he intended to close the *BQR* with the October, 1840, issue, he had printed the "Laboring Classes" essays when he did without regard to the pending presidential election of November, 1840 (p. 519). He went on to say that now, since the storm was aroused, he neither could nor would suspend publication. To accept Brownson's statement, which *is* self-serving, may strike a reader as overly ingenuous. Yet corroborative evidence exists. Anne C. Lynch, literary gadfly, and quondam friend of Edgar Allan Poe, indicated that she knew of his intention in a letter to Brownson, July 12, 1840. She added a nugget of information which she had come upon in some depths or other: "[*BQR*] is more read than any other periodical in the reading room at Philadelphia." The letter is in the Brownson Papers, AUND.

115. Those terms include, of course, the identification of democracy with the Christianity of Jesus: "Democracy . . . is the application of the principles of the Gospel to man's social and political relations. . . . Our great object has all along been to Christianize the democracy, and to *democratize* [his italics], if we may use the word, the Church" (*BQR*, III, 4 [1840], 430). The point seems to be, however (and Brownson himself cites *BQR*, I, 2 [1838], 216–218), that where the Protestants started with a Church and subsumed the state, Brownson started with the state and subsumed the Church.

116. *BQR*, III, 4 (1840), 480–481; p. 444.

117. *Ibid.*, p. 482.

118. *Ibid.*, p. 488. The second answer seems much more Jeffersonian than the first. Brownson's theory is dependent on the reasoning of the Saint-Simonians. See *BQR*, III, 2 (1840), 221.

119. *BQR*, III, 4 (1840), 507. Cf. *BQR*, IV, 3 (1841), 390–391. Here Brownson reviewed a pamphlet attacking his hereditary-descent-of-property argument, and admitted quite calmly that he had never

expected his idea to be adopted, merely discussed. It would have been "Quixotic" to expect its adoption, "repugnant" as it was to "prevailing conditions." Perhaps, he added with an edge, its adoption might come in "a series of ages." Meanwhile, he was pessimistic in 1841 about the possibility of aid to labor beyond working earnestly to help it to attain a fairer share of the return of its own labor (p. 391).

120. *BQR*, III, 2 (1840), 221. Even in 1840 April was farther from the November elections than July.

121. See draft of a letter, Brownson to Victor Cousin, September 6, 1839, AUND.

122. The first "Laboring Classes" essay was ostensibly a review of Thomas Carlyle's *Chartism*.

123. *BQR*, III, 4 (1840), 513–518. The review follows the second essay on the "Laboring Classes," and is defiant in the extreme. Cass had written in horror of the ideas of the French Jacobins, and had listed some of their "Horrible Doctrines" as examples. Brownson, "the American Robespierre," had been accused of deriving his views from those nervously exposed by Cass. The editor denied it (p. 516). But Brownson had great praise for the French Revolution ("one of the most glorious events in human history"), and for the Jacobins, and maintained that he planned a novel—to be called *The Jacobin*—to immortalize the glories of the *sans-culottes*, with Robespierre, a man to respect, as hero.

Much of this is, of course, bravado, swaggering and splenetic; the criticism his work had garnered had bitten very deep. But, however acerbic his manner, however unchained his temper, one may cite it as among his most inflammatory pieces, and then deny that it is at all typical. It is, in short, *ad hoc* rebuttal, and little else.

124. Bury, *Progress*, p. 271.

125. See Wellek, "Minor Transcendentalists," p. 672.

126. For a brief comment on Eliot's opinion of Brownson, see Russell Kirk, "Catholic Yankee: Resuscitating Orestes Brownson," *Triumph* (April 1969), 24. See also Guttmann, *Tradition*, pp. 92–99; *passim*.

127. Schlesinger, *Brownson*, p. 111.

3

BOSTON QUARTERLY REVIEW, 1841-1842

THE SHOCK OF DISILLUSION works strongest in weakest spirits. Under its burden some men have despaired, some have crumbled, some have become so cynical as to doubt the value of anything but disillusion—while the tough-minded probe painfully, looking for the error, for the missed step at the moment of choice. And some of these latter, the genuinely able men, dig to the root, and, if it be found necessary, build again the structures of their thought sometimes with new material, sometimes through the re-employment of the old, broken pieces. But, when built, the edifice is new, however ancient and honorable the tradition in which it is built, and the building, like Hemingway's people, may be stronger at the broken places.

When, in 1840, the last of the hard cider had done superbly its appointed task, and when the uproarious carnival of democracy was a memorial (and memorable) headache, Orestes Brownson found himself amid the ruins of his "democratic" assumptions.[1] For if the people in whom, abstractly, he had placed so much confidence would so easily be moved to the level of "mobocracy," as he was to call it, where was there reason to hope longer even in the view of limited popular sovereignty which he had so laboriously worked out during the four previous years of his writing in the *Boston Quarterly Review*?

But there was little time for immediate sorting out, and the sifting of the broken pieces for the January, 1841, *Review* called for preparation. Consequently, it is not surprising to read in that number (the first after the election) that, while Brownson feared the worst, while he had no "unbounded confidence in the actual virtue and intelligence of the people," he still felt that his democratic faith was sustained at the root by the American Idea, and by the increasing importance of a relatively defined "overruling Providence" which had selected America as the chosen land. This so-called democratic faith seems placed more explicitly in God than in men or any aggregation of men, but it cannot be thought new that Brownson should associate his theological faith, relatively vague as it was, and his political faith, which was only somewhat less vague.[2]

While Brownson still felt that the principle of an ideal democracy was defensible,[3] he seemed now to waver slightly in his earlier enthusiasm for the Idea of Progress. This seed of doubt would grow and develop to the point at which it would help undercut the influence of Victor Cousin, and aid in making way for Brownson's acceptance of a new mentor, Pierre Leroux. Leroux, to whom Bury assigns partial credit for the coining of the word "socialism," was a "humanitarian communist . . . [whose] devoted pupil [was] George Sand."[4] Although Leroux, too, was a believer in Progress, his personal theory of "Communion" greatly influenced Brownson, as we shall see, and started a trend of thought in the American's mind which would lead him to the Catholic Church in 1844.[5]

Further, Brownson would feel called upon to establish for himself finally the historical relation of Progress and Providence, an accommodation which seventeenth-century thinkers had thought impossible. On this point Bury writes:

The Cartesian mechanical theory of the world and the doctrine of invariable law, carried to a logical conclusion, excluded the doctrine of Providence. This doctrine was already in serious danger. Perhaps no article of faith was more insistently attacked by sceptics in the seventeenth century and none was more vital. . . . It was . . . the theory of an active Providence that the theory of Progress was to replace; and it was not till men felt independent of Providence that they could organize a theory of Progress.[6]

Yet in nineteenth-century America Orestes Brownson found a need to reassociate Providence and Progress, and in doing it he seemed to be denying much of the optimism of two centuries before.

Brownson's growing disaffection for the assumptions of democracy and of Transcendentalism, his adoption of Leroux, his search for the historical base of the doctrine of Providence, his deepening conservatism were to absorb much of his thought in this critical year. All of these issues have both an individual and cumulative effect upon his concept of the American Idea in all its aspects.

For the American Idea in 1841 was still very much alive. The American Experiment, that practical testing-ground which had suffered, in Brownson's view, a shattering defeat in 1840, was borne up early in 1841 by the still-viable American Mission, with which, now, the American Dream seems to coalesce in what appear practically Jeffersonian terms:

We contend that the mission of this country [to which the proper American Experiment should be dedicated] is to emancipate the proletary, to ennoble labor . . . and make every man free and independent. Under the material relation, we ask that every man become an independent proprietor . . . able by his own moderate industry to provide for the wants of his body; and under the spiritual relation, that he can be free to develop harmoniously all his faculties, and have access to the highest culture the community can furnish. . . . There shall be no division of society into working men and idlers, employers and operatives. . . . We would have all men work each on his own capital . . . on equal terms with his brothers. This is the end we aim at; this is the mission of this country, and to this should all the measures of government directly or indirectly tend.[7]

The Dream would not be realized *instanter*; but patience and justice could so inform governmental action, and, more important, social endeavor, that public sentiment might be exalted to the point at which society "with resistless force" would find its true and proper end. And this had to be done without the submersion of individual rights in the flood of the mass.[8]

Political democracy was a step to the more important end of social democracy as the Locofoco party was aware.[9] Yet in effecting social remedy, Brownson cautioned that the problem of social injustice would never be fully solved, and that man's capabilities, as he now viewed them, "reach to progress but not to perfection."[10] The two-fold nature of man (one set of instincts and faculties centering in himself, and the other outside of himself) could, if harmonized, lead to a social balance. The first set, that of individuality, was "the element of liberty and progress." If it was destroyed, society became supreme, and Order killed Liberty. If the second set was muted beyond the danger point, Liberty killed Order, and, in fact, liberty conceded its own murder to anarchy.[11] Continuing to reject the rigidly rational social planning of Owen and Fourier, Brownson maintained at this point that institutional government could not be dispensed with in any practical scheme, for it is "the great and indispensable agent of reform."[12] Two conclusions, thus, were drawn: 1. man was to reach his goal *in* society; 2. society could discharge its office[13] by the agency of government only.

The importance, then, of one's definition of democracy became vital. If one meant by the word the "absolute numerical majority," the political party in the majority became the true and only democratic force. Voted out, as the majority shifted, the defeated group's measures and principles became anti-democratic. Thus, little stability of government was afforded, the principle of legislative *stare decisis* became a mockery, and society and the individual were at the terrible mercy of their own caprice.[14] What was needed was a body of codified law, the written Constitution. Ultimately, social progress was dependent upon this concrete legal instrument: the safety of change could be grounded only upon permanence.[15]

The religious motivations and shifts of Brownson's mind can be seen very well in three essays or reviews which he published in the *Boston Quarterly Review* for 1841. These are his review of *The Dial,* his review of Emerson's *Essays* which had been published that year in Boston, and the essay on Theodore Parker's "Discourse on the Transient and the Permanent in Christianity."[16]

The Dial was to Brownson the "organ of the Transcendentalists, or exquisites of the movement party,—radicals, indeed, of a most ultra stamp . . . who would *radicalize* in kid gloves and sattin [*sic*] slippers. The Dialists belong to the genus *cullotic,* and have no fellowship with your vulgar *sans-culottes.*"[17] Irritated by what he considered their unnecessary assumption of their own excellence, and by their lack of "robustness," Brownson considered the verse printed in *The Dial* as prose, and the prose merely verse, although he had great if not unqualified commendation for Emerson's poem "The Problem" and for an essay by his old friend, George Ripley.[18] In further general praise he wrote: "Its authors seem to have caught some partial glimpses, and to have felt the movings of a richer, higher life which carries them away, and which as yet they have not been able to master. . . . One cannot help feeling that these after all are the men and women who are apt to shape our future."[19]

The Dialists appeared to have a serious, solemn purpose as yet half-consciously realized. Part of that purpose was the American Mission: "Though we often find them too ultra for our belief . . . yet we view their movements with deep interest, and hope from their labors much to lead to a new and higher life, for the individual and for the world."[20]

Brownson's full-scale review of Emerson's *Essays* was one of the leading articles of the July, 1841, *Review*. His great regard for Emerson as a writer who forced his reader into new and lasting perspectives[21] did not eclipse the fact that the reviewer denied the essayist the role of philosopher; to Brownson, Emerson was rather a "seer." Brownson wrote respectfully of Unitarianism ("as we would always of the dead"), and found that its root cause and that of deism and atheism in France were generally the same;[22] a major difference was that in France, though not in the United States, the ideas were pushed to their logical conclusion. D'Holbach's *Système de la nature* was judged, therefore, as more intellectually honest than the work of Andrews Norton, the Unitarian leader in Massachusetts. The ascetical Calvinism in the early colonies, if ever really practiced, had descended in importance in proportion as the wilderness was peopled. Eventually it had become a professed but dead faith, and its dispatchers, the Unitarians, thus rendered a notable service: "[Unitarianism] was an effort of those who could not live in a perpetual lie, to reconcile their theology and their religion to their philosophy and their mode of living."[23] Yet by liberating inquiring minds Unitarianism dug its own grave, for it invited such minds to investigate its own bases. The seekers rejected it, and fell back upon the religious sentiment of their nature, while seeking a more spiritual philosophy. "In this state of transition from materialism to spiritualism, from Unitarianism to a modified orthodoxy, if we may be allowed the expression, our Unitarian community now is. This transition is represented in certain of its phases, in the book before us [Emerson's *Essays*]."[24] These essays were seen then as significant of a religious movement toward a religious future, and the men involved as "the real benefactors of their age and country."[25]

The essays had about them a "sacredness . . . a mystic divinity,"[26] especially when Emerson donned the robe of seer. As "the Reasoner," however—and here Brownson adroitly shifts the ground of criticism—Emerson represented a philosophical system, however amorphous, and, though Emerson himself affects to eschew systematic presentation, it was through such presentation that all the greatest philosophers theorize.[27] Emerson's system, if that was the word, was Transcendentalism which to him and to his followers represented the universe truly. To Brownson the present philosophical current in America (that subserving Unitarianism) did not truly represent the true universe for it explicitly ruled out the world beyond space and time; yet it was precisely to this world that Transcendentalism directed itself through the reason (taken as the principle of intelligence rather than a logic), and found its home in immensity (i.e., not space infinitely extended, but the negation of all space) and in eternity (i.e., not time endlessly continued, but the negation of all time). God exists not in but out of time—He *is* in the Eternal Now. Man's ideas of truth, justice, beauty, and goodness were independent of place and time, and were independently "transcendental." Here, too, were the great principles of the Christian religion. In short, "Transcendentalism in its good sense, as used in our community, means the recognition of an order of existences which transcend time and space, and are in no sense dependent upon . . . or affected by them." And man had the power "by direct cognition, or intuition" to know this world. In this sense, all who believed in God and the reality of the spiritual world were Transcendentalists; Emerson's philosophy thus far was sound and "we go with him heart and soul."[28]

But the Transcendentalist ruled out a role for the senses in this "metaphysical" world. Though real and substantial, that world might be apprehended only by the reason, used as the principle of intelligence, "which is partly analogous to what Mr. Emerson's philosophy calls 'Over soul'."[29] To Brownson this doctrine was dangerous for reasons which should have been familiar to any reader of *New Views*: men were thus in danger of losing sight of the world of the senses, for one aspect of the universe would be disregarded and thinkers would find themselves in the pit labeled "Idealism."[30] Brownson argued that, since the world of the senses was "manifold and diverse" and that of reason "one and essential," and, since in the Transcendentalist world one rose to the principles of things which "in a certain sense" are the things themselves, the diversity noted by the senses becomes no real diversity "but merely phenominal [*sic*] and illusory";[31] it followed that there was, then, no distinction between cause and effect, and the "universe was identical with "God." This was pantheism.[32] Thus the Transcendental view was only partial, according to Brownson, and in its weaknesses, leaders such as Emerson fell into ideal pantheism by not giving proper weight to the sensible world. They tended to deny diversity in their eagerness to acknowledge an all-encompassing unity.

Brownson argued, however, that while unity was real, so, too, was diversity, for God Himself is a Unity containing the principle of diversity. He is at once both unity and diversity, as the doctrine of the Trinity shows. To deny diversity was to skip half the world, and set it in a prism where all differentiation was transformed into a God, or godly revelation. The resultant evil was as great as atheism. The relationship of God and the world was one of cause and effect, not of identity, as the Transcendentalists would seem to have it.

Brownson was not convinced that "Ideal Pantheism" could have much future in America where the society was activist, and where minds were too practical for "so refined a speculation." "The practical tendencies" of Americans tended too far to the material, and perhaps it was true that "Mr. Emerson's strong statements are needed to rectify . . . over-attachments to the material order."[33] Emerson's essay on self-reliance, indeed, may point "a lesson which it were well for us all to learn and practice—a lesson which is perhaps more appropriate to the American people than to any other Christian nation; for [no] other Christian nation is so timid in its speculations, so afraid of solving for itself, independently, the problem of the destiny of man and society."[34]

Brownson's other objections to the essays were made on familiar grounds. He deplored the lack of importance of the political state which he noticed in them, for he felt strongly that Emerson was consciously neglecting the vital necessity of an organized society without which there could be, as Brownson saw it, no possible development of the individual. Brownson had said repeatedly that man had to be perfected in society; the Transcendentalist essays of Emerson seemed to dismiss what was to Brownson one of the primary facts of life. The rejection removed the essays from practical consideration by serious men, for while these works were interesting and attractive, and belonged to the realm of "poetry" or of proverb, they laid, as Brownson viewed them, no solid base either for social ethics or for social action. With these weaknesses at the base, they could not support heavier thought in higher philosophical realms.

Moreover, the implied lack of patriotism in the essays offended Brownson's sense of the national Idea. Brownson's nationalism, which the Transcendentalists seemed to challenge, was inescapably fostered in part by his high conception of the origin of this country and of the end for which it seemed that God had designed it.[35] This faith took the shock of 1840 in apparently steady stride, whatever the damage in his eyes to the efficacy of the American Experiment. The current intellectual leaders of New England were now, Brownson thought, in danger of losing their grip upon existential reality, and were, indeed, proposing a scheme which not only was unsound on philosophic grounds, but was rejecting also the Providential destiny of their own country.

In the October issue for the same year appeared an article designed to review Theodore Parker's sermon on the Transient and the Permanent in Christianity.[36] Parker had cited several doctrines here which had been thoroughly congenial to the writer of *New Views* in 1836. For example, Parker made the distinction between the Christianity of Christ (i.e., of the Divine Mind), which was permanent, and the Christianity of the formal creeds and churches, which comprised the transient element of the title. The law of our being, according to Parker, which we only imperfectly comprehend, was progressively worked out as our conceptions of it deepened, and crystallizations of our changing conceptions were left behind. Theology, therefore, was considered subject to constant modification; truth was unalterable: man's apprehension of it, however, progressively deepened.

Brownson heartily agreed with all this; indeed, in all its essentials, it had been his own doctrine since the early 1830s. Parker's unique contribution here, according to the reviewer, was his application of these doctrines, for among the ideas which Parker thought to be transient were: 1. The inspiration of the scriptures; 2. The authority of the scriptures; 3. The person, character, and authority of Jesus. Denying that Parker was a deist,[37] Brownson, in taking up these points, admitted the need for an authoritative interpreter of Scripture; he is "not wanting in proper respect for his Holiness [the Pope], but even his [the Pope's] interpretations of the Bible can be to us only what we understand them to be; and as our understandings are confessedly fallible, what shall preserve us from misapprehending them?"[38] Concerning the person and character of Jesus, Brownson argued that, while the Savior is God, he is such only in intimate union with Humanity "which we can distinguish though not separate from God, viewed as pure essence, and as pure cause and force." God in this sense is something more than a "Hebrew youth," or a "Galilean peasant." "The name Jesus does not stand in our hearts for the Son of Mary, but for God in his intimate connection with man, for the manifestation of love, and we would not have it dimmed or tarnished by any earthly or merely human association."[39]

Brownson's main argument with Parker at this time would seem to be based upon the ground of religious sentiment.[40] As Brownson explained the difficulty elsewhere, the religious sentiment was for Parker the starting-point for reducing religion to sheer "naturalism": to rid the body of worship of the rags of supernaturalism. To Brownson, the religious sentiment indicated that religion was in accordance with nature and reason, and therefore was the starting-place for the acceptance of supernatural revelation.[41] Parker,[42] Brownson now saw, was in the way that Emerson wanted to walk—that is, in the path of pantheism or atheism.[43] And thus between the two essays on Parker (October, 1841, and October, 1842), "one can trace," according to Alvan Ryan, "the movement of Brownson's thought from Transcendentalism to a repudiation of most of its characteristic doctrines."[44]

There is no mistaking the conservative tone which emerged toward the end of the first essay on Parker,[45] an essay, it must be admitted, followed a few pages on by the "Orphic Sayings" of A. Bronson Alcott.[46] But, perhaps much the most significant remaining piece in the October issue of 1841—at least, for our purposes here—is Brownson's brief review of the two volumes of George Bancroft's *History of the Colonization of the United States,*[47] which Brownson praised, excepting only Prescott's work on Ferdinand and Isabella, as "the only real historical work this country has produced." Bancroft was compared favorably with admirable historians such as Gibbon, Heeren, Guizot, and Thiers, and is found to be their equal. A "high merit" of Bancroft's work drew this comment: "[The *History*] is written under the profound conviction, that Humanity, in its progress through the ages, is developing and realizing a grand *providential*[48] idea. . . . Each age, each nation has its essential mission assigned it in advance in the grand scheme of Divine Providence, a scheme which embraces all its ideas and events, from the most comprehensive to the most minute."[49] The continuing relation of Providence, progress, and the national idea should be carefully noted:

This country has its Idea, and its mission. Its idea is Liberty . . . for man, under both his spiritual and material relations. Its Mission is the practical realization of Liberty in this broad sense for the human race. *Hence with us all* EVENTS *are significant or insignificant according to their bearing on Liberty.*[50] Following out this Idea, Mr. Bancroft groups all the details of our history around the Idea of Liberty. . . . Mr. Bancroft not only writes his history under the influence of the true American Idea, but he takes that Idea in a large and generous sense. . . .[51]

After this critical lagniappe, Brownson indicated wherein his own view of the American Idea differed significantly from Bancroft's. Predictably, the difference turned upon the point of whether, in the discussion, the people are to be considered individually or collectively. Bancroft's tendency to welcome whatever tended to enlarge the power of the people in their collective capacity "as an event auspicious to liberty" could not, in Brownson's view, be sustained. For that position argued for absolute government, and, since it was thus tyrannical, it obviously offended against liberty. Brownson repeated here the controlling theme of this essay—namely, that if the numerical majority (the people taken collectively) was sovereign, then the individual was, in fact, "no free man, but a slave."[52] Writing with impressive perspicacity, Brownson concluded, "Unite men in a corporation, and they will applaud themselves for doing in their corporate capacity, what they would shrink from with horror as individuals. Enlarge your corporation till it becomes a State, and you have increased the evil, not diminished it."[53]

Thus, by the end of 1841, the American Idea was still something which could elicit the highest praise from the *Boston Quarterly Review*. But the American Idea was not to include that which would destroy it: the reservation was an old idea of Brownson's, but the election of 1840 forced the difficulty forward again to the point at which the warning became a very important feature of his thought as outlined in his *Review* for 1841.

1842 seems to have been a pivotal year in Brownson's intellectual life. According to his own testimony, for the first time now he spoke as a "teacher not an enquirer"—that is, he claimed in 1842 to put forth positive doctrines which, he said, he may "profess to *know* to be true, and by them henceforth [I will] live or die."[54] Again, he professed to provide an outline of his whole theory in a series of articles published during 1842.[55]

In any event there is evidence, first, that between November, 1840, and December, 1842, pivotal changes had taken place in Brownson's thought; and second, that those changes, which were in fairly vague process during 1841, became central to Brownson's development and ultimate conversion to the Catholic Church in 1844. It must be mentioned early that the essays which appear in the *United States Magazine and Democratic Review* in late 1842 and throughout 1843, and those which appear in the new *Brownson's Quarterly Review* for 1844, are dependent to a great extent upon Brownson's shift from the eclecticism of Victor Cousin to the "synthetic philosophy" of Pierre Leroux, a change signaled by the adoption of Leroux's principle of "providential men" and the doctrine of "Communion" in the July, 1842, issue of the *Boston Quarterly Review*.

Brownson opened the magazine for the year by reviewing his own *New Views* of 1836.[56] Early in the article he wrote of the "sudden inspiration" under which he had written the original in 1836; this force accounted, he felt, for its tightly written character: "More is meant than appears, and more than most readers can find, till they have learned in part the author's views from some other source."[57] For example, God was still distinguishable but not separable from man and nature; Jesus, the Son of Man, was "a finite representative of the infinite God," and to reverence him was to reverence man—the only way we can truly reverence God. Thus Brownson had built the base for the religion of Humanity. Jesus, too, was Son of God, yet not separable nor separated from the sons of men; all men were sons of God.[58]

Developing the "materialism–spiritualism" antithesis of the earlier piece, this 1842 review assumed for the pre-Reformation Church a post-Manichaean or post-Gnostic insistence upon the dual living principles of Good and Evil.[59] This influence had led to Church insistence upon the other-worldly, and forced a split between Church and State—a "monstrous anomaly"—as civil society was abandoned to Caesar.[60] Yet it had been only through the Church's power and authority that civilization was effected, and the royalty and nobility kept in line. However much "Aristocratic Protestantism," which could never control the civil arm, might weep over such power, the victories of a Becket and a Hildebrand were victories for humanity, and the people owed their existence to the Church's doctrine of man's equality and progress.[61] The Protestants had merely built upon the Catholic foundations.

Yet, by its separation of spiritual and material interests, the Church had set a term upon its own progress; further, though once the "suzerain of the State, it was forced to become . . . its vassal."[62] The State became supreme; and the spiritual came to be dominated by the temporal. What was needed now was a rejoining of Church and State, in order that, by creating a heaven on earth, man could be offered his supreme chance for heaven in eternity. The new church could not be the Catholic Church, for that would represent not progress but retrogression; what was needed was a new church fitted for a new time. Again, "man by the fact that he is endowed with a sensible nature can be inspired, and it is by *inspiration* that his progress is mainly effected."[63] God raises up "providential men" (e.g., Moses, David, Isaiah, Paul, Jesus) to inspire Humanity; these men and their modern counterparts were the channels of divine communication, so that the race and individual would push progress onward. The Church of the Future, of Progress, will reconcile spirit and matter, absorb the state, and be "a truly Catholic Church, truly universal."[64]

His essay on "Constitutional Government"[65] reflected his deep preoccupation with the tension between order and liberty. Brownson, after reaffirming his view of the necessity of society, of the mission of society, and of the indispensability of Government to ordered progress, made his now familiar distinction between the *end* of government (Eternal Justice) and the *form* of government (the means to that end). Here for the first time, however, Brownson asserted what was to become a reiterated doctrine: no single form of government—that is, monarchy, or aristocracy, or democracy— was *in se* superior to any other as a means to Justice. The American Experiment, for example, had thus far proved only that democracy *could* be sustained; America had as yet done no more for individual liberty than the best of European governments.[66]

The still unsolved American problem had these aspects: 1. how to elect the fit few—and no others—to govern, when suffrage could not be restricted; 2. how to restrain the potential tyranny of the majority, or, by implication, the devious minority; 3. how to avoid "centralism" in government.

Brownson suggested one omnibus solution, and it was one shaped to the tension of order and liberty in a democratic state: a veto-power upon power. What would result would be two mutually vigilant forces within the state: the government, and a power "naturally and peaceably arresting the actions of the government whenever it attempts to play the tyrant."[67] Brownson's concept of the American

Experiment, it seems, had without doubt a conservative strain.[68] The objection to unlimited democracy as to any form of unlimited government demanded a "constitutional government" which, in turn, required an inherent preservative of the institution itself. This was "the main problem in the organization of government," for without it there was no hope for true minority rights, and, therefore, ultimately, no hope for the "supremacy of man." This, wrote Brownson, was "the extent of our anti-democracy," for if the problem was not solved, the American Experiment would be a "splendid failure."[69]

An extension of these doctrines[70] is to be found in his article on the Distribution Bill wherein Brownson admitted that he had altered his views, not with relation to the end of government, but with regard to the "means by which that end is to be secured."

Central to the problem of Brownson's reappraisal of his views was his article in the January, 1842, *Review* entitled "Reform and Conservatism."[71] Herein he quite plainly argued that there could be no true reform where there was not a firm hold upon tradition, since the true reformer "retains ever a hold upon the past. . . . The past has flowed into him. . . . He is the past as well as the presentiment of the future." The past being part of him, he could deny it only if he denied himself.

The question then became, what of the past should be retained? Brownson answered, only that which still lived: "This is the only real past. This is what we term tradition . . . [which] constitutes our past progress . . . and is the point of departure for new progress. . . ."[72] Jesus, for instance, was not a dead monument, but is alive in the bloodstream of the race, and, "in order to slay Jesus and the Apostles, you must annihilate the race."[73] The race progressed as well as the individual,[74] and the double progression was achieved chiefly through the enlargement of human nature itself, for "we are a synthesis of what has been and what is to come."[75] Brownson no longer desired any structured or "systematic" eclecticism which, willy-nilly, recognized too much the monuments of the past precisely because they were *there*. What was needed was a living synthesis. He admitted a prior lack of clarity on this point, a deficiency attributable to his own mental confusion: his readers could not understand how Brownson proposed to conquer the future by running away from the past. Actually Brownson admitted here that he had meant to bind "the past and the future into a living unity. . . . By our doctrine we retain the past because we live it; live what has been as well as forefeel what is to be. Here is a genuine synthesis." Since every man was engaged in this synthesis through his presence in history, the question was not whether there shall be progress, but simply "what is or what is not progress?"[76]

Brownson now saw only a superficial difference between the "movement" and "stationary" parties, a difference of judgment rather than of tendency. For example, the Church had contributed the idea of the perfectibility of individuals (sanctity); the reformers and the *philosophes* added the idea of the perfectibility of the race: "We [i.e., Brownson] believe neither in the infallibility, nor the sinlessness of the race. We believe only in its capacity for progress, in its perfectibility; not in its perfection, nor power to become perfect, but merely to approach perfection."[77] This approach would be achieved through "special inspiration" conveyed through the agency of "providential men." And, at this point, Brownson defined what he meant by Providence in this state of his developing career:

God . . . is near us, not merely in the fixed and uniform laws of nature, but . . . in his providence, taking free and voluntary care of us, and tempering all events to our strength and condition. God is not . . . fate, an iron necessity . . . but a kind and merciful Father. . . . We see a special as well as general providence in the history of individuals and of the race. . . . Christianity is no natural production. . . . We confess our utter inability to explain the past history of the race on *the theory of natural development* . . .[78] that history is all bristling with prodigies . . . inexplicable . . . save on the hypothesis of the constant intervention in a *special*[79] manner, of our ever watchful Father.[80]

God's Providence, which was exercised through special messengers particularly endowed by the Holy Spirit, initiated the race into higher and higher degrees of moral and social life. Humanity, then, was the child of God. "We have thought differently in our day;[81] but let this confession, written while tears of contrition and joy are falling fast, plead our pardon."[82] Brownson rejected now a "transcendental theology," and planned his still constant hope for "progress" upon the will of God manifested through inspiration in the world.

In his review of his own *Charles Elwood*,[83] Brownson insisted quite clearly that, although man had a natural capacity to aspire, he did not naturally aspire—that is, he was not naturally progressive; consequently, he needed some quickening elements foreign to and

outside of himself. The aspiration needed, therefore, for the furtherance of the American Idea must come from a source outside man's
own powers—in short, from God. The generally accepted but seldom
probed American assumption of a necessary liaison between Christianity and democracy was, in Brownson's thought, coming to have
a firm root in the theories just outlined.[84]

In June of 1842 there was published Brownson's letter to Dr.
Channing entitled "The Mediatorial Life of Jesus."[85] In this letter
Brownson undertook to prove that 1. man cannot commune directly
with God, and that man has need of a mediator; 2. to mediate
between God and man, the mediator must be truly of both natures;
3. Jesus is this mediator, a savior, a redeemer, giving his life "literally not only for [man] but to him"; 4. men live their "normal"—i.e., their eternal—life only in proportion as they live the
"identical life of Jesus."[86]

Man's access, therefore, to the source outside himself (the central
pillar of Brownson's entire theory at this point) was based upon
Jesus.[87] Christianity centered in Jesus as God-man, and this for the
editor now was the central fact of human history.

In July, the lead article of the *Boston Quarterly Review* was
Brownson's review of Pierre Leroux's *De l'humanité*.[88] While the
concentration here can only be upon Brownson's adaptation of
Leroux's theory of "Communion," the essay itself can be studied
as well for an explanation of either the expansion or the rejection
of the views which Brownson had previously held. His discussion
of Saint-Simonism is of great interest, as is his disagreement with
Leroux upon the psychology of man;[89] and one could with profit
examine his association of Leroux with Leibniz, Pascal, Perrault,
Fontenelle, Bacon, Descartes, Lessing, Turgot, and Condorcet with
regard to the Idea of Progress.[90] Yet it is to Brownson's comments
on Book II of *De l'humanité* that present focus must be directed,
since Brownson's theory of communion, and of the solidarity of
the race, both adapted from Leroux, became the philosophic and
historical matrices of his thought at least until 1844, and, with
variations, either consciously or subconsciously for the remainder
of his life.

According to Brownson's version of Leroux, man, of himself,
remained in a latent or virtual state until he actualized himself by
that which was not himself. He could not be conscious without
acting; he could not act without an object which he is not, and

could not furnish of himself. Love, for example, the joint product of the lover (man) and beloved (the object), was actualized in loving, which in turn was man's life. This life, consequently, was partly in and partly out of man himself (the "me") and partly in that which was not himself (the "not-me"). All man's capacities—and love might remain as the example—became actual, then, only by means of appropriate objects; the actualization or manifestation of these capabilities—the "intershock of the me and the not-me"—made up man's life, for he could live only insofar as he had an object, since his life was partly subjective, partly objective.

The "not-me" consisted of the world and other men, and these form the objective portion of a man's life only by means of an uninterrupted *communion* between him and them. His right to this communion was commensurate with his right to live: "it is the necessary, the indispensable condition of his life."[91] Further, man needed this communion under the three forms of family, country, and property. These needs corresponded to the needs of his nature as man. The *destiny* of man, on the other hand, the design of man's Creator in man's constitution, was not to place man in unlimited communion with all men; such a situation would annihilate man, since it resembled the finite seeking in vain the infinite. However, while in fact his actual communion was limited to certain of his like, he did have the right to communicate with all men and all nature. This right and its recognition was man's liberty.[92]

The evil of past societies had not been caused by man's innate depravity, but by the lack of recognition of man's free development and progress in these three areas of communion, and by the enmity which had been suffered to exist among the three themselves. To live "*is to manifest one's self; and one cannot manifest oneself without an object, and this object is our brethren.*"[93]

The progress of the individual could, as he now thought, be effected only in the progress of the race, of social institutions, and of surrounding nature, and, as Brownson took pains to point out, this view was unacceptable to the Transcendentalists who saw man as "an aggregate of individual forces" coexisting without necessary union or mutual dependence: their idea of reform, therefore, dependent as it was upon the isolated wills of men, upon individual improvement and self-culture, was, in its turn, unacceptable to Brownson.[94] To him, man could not be his own object, nor was his life all in himself, and wholly subjective.

The Church, consequently, must enlarge its ideal: the progress of the individual must be sought in the progress of men in their relation with humanity—that is, in the "amelioration of the several forms under which man communes with other men. . . . Our individual lot is bound up with that of Humanity, and whatever be its degree of excellence or depravity, that degree must be ours."[95]

The problem of evil was, then, the problem of a violation of communion, of the law of unity and fraternity, and was caused by a family caste, or a national caste, or a property caste. A solution was to be sought through organization of the state so "as to permit us to develop ourselves and advance in its bosom, without being oppressed . . . [for example] within the narrow enclosure of our country," or family, or property.

The unity of all men in the one life of humanity is what Brownson meant by the "mutual solidarity" of the race. Since life resided jointly and inseparably in the subject and object, and since subject and object were not alone in immediate and naked juxtaposition, but were mutually acting and reacting with other subjects and objects—since these were facts, all was therefore soldered together.[96] The actual object of each man was *his* family, *his* country, *his* property; the *virtual* object (the possible object toward which he aspires or is free to aspire) was all men.[97] "Each man," wrote Brownson, "is an undivided and an indivisible part of the life of all men, and the life of all men and of each man is an undivided and indivisible part of the life of each man. Thus is each in life *soldered* to the whole, and the whole to each." To help achieve true mutual solidarity—"the realization of true Gospel charity"—is "our work for the future."[98]

This, in sum, was Brownson's theory of communion as he apprehended it in 1842. As much as anything else, it marked an important milestone in his intellectual career, for, among other things, it gave a base to a properly understood democratic ideal, a personal philosophic base to Christian charity, a logical analogue to the doctrine of Providence, a solvent to the harassing problem of Progress, a guide to government, a key to history; the doctrine, finally, pointed up—it does not seem too much to say it—the feeling of a vague need for an instrument of divine grace to sustain the race.[99] Further, if America was still the highest point which the race had reached, the theory gave further depth to the indispensability of the American Experiment, and stronger impetus to the American Mission.

Moreover, it is interesting that Pierre Leroux—who had developed his thought under the intellectual tuition of Saint-Simon, the *philosophes,* Bacon, Descartes, and the great progressives who had for the most part believed in the *natural* progress of the race—should have been as strong an influence on Brownson as he was. For he helped clarify the thought of the American editor who himself was so important to the development of the theory of Progress in the country where some of Leroux's own mentors had looked for ultimate progress within the American Dream. Through his theory of "Communion" and of solidarity, Leroux aided Brownson to see the historical relation of mankind, perhaps for the first time clearly. Brownson was to clarify for himself the idea of Providence which up to now he had accepted apparently through the filter of Cousin's thought. So far as Leroux's ideas led to a clearer notion of a supernatural Providence which, as we have seen, would negate the bases of natural progress, just so far did Leroux's influence upon Brownson undercut the prior influences of the early progenitors of the American Dream.

Brownson's final *Review* for the year (October, 1842) was taken up wholly with a second article on Theodore Parker. Though space dictates a truncated discussion here, it may be enough to suggest that Brownson clearly asserted[100] that supernatural revelation was an absolute necessity since "Religion is the highest authority we acknowledge";[101] Christianity could not be separated from Jesus who had instituted it, and who had lived in direct communion with God.[102] Men could commune with Christ only through the true Church, i.e., "Catholicism without Papacy."[103] An authorized interpreter was needed—the Church—and it is *"absolutely* necessary to the salvation of the race and of individuals, and we contend that it has supreme authority in all that pertains to human life."[104] This true Christian Church, the living life of Jesus whose indwelling life was the Holy Spirit, was an assembly of men and women grouped around Jesus, around "the real living of our Lord."[105] Jesus saved by his communion, by communicating his divine life to humanity. Men must submit to the authority of this Church since it was the Ideal revealed to us, and the Ideal (i.e., Justice) "is necessarily sovereign."[106]

The highest freedom was Order, the maintenance of which is effected through Government whose true source in turn could be only from above those who are governed. God chose to inspire men through the Church, the living body of Jesus: therefore, the Church had the right to decide authoritatively in all matters whatsoever touching human life. True liberty consisted, consequently, in obeying absolute sovereignty; there was then no danger to be apprehended (from the Church) to liberty by any who loved truth and progress, though it might be by those who loved license and anarchy.[107]

"What," concluded Brownson, "is the easily ascertainable authentic creed of Christ?" It is a creed—

written on the very heart of this century . . . from the terrible French Revolution down to the Chartist outbreak for bread. . . . We almost dare ourselves venture to give its formula. We gave it six years ago, in two words, UNION AND PROGRESS, the mutual solidarity and continuous progress of the race. . . . SEEK TO BE SAVED FROM SIN AND TO SECURE THE BLISS OF HEAVEN HEREAFTER, BY DOING THY BEST TO CREATE A HEAVEN FOR ALL MEN ON EARTH. This . . . is in substance the genuine, the authentic creed of the Church of Christ in the nineteenth century. . . . The so-called churches of Christ are the real, the living body of our Lord, so far as they adopt this Creed, enjoin it and command obedience to it.[108]

Progress was still to be Brownson's banner, but there was recognition now that liberty needed to be organized or it deteriorated into license; liberty needed to be "ordained by authority, or it was no basis, no safeguard, no guaranty."[109]

Thus wrote Orestes Brownson in 1842, two years before his conversion to the Catholic Church. Thus, too, was strengthened in Brownson's mind a new conception of liberty which, as the objective of government, became for him now an integral part of the American Experiment.

During the years 1841–1842, therefore, it seems clear that in the reappraisal of his own views forced upon him by the election of 1840 Brownson still held firmly to a concept of the American Idea. His faith was now reinforced by four beliefs. First, he recognized the growing importance of the relation between the ideas of Providence and progress; again, he made the admission that progress, but not perfection, was the goal of society. He continued to insist upon an equipoise between order and liberty in the state, and he had concluded that the American Idea could only be worked out in a democratic society—at least through the use of a veto upon the power of majoritarian rule. That veto was to be the written constitution which would safeguard individual rights, contain the radical impulses of innovators, and avoid centralism in government. There is in all this increasing evidence of a sustained conservative element in Brownson's thinking.

Among his criticisms of Emerson and the Transcendentalists generally, Brownson now scored the group for its implicit dismissal of the importance of the state which was the only temporal agent, as Brownson saw it, for the fufillment of the American Idea, that high providential destiny of America. Through his theory of sovereignty, the state, properly understood, could be the agent of the power (God) absolutely necessary for man's progress. The impetus to such progress had to come from outside man himself, for man was helpless to achieve his own progress. On this point he rejected pantheism, which he took to be the solution of the Transcendentalists; he could not accept the monistic view that matter was its own energizer. A personal God was to Brownson the only answer.

Brownson's praise for Bancroft's support of the American Idea was diluted chiefly by the former's distaste for the tendency, as he saw it, in Bancroft's thinking to support majoritarian rule. For, as Brownson argued in 1842, the end of government is Justice; any form of government which would achieve that end was satisfactory. The belief that the progress of society demanded democracy as an earnest of its latest development was waning, and evaporating with it was Brownson's original optimism which had joined protestant Christianity necessarily with democracy as the two indispensables of the American Idea.

In the letter to Channing he represented Jesus Christ as the necessary link between the eternal and the temporal worlds, and the Incarnation became in a sense a kind of leverage principle for belief in progress and a proof of Providence. Through the adoption of Leroux's theories of "Communion" and of the solidarity of the race, Brownson's sense of tradition was shored up, and scope was given to the doctrine of Providence (and of providential men), though he had not yet fully explored this pivotal concept. Further, Leroux had provided a solvent for some of the problems raised by the idea of progress. Brownson had come to believe that ordered progress, which America was to lead, could come most quickly and efficiently through a kind of Catholicism without the papacy. God was His own Pope. It was to Him directly that requisite order and true liberty traced their necessary dependence.

These essays for 1842 are the last Brownson published under the masthead of the *Boston Quarterly Review*. That periodical closed its life with the issue of October, 1842, and, after selling his rights to the title to the editor of the magazine he now joined, Brownson became associated with John L. O'Sullivan in the publication of the *United States Magazine and Democratic Review*.[110]

NOTES

1. *The Convert, Works*, v, 120–121.
2. *BQR*, IV, 1 (1841), 69.
3. *Ibid.*, pp. 69–72.
4. Bury, *Progress*, pp. 318ff.; see also p. 234 n. 1.
5. Malone, *The True Church*, pp. 60–69.
6. Bury, *Progress*, p. 73. See also pp. 74–77.
7. *BQR*, IV, 1 (1841), 81–82.
8. *Ibid.*, pp. 83–84. For instance, Brownson called for a new party, the "Constitutional Party," a coalition of "The smaller states, the slave-holding states, and of the real democracy of the country" to defend individual rights by defending States' rights (pp. 90–92). For further emphasis on this point see *BQR*, IV, 3 (1841), 357–368.
9. *Ibid.*, pp. 114–117.
10. *BQR*, IV, 3 (1841), 267. The fabric of the perfectibility of man was shredding.
11. *Ibid.*, pp. 268–269. Brownson notes in *The Convert* that at this time he "came to the conclusion that the condition of liberty is order, and that in this world we must seek not equality, but justice" (*Works*, v, 121). Though *The Convert* was published in 1857, it seems to me that the conclusions mentioned here are implicit in the bulk of Brownson's work prior to 1840. If that opinion is valid, then those who lean heavily upon *The Convert* can easily misinterpret Brownson's emphasis here.
12. *BQR*, IV, 3 (1841), 276.
13. And the office of society is to maintain for each individual member his entire individuality. This implies the sustaining not only of one individual against another, but also of the individual against society itself. Equal rights are God-given, not man-made. The affording of effective guarantees for the individual against the invasion either of other individuals or of society itself is the "only difficult problem in political science" (*ibid.*, pp. 277–278).
14. Universal suffrage or education were really not remedies here. Men today, Brownson thought, were often forced to vote against their own interest. Further, policies of political parties represented the will of the minority controlling the majority of the party, a will

which, instead of that of the majority of the people, ultimately decided (*ibid.*, pp. 280–281). Brownson here was, perhaps, indebted to Calhoun (*ibid.*, p. 286).

15. "The Senate is unquestionably a conservative body, and wo [*sic*] to the state that has not somewhere in its organization a conservative body . . . [which] gives stability and something of systematic unity to the action of government" (*BQR*, IV, 3 [1841], 368–369). Interesting also are his added comments on those who "scream democracy from morning to night," and upon aristocracy seen now as "a natural element of every society." The aristocracy, of course, is one of talents (*ibid.*, p. 370).

16. *BQR*, IV, 1 (1841), 131–132; *BQR*, IV, 2 (1841), 258; *BQR*, IV, 3 (1841), 291–308; *BQR*, IV, 4 (1841), 436–474.

17. *BQR*, IV, 1 (1841), 131–132. There is a note of seriousness under the heavy-handed banter. Brownson's emphasis upon "radical" and "ultra" reflected again his growing conservative stamp. A radical, it seems, was dangerous with or without shoes.

18. *Ibid.*, p. 132.

19. *Idem.* Again Brownson seems to be rather following a thought to its logical conclusion than expressing any preference for such a conclusion.

20. *Idem.* This "new and higher life has been quickened" in Ralph Waldo Emerson especially, said Brownson in a preliminary and brief review in *BQR*, IV, 2 (1841), 258.

21. In 1839 Brownson had seen both Emerson and Carlyle, members of a cult who pursued "obscurity" of language, as "leaders of women and literary amateurs" (draft of a letter to Victor Cousin, September 6, 1839, AUND).

22. *BQR*, IV, 3 (1841), 294.

23. *Ibid.*, p. 296.

24. *Ibid.*, p. 297.

25. *Idem.*

26. *Ibid.*, p. 298.

27. *Idem.*

28. *Ibid.*, pp. 300–301. Brownson labeled those who deny such a world "skeptic, materialist, atheist."

29. *Ibid.*, p. 301.

30. *Ibid.*, p. 302.

31. *Ibid.*, p. 303.

32. *Idem.* Brownson did not call Emerson a pantheist, but indicated that his tendency was toward pantheism (*ibid.*, pp. 303–304).

33. Brownson had high respect for Emerson's ability in the use of example. In the most diverse things Emerson found unity, and the resemblances he observed in nature were generally "just," for Emerson had great power here. And, Brownson added, such identity *did* run through nature.

34. *Ibid.*, p. 305.

35. *Ibid.*, p. 306–307.

36. *BQR*, IV, 4 (1841), 436–474.
37. Brownson's definition: "A deist is one who while he admits the existence of one God, denies all supernatural revelations from him to man. The essence of deism consists in this denial" (*ibid.*, p. 443).
38. *Ibid.*, p. 456.
39. *Ibid.*, p. 472.
40. This difference is extremely clear in the October, 1842, number of the *BQR*, the whole of which is given over to a further discussion of theological differences with Parker. For the importance of these two articles on Parker, see Alvan S. Ryan, "Orestes Brownson: The Critique of Transcendentalism" in *American Classics Reconsidered*, ed. Harold C. Gardiner (New York, 1958); R. W. B. Lewis, *The American Adam*, pp. 174–193.
41. Brownson had argued the importance of the supernatural, two years before. In the draft of the letter to Victor Cousin he had written, "no philosophy will be acceptable to us for a long time which does not recognize the supernatural, and by teaching us to find it *in every man* gives us a firm basis for our faith as Christians and as *democrats* [italics his]" (Brownson to Cousin, September 6, 1839, AUND).
42. *Idem.*
43. *Works*, V, 152–153.
44. "Critique," p. 110. Brownson, as has been shown in the comments on Emerson's *Essays*, was moving away from the Transcendentalists much earlier. However, that Brownson was still acceptable to "Transcendentalists" generally is indicated by an invitation extended to him to preach at Philadelphia in a "transcendental Christian Church," whose pastor was the Rev. F. A. Eustiss. See the letter, William D. Kelly to Brownson, December 18, 1841, AUND.
45. *BQR*, IV, 4 (1841), 474.
46. *Ibid.*, pp. 492–494.
47. *Ibid.*, pp. 512–517.
48. My italics.
49. *Ibid.*, p. 513.
50. My italics, except for Brownson's stress upon "EVENTS." Cf. Brownson's comment, *The Convert*, *Works*, V, 121.
51. *BQR*, IV, 4 (1841), 513–514.
52. *Ibid.*, p. 515.
53. *Ibid.*, p. 516.
54. *BQR*, V, 3 (1842), 384; italics Brownson's.
55. These articles are *BQR*, V, 1 (1842), 1–26; 27–59; 60–83; 84–118; *BQR*, V, 2 (1842), 129–182; *BQR*, V, 3 (1842), 257–321; *BQR*, V, 4 (1842), 385–513.
56. This tack seems clear objective evidence that Brownson was consciously reviewing, not so much this one pamphlet, but the whole basis of his thought. If this is true, then there is inferential evidence that he is very conscious of having reached a turning-point in his

intellectual life. There is evidence that he would conduct such a review more than once before 1860, certainly in the years 1856–1857.

57. *BQR*, v, 1 (1842), 5.
58. Jesus, as the reader will note, while remaining man as he had to Brownson in 1836, was becoming of central importance to the proof of the religion of Humanity, and to the ultimate relationship Brownson will find between Humanity (considered both as individuals and as the race) and the Godhead. That relation—mediatorship—will be stated in relatively unequivocal terms for the first time in Brownson's "Mediatorial Life of Jesus," published on June 1, 1842. In *BQR*, v, 3 (1842), Brownson reaffirmed the divine sonship of all men but now only *"mediately,* through Christ" (p. 384).
59. Brownson acknowledged that the teaching had been condemned, but asserted that the proposition had a strong after-image which mightily affected the Church's attitude toward social reform (*BQR*, v, 1 [1842], 11).
60. Brownson praised the civilization formed and fostered by the Church up to the fifteenth century, especially during the period "called by narrow-minded and bigoted Protestant historians the dark ages" (*ibid.,* p. 13).
61. Among the accomplishments of the Catholic Church Brownson listed the foundations of modern civilization; the humane and gentle spirit which informed society; the aid given to the preparation for universal education by its early sponsorship of schools and universities; the emancipation of the slave; the doctrine of the equality of men before God; the Church's lack of class consciousness in choosing priests and popes; its denunciations of malefactors of great wealth. The tone here was that of an American Burke.
62. *Ibid.,* p. 15.
63. *Ibid.,* p. 20. Here is the incursion of the supernatural into the natural. The reader will recall Brownson's insistence in 1842 that *New Views* (1836) had been written under "inspiration." Leroux's doctrine of "providential men" which follows in the text above was a refining of Brownson's answer to the question "How does supernatural influence enter natural life?" The editor's answer here, however, was not final. That was to come in a year or two.
64. The emphasis here seems to be that the Church will be the state—i.e., that the absorption will be effected the other way around (*ibid.,* p. 25).
65. *BQR*, v, 1 (1842), 27–59.
66. *Ibid.,* p. 30.
67. *Ibid.,* p. 40.
68. This "conservative" thread, as has been stressed, had been present, with varying emphases, in the *BQR* since its inception.
69. *Ibid.,* p. 59.
70. *BQR*, v, 1 (1842), 84ff. Cf. pp. 86–89 for a deep commendation of Calhoun, and for what seems a clear prediction of what might be called the "evolutionary" concept of the Constitution.

71. *BQR*, v, 1 (1842), 60–84.
72. *Ibid.*, pp. 63–64. The argument is reminiscent of the upholding of the "permanent" in Christianity—the argument of *New Views*.
73. *Ibid.*, p. 64. The matter is important. Tradition is now the line of communication between generations, and the way in which the race is linked through individuals. The idea is implicit in Brownson's acceptance of the theory of communion, of his views of Providence, and of his letter to Dr. Channing, "The Mediatorial Life of Jesus."
74. This view was modified somewhat in the essay on *Charles Elwood, BQR*, v, 2 (1842), 155.
75. *BQR*, v, 1 (1842), 68.
76. *Ibid.*, pp. 69–70. One may note Brownson's recognition now of the "vital" importance of religion in the probing of being. The current insistence upon the point marked the rejection of Benjamin Constant's notion which Brownson had previously held—i.e., in Arthur Schlesinger's words, that religion was "the shadow of [man's] desire." It represents, too, Brownson's approach to a philosophical moderate realism, since he had been forced some years previously to look for a logical basis for the view that the object (what he calls the "*non-moi*") had existence apart from the "*moi.*" One of Brownson's chief objections to Transcendentalism, for instance, had been its tendency to subjectivism. For the influence of Cousin, and later Leroux, in the working-out of this problem which was to have further point in the development of Brownson's hotly debated "ontologism," see Schlesinger, *Brownson*, pp. 124–128; 142–143. Ryan, "Critique," pp. 102–113; *BQR*, v, 2 (1842), 139–152; *The Convert, Works*, v, 74–99; 109–140.
77. *BQR*, v, 1 (1842), 75.
78. Italics mine.
79. Italics his.
80. *Ibid.*, pp. 77–78.
81. Reference is, it seems, to the period prior to 1836, and then to the time when Brownson was under the influence of Victor Cousin. He has been citing "providence" and "progress" together throughout since 1836. But his sense of providence had been Cousin's, and he will explain the difference between that and his new view of providence in an 1843 article in the *United States Magazine and Democratic Review*.
82. *BQR*, v, 1 (1842), 78. This theory of providence and of providential men was, by Brownson's own admission, a pivot upon which his thought turned, for it meant that "I was no longer chained, like Prometheus, to the Caucasian rock, with my vulture passions devouring my heart. . . . I shall never forget the ecstasy of that moment, when I first realized to myself that God is free" (*The Convert, Works*, v, 140). Yet he modified his current idea of transmission of life through natural generation (for more comes through spiritual generation than he had thought) in *BQR*, v, 4 (1842), 384. The latter theory is more "democratic"; the former, too "aristocratic."

83. *BQR*, v, 2 (1842), 129–183.
84. *Ibid.*, pp. 178–180.
85. *Works*, IV, 140–172.
86. *Ibid.*, p. 157.
87. He now saw that to deny God's providence, for example, was to deny God's freedom (*ibid.*, p. 147). As Ryan notes, a good part of the letter denies Transcendental religious views: man is not divine by nature, Brownson now argued, but is in fact alienated from God. The historical fact of Christ is stressed: Christ is Christianity. It is interesting but predictable that Emerson found the "Mediatorial Life of Jesus" to be "local and idolatrous"; from a letter to Elizabeth Peabody. See Ryan, "Critique," p. 112; p. 290 n. 44.
88. *Works*, IV, 103ff.
89. *Ibid.*, pp. 108–122.
90. *Ibid.*, p. 112.
91. *Ibid.*, p. 116.
92. This argument is certainly important since its immediate relation to political theory is evident. No one, according to Brownson—not scientific man, artistic man, or industrial man—has freedom to restrict this right of liberty; further, no individual man has the right to restrict himself, that is, become a slave to any one of the three (family, country, or property). It will be noticed that, logically and under the aspect of "country," a chauvinistic spirit is undercut, at the same time that the idea of the American Mission is emphasized (*ibid.*, p. 112).
93. *Ibid.*, p. 118; italics Brownson's. The point stressed may not be without relevance to some recent philosophical thought. Indeed, Brownson, in commenting upon the words here cited, wrote: "Our life exists jointly in us and in them, and to injure them is to injure the *objective* part of our life, every whit as essential as the subjective part. This is the richest discovery of modern philosophy, and contains . . . the seeds of a whole philosophical, moral, religious, and political revolution. Let it be pondered well" (*ibid.*, p. 118).
94. *Ibid.*, p. 119. Brownson aimed here, of course, at both Channing and Emerson.
95. *Ibid.*, p. 120. Again, the tone and substance have familiar resonances today.
96. *Idem.*
97. The actual object, then, was concerned practically with the American Experiment; the virtual, with the American Mission.
98. *Ibid.*, pp. 122–127.
99. The gradually clearing perception of the centrality of Jesus in human history which Brownson had set forth in his letter to Channing should be remembered here. Alvan Ryan believes that it was at this period that Brownson "began to examine the claims of the historical Catholic Church" ("Critique," pp. 113–114).
100. Cf. n. 41, this chapter.
101. *BQR*, v, 4 (1842), 453.

102. *Ibid.*, p. 474.
103. *Ibid.*, pp. 476–488. Neither pope, Bible, nor individual reason can be enthroned, though the papacy which died with Leo X (i.e., 1521) would be preferable to the others. But its revival would serve small modern purpose.
104. *Ibid.*, p. 457; Brownson's italics. Parker, wrote Brownson, starting from the Protestant base of private judgment overthrew by this seminal principle the possible authority and sufficiency of the Scriptures (*ibid.*, p. 488).
105. *Ibid.*, p. 497.
106. *Ibid.*, p. 504.
107. *Ibid.*, p. 507. He who is outside "the true Catholic Church" in the sense that Brownson here explained it "is destitute of [God's] inspiration . . ." (*ibid.*, p. 505). Is this another reason why Brownson, immediately after his conversion, held so strongly to the doctrine of *nulla salus extra ecclesiam*? Cf. Maynard, *Brownson*, pp. 152–188. For an opinion opposed to Maynard's and more persuasive, see Thomas R. Ryan, *The Sailor's Snug Harbor* (Westminister, Md., 1952), pp. 43–53.
108. *Ibid.*, p. 507.
109. *Ibid.*, p. 508.
110. *Ibid.*, p. 510.

4

Transition—1843-1844

IT IS CURIOUS that in his autobiography, *The Convert,* Orestes Brownson made scant mention of this new literary association with O'Sullivan's magazine. His chief comment was that, "having for the year 1843 discontinued my Review, I started another under my own name. . . ."[1] Although Brownson's contributions to O'Sullivan's magazine are of some significance (they begin in October, 1842, and continue through the major part of 1843), they have not always had as much critical attention as they might. Schlesinger, for example, practically dismisses them with such terms as "misty" and "the deluge of metaphysics" or "the smoke of metaphysics," phrasing that in itself is a not inconsiderable achievement. In summary, Brownson's ablest biographer notes that "the essays had all the faults of abstract argument. The words were so remote from things that it would have been useless to ponder their truth."[2] Yet it may be that a more careful probing of these essays may yield important clues to the changing character of Brownson's general views, and perhaps even help to explain the metaphysical fire which the deluge damped, and from which, one supposes, the smoke arose.

There is space here for comment upon only one of Brownson's articles of this period,[3] a piece which, following Brownson's custom, is only a tangential review of Jules Michelet's *Introduction à l'histoire universelle* which was printed in the *United States Magazine and Democratic Review* for May, 1843, and continued the following month.[4] It was entitled "Remarks on Universal History," and in it Brownson, who now saw increasingly that the idea of Providence was of vital importance to his developing thought, attempted to find deeper ground for his belief than emotional need or visceral reaction. In the process he subjected his beliefs to the grindstone of his own ranging, discursive intellect. Therefore, instead of reviewing Michelet, he actually exposed his own views of what he called "the Philosophy of History," an approach to truth which, stemming from the Cartesian school, attempted to find the "scientific explication" behind the historical fact—to determine, if possible, the plan or law behind history itself.

According to Brownson, this group of historians of which Michelet was a member assumed that man was made for progress. This is the ground point from which these writers constructed their historical theories, and thus far Brownson seems to have had no disagreement with them. But thus far was not enough. For, Brownson continued, progress was not an end, but a means, and must therefore be subordinated to its own end, an end toward which men themselves must aspire.[5] The major question, therefore, was "what is going to this end for which man was made and by what means or agencies do we go to it? In other words, what is human progress, and how is it effected?"[6]

Brownson studied the possible answers under four headings: 1. The War Theory; 2. The Humanitarian Theory; 3. The Rationalistic Theory; 4. The Providential Theory. He rejected the first three;[7] the fourth he accepted under certain conditions.

Providence was, Brownson felt, the end proposed; however, it was not a Providence understood as Victor Cousin and others had seen it (i.e., "the pantheistic view") but Providence taken in its supernatural aspects (i.e., "the religious view").[8] According to Cousin there were five "elements," five "original ideas," to which as sources all the facts of the life of humanity may be referred. He included industry and the sciences under the term "the useful"; the state and jurisprudence generally under "the just"; the fine arts under "the beautiful"; religion under "the holy," and philosophy under "the true." If and when Providence intervened in the creation of these, did it do so "in the form of a fixed, permanent, and necessary law of humanity; or in the form of a free, sovereign power, distinct from humanity . . . ?"[9] If in the first manner, then Providence is pantheistic; if in the second, theistic.

Giambattista Vico, whose disciple Cousin was, had taught that the action of Providence was fixed and limited:[10] God acted upon the race "but only by it in its instinctive operations" or "the common sense of nations."[11] The race was divine; man was not. Cousin, whatever his disagreement with Vico, placed the operation of God's

Providence in "the common instinctive wants and aspirations of the race"—that is to say, in its "spontaneous intelligence" which may be ascertained by collecting what is common to the race, what is regular, permanent, and reproduced with each generation. This thinking of Cousin's was, according to Brownson, either pantheism or its nearest relation, though the editor explicitly remarked that Cousin was not a pantheist.[12]

Brownson's central question demanded a sharp distinction: "where . . . shall we find in the facts of human history, not the *separation*, but the *distinction* between the divine action and the human . . . the force properly and strictly human, and the force properly and strictly divine?"[13] If God affected the human condition only in the inherent and necessary laws of human nature, what was the point of prayer, of devotion, of sacrifice? A man, Brownson reminded his readers, did not pray to his own instincts. If philosophy had led to Vico's or to Cousin's conclusions, then religion could only be for the unphilosophical; religion was a fact in human history only for those who did not comprehend the true nature of history.

According to Brownson, the fault here could be traced to the Cartesian deification of human reason, manifested in the individual consciousness. If religious faith, institutions, and discipline were for the unphilosophical, and if reason was the sole agent of philosophy, then reason destroyed the need for religion, as the French *philosophes* saw.[14]

Cousin's theory, Brownson continued, would explain, perhaps, the fixed, the permanent, the uniform in human history; it was helpless before "the exceptional, variable, individual, diverse." Providential men, for example, were not ordinary developments of humanity as tradition or history presented them to us, "for humanity cannot of itself surpass its uniform type." How could one deny the existence of Homer, Moses, Zoroaster, Plato, Confucius, and all the others?

Further, for Brownson, the theory under discussion refuted itself. A belief in a providence "intervening for individuals and nations, and through specially appointed nations and individuals as agents or ministers" was a uniform, universal, and permanent fact of human history; as such, it should be part of providence itself. But the two ideas were mutually destructive. "If the theory be true, this belief must be true; therefore, if the theory be true, the theory itself must be false."[15] The fundamental flaw in this theory, then, was the old Epicurean error—man does not suffice for himself; what is human does not develop solely from humanity.

Now, Brownson pointed out, Cousin had denied freedom to God in His relations with man after the fact of creation. God was bound by the laws of the creature, laws which He Himself had made. Yet, Brownson countered, men were dependent upon God, and upon His active intervention for the conditions of life and motion. This *was* an intervention, and was, in essence, a supernatural intervention, for the condition of life and motion were outside man's nature. Since the intervention was free, it presumed the divine sovereignty. Therefore, "God is free at any moment to intervene in our behalf, to reward . . . to console . . . to redress . . . to punish."[16]

Although Orestes Brownson felt that Bossuet's[17] *Discours sur l'histoire universelle* was defective considered as history, he found in the work an excellent presentation of the true doctrine of Providence, and he regarded it as the first study to examine adequately and systematically the phenomenon of divine intervention in human affairs. It was based upon Genesis, Augustine's *De Civitate Dei,* and Sir Walter Raleigh's *History of the World.* Bossuet's view of Providence, filtered first through the Jewish church, and then the Christian, was true according to Brownson, but only partial in character, since the French thinker was ignorant of the theory of communion, and of the providential men who were also agents of Providence.[18] Bossuet, following St. Augustine, and agreeing with Schlegel's *Philosophy of History,* believed that the end of Providence was the growth of religious empire; Brownson concurred, but found it necessary to add that God's Providence was for all men, not for chosen people solely; the latter he considered agents.

At this point Brownson began his own answer to the question of how progress is effected. Nature, Humanity, and Providence, he wrote, were the three elements at work in human history. Nature was not a "mere passive theatre" of man's activity[19] but an active, progressive force; all substance was immaterial and possessed inherent activity, and God was "actually, eternally, and universally a cause . . . who is realizing his own infinite ideal in space and time."[20] But space and time contained only the finite: creation was an imperfect realization of the divine ideal.

Yet, since God is infinite, and essentially a creator, Brownson went on, the realization of His infinite ideal was ever coming nearer and nearer, and there was continuous progress of the universe toward it. Nature was progressive, though *not* internally by her own agency, distinct from divine agency, but "by virtue of the continuous creative effort [by God]."[21] God's great business, then, would seem to be not only creation, but ineluctable re-creation.

Humanity did not develop in itself in answer to its own inherent needs. Yet humanity in human history was a free, active, productive if limited cause working in conjunction with other causes. Therefore, to a great extent, human history depended upon human volition. Brownson further argued that Providence did intervene in human history to secure the execution of divine purpose, "but it does not follow from this that nothing is to be found in human history not there by the express will and appointment of God."[22] Otherwise, there was no room left for human agency. Since humanity lives and actualizes itself only through individuals, individuals were accountable for individual actions. Inevitably, then, the individuals who composed a nation were, proportionate to their acquiescence, responsible for the merit or blame to be attached to government action. For it was God's providential purpose to leave men free, within limits, and to reward man or to punish him according as he deserves merit or blame. The idea of Providence, therefore, did not countervail the notion of human freedom.

As the Jews once had been, so Americans were now, a chosen people, with a definite work to do for humanity. As a people, they would have God's aid in that task's performance, or His censure for its failure. In default, another people would replace Americans in the divine plan. "Whether we execute this [God-given] work or not will depend on ourselves, on our own intelligence and virtue."[23]

History itself proved the intervention of Providence just as the universal belief in God proved His existence. "Man . . . aspires, and is progressive because he aspires. But man is not naturally progressive, saving progress only as he is carried along with the onward course of the universe itself. . . . Savage tribes are not progressive . . . [rising] by [their] own spontaneous efforts from the savage state . . . into the civilized state."[24] Man and nature, thus, were not sufficient for progress into a civilized state, and "civilization itself becomes a proof . . . of the intervention of Providence in human affairs. History becomes . . . a proof of Providence."[25]

These three, then—Nature, Humanity, and Providence—intervened, intertwined, and cooperated following an original law "eternal and *essential* in the infinite mind or LOGOS."[26] This idea of an original law reinforced Brownson's optimism that for men a scientific exposition of history became possible—that is, an explanation of the historical law which informs and governs the facts of history; the facts themselves, of course, must be learned empirically.

Thus, Brownson concluded, the course of history depended to a large extent upon the free action of individuals. The "room" for human virtue was "in the span we allow in history to human freedom"; the *motive* was "obedience to God, and the welfare of humanity . . ."; the "sanction," a continuing Providence which rewarded or punished us either as a people or as individuals, according as our acts were good or evil. What was demanded was a "strict obedience to the perfect law of liberty," that is, obedience to the authority of God as Sovereign, who, with nature, is the enabling force for men to do all things.[27]

As far as Brownson was concerned, all this established Providence firmly as the law of history, or what he called at this time the philosophy of history. As he now conceived it, the law of Providence was actually a key—perhaps the major key—to his current thought. His law of communion, his conviction of the need and possibility of social amelioration, of the indispensability of government for its achievement, and, of course, of man's aspiration in nature, both as an individual and as a race, were all affected by his intensified awareness of what he saw as the ways of Providence. For one of the few times publicly, he had formally probed providence as *the* teleological principle, and saw that it was not only good but true. God wanted progress since, as Creator, He had made both nature and humanity, and had planted in man those aspirations which, in tune with His own volition, helped man to climb. The Creator, too, had made use of a chosen people, as He had done of individual providential men, and there is more than a strong hint in this pivotal essay that Americans were such chosen people whose work was God's work.

Since God's will both in itself and as it is reflected in the natural law worked toward the fulfilling of the Divine Ideal, then in consequence, man, an aspiring being, was a progressive being. Brownson visualized America as a specially chosen land of aspiring men; it became for him a kind of providentially dedicated country, and its "experiment" remained closely associated with the world beyond the natural, yet was dependent upon man's free will for its success. If Americans could not do the work, others would. But if this special breed of men were successful, the American "mission," the spreading of the good news, was to be the climactic task of this modern chosen people. The word "mission" implied a sender and a sent, and it was the sender who raised the American Idea far above the natural order in its origin. Other men of Brownson's time cited Providence continually in connection with Progress and the American Idea; Brownson, at least to his own satisfaction, proved the intense, vital relation.

His connection with the *United States Magazine and Democratic Review* ceased in October, 1843. Brownson then began another review whose first issue was dated January, 1844. This work, *Brownson's Quarterly Review,* which was to contain much of his significant writing for the remainder of his life, was so-called because it was to be quite literally Brownson's review.[28] He now felt that he had matured, that his more ordered mind had firmer root in more profound conviction. "I have my doctrines determined," he wrote, and argued that his aim was no longer (as it had been in the *Boston Quarterly Review*) to excite inquiry, but to give positive instruction.[29] And that instruction, which often was to take the form of a review of his intellectual progress since 1838, found expression not only in a doctrine of "development" of Church teaching from the original "germ" contained in the Gospel, but in what seems a partial rejection of the view of ancient tradition and primitive usage. His doctrine of progress and of the putative "mission" of the Church seemed to demand in January, 1844, some theory of development.[30] Since the Church was progressive in a true sense (his "Protestant education" had confused him on this), he found the Catholic Church, "theoretically considered," all he had intended his "new Church" to be in 1836.[31]

Yet that Church, no longer the sole depository of divine life, should shrink from the *nulla salus* doctrine. Since there are individuals outside the Church who shared her mission for progress, the Church must rehabilitate herself, and aid the reorganization of the Christian World "regarded as a polity."[32]

Brownson argued for the "Law of Continuity," which demands that "the Present and Future must be always regarded as intimately linked with, and evolved from, the Past. I accepted . . . the Traditions of the race; but . . . with a reserve in favor of progress."[33]

Tradition, he wrote, was a "patrimony," to be edited and improved through the continuing inspiration of the Church, a task quite as important as the preservation of past inspirations. Now it was this attitude toward tradition (not entirely variant from his past views) which, while underscoring the true law of progress as he saw it, separated Brownson from the "ULTRAISTS" who abounded in his time.[34] "The attempt to reform the world, and to regain the long lost Eden, by *human* agencies, *human* philosophies, political economics, workhouses, and 'cash payments,' has been made and failed, and always will fail. . . ."[35] The Kingdom of God on earth "is the only possible medium of preservation and growth."

It seems clear by now that Brownson's "conservatism" had some relation to what he saw as the corruption of the American Dream which had been effected by the venal government of demagogues who in turn had corrupted the people who supported the government. This attitude was, of course, one partially derived from the traumatic experience of 1840. To Brownson in 1844 it seemed vital that the American people accept a Catholic Christianity as he now understood it; to this must be added an acceptance of tradition, that is, the preservation of the good and true inspirations of the past.[36] Unless this twofold necessity was recognized, America could lose forever the opportunity given it to lead the cause for the amelioration of man's social condition on earth. The danger came chiefly from the pernicious doctrine, as Brownson continued to regard it, of popular sovereignty, and from the indiscriminate extension of suffrage and of a superficial public education.[37] The absolute necessity for civic virtue's proceeding from the private virtue of citizens is of especial interest and importance here. Implicit in Brownson's thought seems to have been the assumption that power will force *some* kind of order.[38] Liberty under law, the only real liberty as he saw it, was the only answer to the dangerous use of power. Given the centrifugal tendencies of a democracy (in Brownson's use of the term), the popular power could easily deteriorate into a condition very like anarchy, and the need for an outside coercion be introduced. America could meanly lose the last best hope of earth.

To achieve the kind of liberty which the times demanded, and to safeguard the republic from those who under guise of saving her would destroy her, Brownson insisted that America recognize and honor the cultivated few rather than stupidly concede the superiority of the mass mind. He traced such majoritarian trends to a false Kantian philosophy,[39] and to that "false theology" which postulated divinity for man, and the political democracy deriving from that assumption.[40]

Since progress was the result of a long and painful elaboration which all were to further according to their capacity, it was specious and dangerous to argue that all men would make the same contribution. Indeed, the common mind was incapable of understanding the profound comprehensive views of truth—moral, political, scientific, religious—which were needed to do the world's work of progress. One might work for the masses; one need not defer to them. Since education determined the class, and since an educated class was indispensable to the proper functioning of the American Experiment, it is to the elite class that men must look for the salvation of the country.

It was at this period of his development that what some have seen as Brownson's deepening conservatism combined with his shrewd insight to effect a remarkable anticipation of the well-known studies of Max Weber, R. H. Tawney, and others, on the relation of Protestantism and Capitalism.[41] Indeed, Brownson now considered the sad condition of the American laboring classes as the result of the Protestant rejection of the Church; the idea of authority, which had also been denied, could no longer restrain the natural selfishness of man who was free to regulate individual and social matters upon "the dictates of [the] self-interests of individuals and governments, instead of the dictates of Christian duty and love."[42]

During the middle ages, and prior to the Reformation the Catholic Church, by insisting on Gospel charity, on the merit of good works, and especially on the *merit* of voluntary poverty, and self-denial, had confined within some bounds the accumulative propensity of our nature, modified and restrained the empire of capital, and compelled it, through considerations drawn from a future life to make rich and ample provision for the poor.[43]

Jeremy Bentham, too, fared roughly at Brownson's hands. The *Review* had little use for Utilitarianism, and of its leader Brownson wrote in these terms:

. . . intolerable stupidity, ignorance and dogmatism of that prince of Utilitarians . . . a man innocent of all philosophical conceptions and . . . tendency, wise in his own estimation only . . . obstinately ignorant of the wisdom of others,—an exaggeration of the very worst features of John Bull, crying out against cant and humbug, and all the time the prince of canters and humbuggers, and the most egregious dupe of both. . . . His mind was a confused jumble, and he never succeeded in getting even one tolerably clear notion of the science of morals, either in its principle or in its details.[44]

There could be little excuse for this sort of ranting if it represented a mere exercise in concentrated abuse. But it might be remembered that Bentham (and Richard Hildreth whose book was under review) represented all those elements which were now so antipathetic to Brownson that, in his passion, he sometimes identified the man with the idea. But there is no mistaking here his abhorrence of the budding pragmatism which, after the Civil War, would ride triumphantly over Transcendental misgivings, governmental ineptitude, and an American ethic in some ways so devitalized as to become mere etiquette. Perhaps Brownson sensed the trend even this early, for his pessimism, a feature usually associated chiefly with his later thought, is not absent from his Review in 1844.

At this point in his life Brownson began taking instructions for entrance into the Catholic Church. The move was begun with Brownson's visit to Bishop Benedict Fenwick of Boston in May, 1844. Fenwick entrusted Brownson's education to his coadjutor, Bishop J. B. Fitzpatrick, and in October, 1844, the editor was received into the Catholic Church.

It must be remembered that, with the important exceptions of the article on Hildreth (Brownson's Quarterly Review for July, 1844), and the continuing article on Kant which was featured in the three issues from April to October, 1844, all the material discussed here had been written prior to Brownson's receiving formal instruction in his new faith. Indeed, as we have seen, the first issue of 1844 had specifically rejected the need for joining the Catholic Church, and had argued the "New Church" doctrine of 1836, with its attendant accent upon Progress, though his doctrine of progress was now one which specifically demanded supernatural and specific intervention through Providence. The assurance with which he appeared to argue in January did not last through May.

In any event, his growing conservatism was stated in rigid terms in July, 1844, about two months following the initiation of his religious instruction. The tone of the article entitled "Come-outerism or the Radical Tendency of the Day" is by no means surprising to any careful reader of the *Review*. He betrayed here his concern for those "democratic" elements whose assumptions seemed to him unrooted, and who, in their fervor for Progress, might well be unwitting subversives of the true American Experiment. Positions were hardening, as Brownson saw it; limited to two, they were so irreconcilable as to be polar. Middle ground denied, there were only "conservatives" and "revolutionaries." And, from this point on, "revolution" was never idly used; indeed, words such as "democracy" and "liberal" could seldom shed for him the cloak of the Jacobin.

American institutions, the results of the original condition of equality in this country, were impotent of themselves to preserve the freedom which had sponsored them in the beginning. The conditions of the country generally in 1844 were characterized by the lack of real religion; America had "galvanic motion but no genuine religious life." Reform movements, not surprisingly, were omnipresent; the "Come-outers"[45] represented in their best quality a spirit of protest against the disorder of the day in America. Yet this reform spirit was itself a revolutionary one—"the Protestant spirit of the sixteenth century of which the French Revolution was only one of the necessary expressions." The Come-outers were in fact the "Jacobins of the eighteenth century, the Independents and Fifth Monarchy men of the seventeenth, and the Protestants of the sixteenth."[46]

Brownson suggested that one could, on the one hand, accept the existing order, and, through methods which that order could authorize or tolerate, seek the correction of abuses. On the other hand, one might resist the existing order, negate its laws, and try to introduce an entirely new order. The first method Brownson called conservative, the second, revolutionary. The editor now chose the first;[47] to elect the alternative would be to assume that any "man has the right, *on his own individual authority* to attempt . . . [the] destruction [of the old order]. . . ."[48] Any such assumption was indefensible.

This revolutionary force, an arm of Satan at war with religious spirit, had broken loose in ecclesiastical affairs in the sixteenth-century revolt against authority, had passed into civil affairs, and culminated in the bloody French Revolution. Voltaire was the historical son of Luther.

The problem in America was that "we affirm a principle, follow it to a certain extent, in regard to certain things, and condemn all who, believing in the soundness of the principle, would carry it out in all its legitimate consequences. Now this is miserable folly and poltroonery."[49] How could a man be "revolutionary" in politics and conservative in religion?[50] A sound principle bears analysis.

The good people of the country, the practical people, the worshippers of common-sense, the *via-media* folks, who believe the panacea for all ills [*sic*] is compounded of equal doses of truth and falsehood, courage and cowardice, wisdom and folly, consistency and inconsistency will admit nothing of all this. They will permit us to condemn results, when we must not touch causes; the consequences, when we must respect the principle. When the principle goes a little farther than the mass are prepared to go, but still in the direction they are going, we may condemn the extreme, but not it. We may declaim against come-outerism . . . and the great multitude will applaud; but let us trace come-outerism to its principle, let us condemn that principle, and set forth and defend in opposition to it, the only principle on which we can logically and consistently combat come-outerism and . . . we ourselves are condemned.[51]

The man who wins the mob is he who "provided he does not leap too far at a single bound,—calls for liberty, reform, progress, man, humanity against oppressors—denounces state, authority, the Church and its pretensions."[52] Either revolution or conservatism must prevail: the advantage in America "is now all on the side of the radical tendency, however much it is decried in colleges and saloons."[53] Yet, although honest men may differ on the subject, a decision was imperative.

Essentially the same criticism, though one utilizing different terms of debate, was recorded in the October number wherein Brownson again took issue with the disciples of Charles Fourier.[54] What is noteworthy in this article is, first, Brownson's accent upon the nature of the Fall and original sin and their implications for the theory of Progress; second, his criticism of Fourierism as a relict of rational deism.

According to Brownson, Fourierism could not make good its claim upon Christianity, since the latter was stable and certain, not capricious and therefore "varying with each individual interpreter."[55] Its standard was "the word of God, as preserved and interpreted by the Church"; it taught that evil comes from within, "from man's abuse of the freedom essential to his being as man . . . [whose nature] in consequence . . . has become exceedingly disordered, his appetites and affections depraved, his moral tastes vitiated." Fourierism, on the contrary, assumed that human nature was perfect, that man's instincts, passions, and drives were essentially holy, and "that the evil in the world comes from causes extraneous to man [which] . . . restrain [and] repress his natural instincts and passions and hinder their free full harmonious development."[56]

It was idle, Brownson remarked, for such people as Parke Godwin, a Fourierist, to have argued the *original* perfection of human nature, and the loss at the Fall of this holiness. This was not Christianity, for Godwin also must hold as a Fourierist that the *essential* holiness of man survived the Fall. Further, the corruption Godwin admitted was not a corruption of man, but of the theater in which man played his part—that is to say, the actual condition of society.[57] The Fourierists recognized seven phases in the life of Humanity: "namely, Birth, Infancy, Youth, Maturity, Decline, Decrepitude, and Death. Maturity is the Apogee or Plenitude; Birth, Infancy, and Youth belong to the *ascending* scale; Decline, Decrepitude, and Death to the *Descending* scale."[58] The Fall, according to the Fourierists, took place in the "Dentition" period (roughly, the Infancy of Man)—that is, on the ascending scale at a time, in brief, when man was on his way to better things. This was not only not Christian doctrine, it was illogical on the face of the argument.

Brownson supplemented his criticism by an examination of the Fourierist doctrine of Attraction,[59] a teaching which assumed the perfection of human nature, an essential of all Fourierist doctrine, and one which was the base upon which its author built his system. The editor followed with an implied criticism of Fourierism as deistic.[60]

Fourierism, Brownson concluded, was dangerous principally because it declared the Church unnecessary. For thus it must mistake the evil of man's nature for its effect—the evil in society—and it attempted to cure the latter while ignoring the former. In so doing, it denied to man the grace of God:

Here is their fatal mistake. . . . No human arrangements, no industrial and unitary combinations, can deliver us from the body of this death. Nothing can deliver us but the grace of Our Lord Jesus Christ, the benefits of His mission and death personally applied by the communication of the Holy Spirit. . . . And till we receive this grace . . . it is in vain we attempt social ameliorations. They will all prove abortive.[61]

The notions of original sin and the need for redeeming grace with which time and history had played havoc were being brought back again into sharp intellectual focus in New England. The need of understanding both would henceforth become implicit in Orestes Brownson's view of the American Idea.

To Brownson now, man was a wounded and therefore limited creature who, for the demands of order as well as true liberty, needed society, and that society was impossible without government. Government could not be carried on without some instrument which incorporated the truths of the natural law, and, in America, that instrument was the federal Constitution. The problem of ultimate sovereignty was not to be decided by presupposing "natural rights" wholly based in man simply because he was man. For ultimate sovereignty resided in Justice, or God; man's political sovereignty was a mediate power deriving from the ultimate source, and was limited to the people acting not as individuals, but as a definite people, a nation. A mob had neither sense nor sovereignty.

God is both within and without the world of space and time, but is separate from that world—a view which countered what Brownson thought to be the pantheistic tendency of Transcendentalism.[62] The Creator is brought ultimately to his people—i.e., all Humanity—through the mediatorship of Jesus Christ, who united two natures in one person and who became the instrument of mercy which reforged the links of the worlds of grace and nature. Historically, men were united (in a horizontal sense) through the theories of "Communion" and the solidarity of the race, and this union was true of men in their own time and as a race throughout history.

Both theories could be held only by assuming the active and continuing Providence of God which, therefore, accounted for the relation of the individual to the race, and supplied essential purport to the idea of Progress. What in Brownson's thought was still lacking prior to 1844 was a continuous agency of grace[63] dependent upon God (i.e., the sacraments) through His Son, Jesus, and, mediately, through the Apostolic succession. The Catholic Church was now more and more plainly what he had been seeking under the term, the "New Church."

Progress, once the irresistible law, the end of the American Dream, the proof of the Experiment, the agent for the Mission, now faded as the central purpose of existence. While it was still true that progress remained as the work of the Church whose mission was the evolution and realization of the true principles of the Christian dispensation, and while the work "constitutes the continued progress of mankind,"[64] yet progress can be achieved *"only by virtue of a wisdom and a power not [man's] own."* Any assumption that man has the inherent power of progress, or innate capacity for improvement, was to Orestes Brownson in 1844 "all Moonshine."[65]

Progress depended upon Providence; as far as the latter had a higher end which is not mundane, then Progress in its true sense would tend not to the world of time, but to the timeless. Brownson had been forced by his reason to accept the idea cited succinctly in the phrase "every generation is equidistant from eternity."[66] The effect of such a truth upon the American Idea as Brownson once had held it may be remarked as this book proceeds.

What may be recognized finally is the ironic fact that Pierre Leroux, whose thought had developed from the *philosophes,* from Bacon, Descartes, and the great progressivists, should so influence Orestes Brownson. For Brownson, juxtaposing the lessons learned from his French master with the idea of the solidarity of the human race, saw in the process the historical relation of mankind. That the sequent train of thought should help construct for the American progressive a theory of Progress, generating through Providence, which would negate the bases of inherent natural progress, constituted a denial of some dearly held assumptions of early dreamers of the American Dream.

NOTES

1. *Works,* v, 161. The new review was, of course, *BrQR,* begun in January, 1844.
2. Schlesinger, *Brownson,* pp. 156–159. Had the same reasoning been applied to Kant (or to Schelling or to Swedenborg) American literature would have had a calmer if less interesting course. Schlesinger's comment that only Catholics could understand Brownson here may be correct; it is true, however, that others could understand that Brownson was tending toward the Catholic Church, and an old friend clearly warned him of this consequence (letter, Isaac B. Pierce to Brownson, July 28, 1843; Brownson Papers, AUND).
3. It might be said that, upon the whole, his conservative trend continues in these articles; that what appear to be his "attacks" upon the democratic principle are merely the logical extension of principles already enunciated. The article on Providence (*Works,* IV, 361–423), a discussion of which follows above, is, however, to my knowledge, the only full-scale one he ever attempted on the subject. Certainly this

seems true for the years 1836–1860. Its importance at this time can be gleaned, it is hoped, from previous comment here.

4. Pp. 457–474. The material is reprinted in *Works*, IV, 361–423. For a cogent commentary see Thomas R. Ryan, "Orestes Augustus Brownson and Historiography," *The Irish Ecclesiastical Record*, 85, No. 1,057 (January 1956), 10–17; *ibid.* (February 1956), 122–130. An interesting treatment of another of Brownson's essays at this time can be found in Guttmann, *Tradition*, pp. 83–84.

5. *Works*, IV, 362–364.

6. *Ibid.,* p. 364.

7. *Ibid.,* pp. 364–392. These discussions are clear, interesting, and well worth reading. Their significance is real (though negative) since Brownson is rejecting a large section of opinion which gave rise to the idea of Progress and its attendant optimisms.

8. *Ibid.,* p. 392.

9. *Ibid.,* p. 393.

10. For an interesting comment on Vico, see Karl Löwith, *Meaning in History* (Chicago, 1958), pp. 115–136; for another view, see Martin D'Arcy, *The Meaning and Matter of History* (New York, 1959), pp. 122–132.

11. *Works*, IV, 393.

12. *Ibid.,* pp. 394–396.

13. *Ibid.,* p. 396.

14. This error Brownson called the fundamental vice of modern philosophy (*ibid.,* p. 397).

15. *Ibid.,* p. 401. Brownson's use of his prime weapon—logic—was beautifully applied here. The theory which he attacked supplied the weapon for its own destruction.

16. *Works*, IV, 402–403.

17. See Löwith, *History*, pp. 137–145.

18. That Bossuet was also ignorant of the Brownsonian theory of "specially appointed nations" is clear from what has preceded (see *Works*, IV, 401).

19. Brownson here refuted a Transcendentalist view, i.e., that man, the actor, naturally aspires, and this aspiration suffices. See Brownson's full rejection, *ibid.,* p. 419.

20. *Ibid.,* p. 412. This statement and the material surrounding it point to the interesting modernity of Brownson's insight.

21. *Ibid.,* p. 413.

22. *Ibid.,* pp. 416–417. These pages contain historical evidence for Brownson's point.

23. *Ibid.,* p. 418. Brownson praises Lessing's view, expressed in *Die Erziehung des Menschengeschlechts,* that God is an educator who teaches timely lessons. The pupil, however, must work, and be responsible, or the educator's work is rendered nugatory.

24. Brownson never lost sight of the importance of this idea. Twenty years later, he made it a basis for his refusal to accept the "natural contract" theory in *The American Republic.* See *Works*, XVIII, 30–31.

25. *Works,* IV, 420.
26. *Ibid.,* p. 421; italics are Brownson's.
27. *Ibid.,* pp. 422–423.
28. *BrQR,* I, 1 (1844), 4. Brownson was not quite candid in this opening statement of his new *Review.* The truth is that the title "Boston Quarterly Review" was now the legal property of J. L. O'Sullivan; transfer of title to the name had been part of the consideration in the merger of October, 1842. Brownson's efforts to regain the name and O'Sullivan's polite refusal to accede are part of the extant correspondence. O'Sullivan, for instance, suggested in a letter that Brownson call his new review "The Examiner" (O'Sullivan to Brownson, October, 9, 1853; Brownson Papers, AUND).
29. *Ibid.,* pp. 5–6. This distinction of purpose Brownson made in several places. While it would appear to be largely true, yet the statement cannot be used as a sword to cut off the early *Review* as not properly reflective of Brownson's thought. This would be to commit Laski's error in reverse. *BQR* is so reflective, if in no other way than in showing his development, as indeed Brownson admitted when he stressed "advancement" of views rather than "change" (*ibid.,* pp. 3–4).
30. *Ibid.,* pp. 10–11. This view is reflected later when he will deny its efficacy in his argument with Newman. There is, however, no systematic working-out of a theory of development in these pages. He does indicate that Protestantism "is a direct protest against the progress of the race, an attempt to keep the Church stationary in her action . . . and is, therefore, anti-christian," though this tendency is more implicit in Protestant principles than expressed in formal statement by the reformers (*ibid.,* pp. 12–13).
31. *Ibid.,* pp. 13–15.
32. *Ibid.,* p. 15. Here, still, was the "New Church" doctrine, though the new emphasis altered the early dress.
33. *Ibid.,* p. 17.
34. *Ibid.,* p. 18. The line is drawn: the American Idea is not "ultra" but, properly understood, traditional. Brownson, therefore, felt he must take the "conservative" side of politics, a side he insisted had been his since 1838. This was especially true "here in this country, at least, [where] the existing order is to be preserved . . ." (*ibid.,* p. 19). The American Experiment was to be upheld; our government was a "constitutional republic," not a "democracy."
35. *Ibid.,* p. 26; italics mine. This "adamic" concept seems to have been particularly on Brownson's mind at this time. In the same issue (January 1844) he appeared to blame mass democracy for the failure of the American Dream which, of course, included the "many peculiar advantages" with which America began—that is, virgin soil, vast new country, great internal resources, remoteness from the "vicious" example of the Old World, opportunity for agriculture, people of simple tastes, etc. Briefly put, the listed advantages add up to the pantisocratic ideal. These advantages Americans had no longer; in-

deed, they had fallen nearly level with the Old World, and away from the stern virtues of their past (*BrQR*, I, 1 [1844], 84–85; *ibid.*, I, 2 [1844], 189–190).

36. See his article "No Church, No Reform," *BrQR*, I, 2 (1844), 175–195. Also *ibid.*, I, 3 (1844), 310–327; 367–385. Still, tradition, through continuing inspiration, was providing new insights whose force not only supported the old, but widened and deepened it.

37. See "Necessity of a Liberal Education," *BrQR*, I, 2 (1844), 194–208.

38. "The law of all government, like that of man himself, like that of the universe of which man is a part, is STABILITY in PROGRESS" (*BrQR*, I, 2 [1844], 226; emphasis is Brownson's). The Constitution, that guarantor of order in a properly conceived America, rested upon "the presence of a higher than human authority . . ." (*ibid.*, p. 242). This was Brownson's present doctrine of ultimate sovereignty.

39. At this time he was conducting a study of Kant's *Critique*. See *BrQR*, I, 2 (1844), 137–174; *ibid.*, I, 3 (1844), 281–309; *ibid.*, I, 4 (18), 417–449. A good brief discussion of his attitude toward Kant can be found in Schlesinger, *Brownson*, pp. 177–179, though professional philosophers may find Schlesinger's easy dismissal of Brownson's arguments a bit superficial, as they may find Brownson's dismissal of Kant premature.

40. This "false theology" sprang from German transcendentalism, and was represented in America by such thinkers as Channing. *BrQR*, I, 2 (1844), 198. See also his review of Richard Hildreth's *Theory of Morals*, *ibid.*, I, 3 (1844), 328–349.

41. This area of Brownsonian prescience has escaped notice, as far as I can determine, except for a passing mention by Alexander Kern ("The Rise of Transcendentalism," *Transitions*, p. 260 n. 55). Kern's reference is to Brownson's *New Views* of 1836; the material there is too general to sustain more than the brief reference given. Further, in 1839, Brownson was praising the "business habits of our country men . . . their money-getting propensities" as an aid to Progress— hardly the Weber–Tawney conclusion (*BQR*, II, 1 [1839], 10–11). But in 1844 his mind seems definitely settled on the point.

42. *BrQR*, I, 2 (1844), 279. Increasingly in Brownson's thought this lack of human moral restraint was becoming associated with a notion very like original sin operating in the deeper recesses of the nature of man. See *BrQR*, I, 3 (1844), 312–313.

43. *BrQR*, I, 2 (1844), 279–280. There is further extension of the idea (p. 280) as Brownson stated that he had come to this conclusion before he had read Bishop Hughes' essay on the same general topic. See also *BrQR*, I, 3 (1844), 326–327.

44. *Ibid.*, p. 333.

45. The name stems from the Biblical injunction: "Come ye out, come ye out from the midst of Babylon, and be ye no longer partakers in iniquity . . ." (Rev. 18:4).

46. *BrQR*, I, 3 (1844), 369–370.

47. His explanation included a history of his own experience; he argued

that maturity and the wisdom of years had brought his position to its current firm stand. Yet, conservative or not, Brownson called himself as staunch an advocate for Progress as was any young radical firebrand (*ibid.*, pp. 370–371).

48. *Ibid.*, p. 371; italics are Brownson's.
49. *Ibid.*, p. 381. Brownson may be thinking here not only of the current criticism for his change of views (as some saw it), but, perhaps, too, of his experience with the "Laboring Classes" essays, which to him were merely logical extensions of the views he held even with many of his critics.
50. Brownson raised a point very astutely here. Though he did not probe it, he was clearly assuming the impossibility of compartmentalizing the various activities of men, thus ruling the effects of one off from the other. His opponents were already in practice doing just that. Later nineteenth-century tycoons who worshipped on Sunday and stole voraciously on Monday would not have understood the point, but their historians would.
51. *BrQR*, I, 3 (1844), 381–382.
52. *Ibid.*, p. 383.
53. *Ibid.*, p. 384.
54. *BrQR*, I, 4 (1844), 450–487. This article is a restatement and a more developed criticism of Fourierism than he had attempted in a prior article (*BrQR*, I, 3 [1844], 310–327). The great importance of Fourierist principles as they were adapted and currently used at Brook Farm seems to demand little comment here.
55. *BrQR*, I, 4 (1844), 451.
56. *Ibid.*, p. 452.
57. *Ibid.*, pp. 453–454.
58. *Ibid.*, p. 458; italics are Brownson's.
59. *Ibid.*, pp. 461–462.
60. *Ibid.*, pp. 465–466.
61. *Ibid.*, p. 486.
62. *BrQR*, I, 1 (1844), 9–17.
63. The theory of "providential men" was not denied, but it was clearly inadequate to the grand purpose.
64. *BrQR*, I, 1 (1844), 10–11.
65. *BrQR*, I, 2 (1844), 189.
66. See Jean Daniélou, *The Lord of History* (Chicago, 1958), p. 101.

5

BROWNSON'S QUARTERLY
REVIEW, 1845-1849

"IT WOULD BE IMPOSSIBLE," wrote a contemporary commentator, "to link [Brownson's] former opinions with his present ones, by any connexion, either logical or psychological."[1] If Rufus Griswold was demanding a point-by-point examination, analysis, and demonstration, then perhaps few will argue with his conclusion. But if this yardstick is to be applied, what American thinker of importance in the middle of the nineteenth century could survive such an examination—Emerson? Thoreau? Whitman? Webster? George Ripley? Horace Greeley? In an age of change, growth and development are almost as ubiquitous as lack of principle. If that growth demands rejection of some or all of one's past, the rejection may still serve, historically, as a link to that past.

If it can be shown that Brownson, or anyone like him, was capricious in his change, or intransigent, or insincere, or otherwise dishonest, then the implications of Griswold's statement deserve to be entertained. If not, then it may be much more important to try to understand the change; the interest at this point should be not in whether Brownson was right or wrong, but in whether, given *his* assumptions, climate of mind, and time, he thought he was right. Sincerity, while no guarantee of truth, is not yet as nervous a word as respectability. As Henry James once remarked, it is a complex fate to be an American.

That Orestes Brownson came under the tutelage of the rather limited Bishop Fitzpatrick in 1845 seems pointless to deny.[2] That he was wholly under that influence is not at all so secure a fact. The rash of apologetical articles which spread through the *Review* in the years following the editor's conversion are to be attributed, it seems clear, certainly in their polemic tone, to that influence. But the equally prolific examinations of American life, and the underlying assumptions of American governmental philosophy and thought are merely a continuation of like articles which Brownson had been publishing since he had begun the *Boston Quarterly Review* in 1838. Indeed, he was careful to show during this period, as will become clear, that certain conclusions now drawn were implicit in the judgments he had been making long prior to his conversion. But the important point here is this: the American Idea— Dream, Experiment, Mission—did not, after Brownson's conversion, become lost in a welter of strictly religious controversy. Between 1845 and 1849, for example, he published twenty or more major articles on the general subject, an average of one per issue for the five-year period. Whatever be the influence of his new religion upon these articles, or whatever the logical disagreements he himself will have with his former positions (say, for example, in *New Views* of 1836), two facts should be emphasized: 1. his preoccupation with America and its position never faltered; 2. given a few pivotal redefinitions or clarifications of the same, there is a definite relationship of his thought on this matter to the material he had written from 1840 to 1844, and, assuming the intellectual change after the election of 1840, to the material before 1840. Indeed, it might be well at this point to cite Brownson's own words:

Then I was indignant at the past, and wished to destroy all existing society and to create a new society modeled after certain notions of social perfection of which I then dreamed. But now I absolve the past, see much in the present to approve, and have no wish to destroy, but to perfect what is already begun. I would not, if I could, blot out the past. I love it too much. . . . I am now much more of a conservative. The age of revolutions is passed by. We live in an epoch, at least in a country, of orderly legalized process. . . . Here is no settled order to break up, no privileged class to break down, no change in the fundamental laws to be effected. . . . There is no need of [terms such as] Conservative and Radicals. Both terms should be abolished. . . . I am then, it may be seen, neither Conservative nor Radical, but a combination of both. . . .

These words were published on July 1, *1836*.[3]

In his probing of the American Idea after 1845, Brownson examined fairly carefully what he conceived to be the implications of his new faith in relation to his old convictions. The study included the mutual contribution of Catholic and Protestant thought to liberty, especially liberty in a democratic society, with the partisan positions, if one may so speak, considered in their mutual relation to the meaning of Christianity. That this involves some study of history is obvious. The idea of Progress—that staple optimism of the American nineteenth century—would be reconsidered under what was now to be a Catholic light as Brownson saw it. Providence, however, was now an axiom to Brownson; there would be no more full-scale discussions of it.

In the January *Review* there were four articles on the general subject, articles which made up the major part of the issue. The article entitled "Native Americanism" was ostensibly a review of Fenelon's *Catholicism Compatible with Republican Government,* and was actually a plea for national harmony in the United States. Brownson, a native American, had no patience with the actual party of the same name which offended against the idea of America—i.e., that here "merit makes the man," and that there should be given "to each one according to his capacity, to each capacity according to his works."[4] The Native American party, which represented Protestant resistance not to the Irish specifically but to Catholicism, worked against the best interests of the country, since the nation, as a democracy, demanded for its very life a virtuous populace. Protestantism had proved itself incapable of promoting such virtue among the people; moreover, it was dead, and no longer an influence, as the clamor of all the reformers (Emerson, the Come-outers, Fourierists, Socialists, Communists) attested. While it was true, Brownson continued, that Protestantism founded America—given the circumstances, it could have done no other—it was now not capable of sustaining such a free society, for it lacked that "unction of the spirit" which would foster virtuous action. The rampant materialism current in America was offered as another proof. Catholicism alone can foster such action, such virtue, without which democracy was a "mischievous dream . . . a delusive dream."[5] Free institutions could not be maintained without a vigorous Catholicism,[6] which was not given to sectarianism, or to a false view of liberty.

Here is Brownson's statement of the American Idea at this time:

We have been accustomed to trace the hand of a merciful Providence in reserving this New World to so late a day for Christian civilization; we have been in the habit of believing that it was not without a provi-

dential design, that here was reserved an open field in which that civilization, disengaging itself from the vices and corruptions mingled with it
in the Old World, might display itself in all its purity, strength and
glory, and work out for man here on earth a social order to which
the good hope to attain hereafter. We have regarded it as a chosen land,
not for one race, or one people, but for the wronged and down-trodden
of all nations, tongues, and kindreds, where they might come as to a
holy asylum of peace and charity. . . . Here was founded, as it were,
a city of refuge to which men might flee from oppression . . . [and]
tyranny, regain their rights as human beings, and dwell in security.
Here . . . every man . . . was to be regarded as man—as nothing more,
as nothing less. Here we were to found, not a republic of Englishmen,
of Frenchmen, of Dutchmen, of Irishmen, but of men; and to make
the word *American* mean, not a man born on this soil or that, but a
free and accepted member of the grand republic of men. Such is what
we have regarded as the principle and destiny of this New World; and
with this, we need not say, Native Americanism is directly at war . . .
[a] going back to the barbarous ages. . . .[7]

Brownson's hopes for the American Idea were high. Yet America
had "virtually failed to accomplish the hope of its founders" and
the Dream and the Experiment would speedily be lost without "some
notable change" in the people; the best that could be hoped unless
that change came was a sinking "into a miserable timocracy, infinitely
worse than the most absolute despotism."[8] Catholicism could be
the savior of this country. The Protestant virtue of philanthropy
had to be raised to the Catholic virtue of charity, or there would
be no true equality, no true love of all men. "We look for our
safety [i.e., of the Republic] to the spread of Catholicism. We
render solid and imperishable our free institutions just in proportion
as we extend the kingdom of God among our people, and establish
in their hearts the reign of justice and charity."[9] The American
Idea, in short, was dependent now upon the disinherited mother
of Western civilization; the Idea itself was not devitalized, but the
underlying principles demanded a more severe scrutiny.

In April, Brownson took up the question of reform, and decried
the idea of regaining a "lost Eden" in America or anywhere else.[10]
Reformers who hope by "free, full, and harmonious development
of human nature" to restore some pristine purity of the individual
man or of the human race were deluding themselves dangerously.
Eden was ahead, not behind, wrote Brownson, and original sin had
killed the first Eden forever. The law now to be imposed, he con-

tinued, was that of the Gospels, *Beati pauperes spiritu*. Man must reform his own spiritual life; there was no other kind of reform possible.

This relatively brief discussion preceded an essay in the July number on "Protestant Love of Liberty," which, in turn, was followed by one in October entitled "Catholicity Necessary to Popular Liberty."[11] By this time, clearly, Brownson had rejected the old religion of "Humanity" of his earlier days, and now associated those old errors with Protestant beliefs in general:

Our modern philosophy, poetry, literature in general, politics and institutions are rapidly conforming themselves to [the religion of humanity], and preparing to embellish, and sanctify, and sustain it. The appeal through all is to the 'mighty heart of humanity, . . . the onward movements of the masses.' Alas! how little do they who are burning incense to 'the masses' . . . know of what horrible idolatry they are guilty, into what depths of sin and misery they are plunging this poor human race they profess . . . [however] honestly, to serve! God forgive us for having been once one of their number![12]

The names of these misguided agents were "LIBERAL, PHILANTHROPIST, and REFORMER," and their number was legion.[13]

In this discussion of the Protestant view of liberty, Brownson argued that Protestantism could offer "no antagonist power to wealth."[14] Furthermore, all the reformers of the sixteenth century were merely political instruments, masks for the power-hungry monarchs who, in reality, had been the originators of the Protestant Reformation. These men were

hostile to religious liberty . . . opposed to the independence of the Church, who wished to bring it into subjection to the state, to make it their ally, their tool in oppressing the masses and fleecing the multitude. . . . This they could not do, so long as they acknowledged the spiritual authority of the Pope, or a common center of ecclesiastical unity. Here is the noble, the *royal* origin of Protestantism, which has the impudence in open day to call herself republican, and the friend of religious liberty.[15]

Recalling like sentiments expressed in *New Views*, wherein the idea of religion as a function of the state was considered "materialism," Brownson submitted that Protestantism had tolerated liberty because her multiplication of dissent had forced her so to do. The American Protestant record of intolerance in Virginia, for example, or in Massachusetts, or even in Maryland, was far from creditable; what religious liberty had existed had been caused not by the liberality of one or more Protestant sects, but by the multiplicity of sects.[16] The record of Protestantism in this country, he wrote in summation, was concern with breaking away from England prior to 1776, and making money thereafter; to prove his point he cited the book *The Simple Cobbler of Aggawam in America* (1645) by Nathaniel Ward, a Puritan clergyman. America could hope for little support from Protestantism in its search for proper liberty.

Before essaying a discussion of Catholicity (he seldom used the word "Catholicism") and Liberty, Brownson in an essay in July had this to say about the Church and popular government:

A new political order seems to us to be rendered inevitable by the popular movements of modern times . . . an era of popular governments. The people are to take the place of the old kings and nobles. Whether this will be a change for [the] better [is] . . . problematical; but that it is to be we regard as inevitable. . . . The Church, which has always been on the side of the people, will hereafter . . . be on the side of popular liberty, and the triumph of the Church and of the people will be celebrated together. . . . The most democratic government, under the sanction of the Church . . . free to fulfil her mission in the Spiritual order will be a good government, and perhaps the best of all conceivable governments. Whatever evils might be apprehended from popular liberty, where we have not the Church, will be avoided, where we have it. . . .[17]

In October he came to the key essay of the discussion, and to the key question: what can guarantee true liberty in a democracy such as America if the dominant religious body is moribund? His answer was forthright, and, it may be presumed, highly irritating if not unexpected to whatever non-Catholic readers of the *Review* still remained.

After defining his terms, Brownson carefully explained his purpose: "The thesis we propose to maintain is, therefore, that without the Roman Catholic religion it is impossible to preserve a democratic government, and secure its free, orderly and wholesome action. Infidelity, Protestantism, heathenism may institute a democracy, but only Catholicity can sustain it."[18]

The government of the United States was not, in its original constitutional form, a democracy but "a limited elective aristocracy," since, as his purpose was conceived, the representative was not to be responsible to his constituents, but to be independent of them.

Yet this original concept was now dead in any practical sense, for, since Jackson, the American government had been, for all realistic purposes, the quickly changing majority-will, employed as a kind of constitution. Nor could there be a return to the original concept, as John C. Calhoun was attempting. The practical question then became, how could Americans sustain the true liberty of the people under this capricious rule of the majority?

Brownson maintained that the essential point was to be found in the very theory of democracy: if the people were assumed to be the first, medial, and final cause, and yet were—as they were—fallible, taken either as individuals or as a group, and since they tended to be governed as much by emotion and self-interest as by intelligence and selflessness, then how could rational, intelligent government be expected from them? The answer appeared to be, in a high civic responsibility fostered by an adequate private virtue, both corporately and individually. Brownson contended that this necessary eminence had not yet been reached by the American people, and never would be if there were to be dependence upon the various agencies which had been proposed.

For example, Brownson asked whether the newspaper press could be depended upon here. Clearly not, since these organs were controlled by limited men who merely echoed popular errors. Nor could popular literature serve, for the obvious reason that it pandered to popular ignorance. It was arguable that education might provide the necessary grounding in virtue. But intelligence, even trained intelligence, did not automatically culminate in virtuous action: intelligent villains or virtuous dupes, save as museum specimens, could hardly suffice in the practical order. Who was to be the teacher, and what was he to teach? Ultimately the choice would be made by the very people who were to be improved, and the dilemma was not exorcised by its mere statement.

Perhaps Religion, then, was the only solution, as indeed it was, since it "is the power or influence we need to take care of the people, and secure the degree of virtue and intelligence necessary to sustain popular liberty."[19] A democratic state was to be governed by the people; religion alone could teach them to administer power wisely. But, to be effective, this religion must be above the people in order to control them; it could not be dependent upon them, for if the people decided what was good, and what the Church should teach, then the problem returned again.

Thus, Protestantism could not be effective, Brownson thought; its three stages of development could be summarized thus:

1. Religion had been placed under civil authority, and was so abstracted from Church control that the prince had determined the faith of his subjects. This condition had obtained, *mutatis mutandis,* originally in America. How could religion control the "sovereign" people? Could the people control the people? The quandary returned.

2. Later, historically, the authority of the temporal government had been rejected, and religion became subject to the control of the faithful. The democratic principle thus had been applied to matters of religion. "The patient directs the physician what to prescribe. . . . The people [here] take care of religion, but who takes care of the people?"[20]

3. The final stage had to be individualism, wherein the individual chose his own beliefs, and "this [condition] makes a man's religion the effect of his virtue and intelligence, and denies it all power to augment or direct them. . . . The individual takes care of his religion, but who or what takes care of the individual? The State? But who takes care of the state? The people? But who takes care of the people? Our old difficulty again."[21] For, Brownson argued, Protestantism ultimately was constrained to teach what the people demanded, and "must follow instead of controlling, their passions, interests, and caprices."[22] It became, then, either an expression of the government, or of the people, and it had, in any case, to obey either the one or the other.

To Brownson, the great danger to the United States was the predominance therein of material interests, and, because democracy was especially sensitive to the passions and interests of the people, what would rule America would be the stronger passions and interests. Thus in America the acquisition of wealth was made easy, and those who gained it would tend to increase it in proportion as they could capture and use the government. The only possible control was somehow to moderate the desire for wealth, and to inspire the people with a sense of justice so that one interest might cease struggling inordinately at the expense of another.

Alive to this difficulty,[23] the Founding Fathers had attempted to checkmate its effect through a written constitution entrusted to the people. As any other restraint upon the people decreased, Brownson continued, the Constitution began to die. John Calhoun's compact theory of the American government—"though unquestionably the true theory of the Federal Constitution"—would never be practical in American society.[24] The question, therefore, still obtained: what sustains popular liberty?

Brownson's answer was that liberty may be sustained only by a religion which "can and will govern the people, be their master. . . . The word [master] must be spoken. . . . But it is not our word. . . ."[25] That religion was Catholicity which, being above the people, could command their obedience; indeed, it had the authority from God to do so. With God its only master, it was a religion made not *by* the people, but *for* them, and it was accountable to God alone, as a catholic, universal, supranational church. That church was both "adequate" and "necessary" to the sustaining of popular liberty, wrote Brownson, adding that he spoke not as a theologian, but as a "statesman." The authority involved was spiritual, not temporal; it was in this sense that Catholicity was suggested: as a religion, a moral not a political power, it could impose a moral restriction upon the so-called sovereignty of the people. The influence of the Church had to be upon "the mind, the heart, and the conscience." It would point out man's proper end, instruct him in proper values, discipline his passions, and teach him the true meaning of charity. "This," concluded Brownson, "is the kind of master we demand for the people, and this is the bugbear of 'Romanism' with which miserable panders to prejudice seek to frighten old women and children."[26]

Brownson's preoccupation with the need for virtue in American life was continued in the next number of the *Review,* that of January, 1846. The second article of that issue, one entitled "National Greatness,"[27] took note both of the American habit of assuming virtue, and of the "lofty notions" they had of past achievements and of future promise. They gloried in their youth, new cities, canals, railways, trade and commerce, schools, universities, their press, hospitals, asylums, poorhouses. Especially did they take pride in their government which reconciled the authority of the state with the freedom of the subject, and guaranteed religious liberty. Alive to the quick injury of denial, Americans were apt to miss the major point. The real question remained: what was the true standard of greatness?

We [i.e., Brownson] answer, that nation is greatest in which man may most easily and effectually fulfil the true and proper end of man. . . . The greatness of a nation is the greatness of the individuals that compose it. . . . No man is truly great who neglects life's great ends, nor can one be said in truth to approach greatness any farther than he fulfils them.[28]

To assess true national greatness, Brownson declared, one must first determine true individual greatness. That judgment turned upon the presumed end of man—that is, the end which Almighty God had assigned to the individual man. If man had only a natural destiny, religion was necessary to morality only as "a sort of police establishment." If the purpose were supernatural, man required supernatural revelation to achieve the supernatural elevation of his nature—i.e., in the order of grace, an end impervious to natural means. Man must obey God's law, and since grace is dispersed by God's law through the Church, man's true purpose could only be achieved by submission to the Church.

Now, if this test of the true end of man and, by logical extension, of the greatness of a nation should be applied to "your Goethes, Byrons, Shelleys, Scotts, Bulwers, Victor Hugos, Balzacs, Eugene Sues, George Sands, Kants, Hegels, Cousins . . . [they] shrink into inconsequence before the simplest Christian who has given his heart to God."[29] As for Americans, their goal was mammon. Their dominant passion was worldly wealth and preferment; to these ends "conspire all our education, science, literature and art. . . ."

Brownson reminded his readers that since the Reformation a "new social order" had developed and had tended in an industrial direction; by overemphasis, it had perverted a greater end by stressing a lesser one, even though its industrial successes had been impressive. With material success as a goal, American reckoning sailed south against the compass. One day history and experience would teach them that, as their laws must increasingly reflect the primacy of wealth and property, there would be a corresponding growth of the inequality of property, with fatal results to the American Experiment.[30]

The reign of the *novi homines* had resulted from an attenuation of religious faith, and the growing "devotion to the goods of time and sense. Consequently . . . wherever we find a popular government[31] we may regard the fatal results we have pointed out as inevitable, unless arrested by the operation of some cause foreign to that [which is] operating in the people and government."[32] Popular government, such as that in America, could function properly only if the people were devoutly Christian; if not, the prospect was for a godless republic, a possibility Brownson greatly feared. With the Church, democracy might be the best form of government; without it it was categorically the worst, "as our own [American] experience . . . will soon demonstrate."[33] In a great industrial nation no one was ever satisfied; all strove for the first social rank. To achieve that, men would neglect the spirit in a lemming-like rush for the material. Finally, "we shall be what were Tyre and Sidon, and Carthage, and what they are now."[34] Brownson took pains to make clear that he was not condemning wealth or industry as such, but the tendency to make material things the "ends for which [men might] live and labor. This is always sin . . . folly and madness."[35]

In the true greatness, then, America was sadly wanting, however she might be advancing industrially. Brownson concluded that

We see the golden, or rather *paper* age of demagogues advancing, and we tremble for our country. To us, the direction things are taking seems likely to prove disastrous. . . . We would not see our [American] experiment in behalf of popular freedom fail; we would see it succeed. It will not fail, it will succeed, if we return to God, put our trust in him, and live for the end to which he has appointed us.[36]

In Article V of the January number, Brownson met head-on the arguments of the nineteenth-century French progressivists, Edgar Quinet and Jules Michelet.[37] In a review of Quinet's *The Roman Catholic Church and Modern Society,* Brownson first summarized the comments of C. Edwards Lester, Quinet's translator, to the effect that Catholicity, led in France by the Jesuits, was a foe to progress. Quinet supported the thesis, and Brownson referred to the French thinker's earlier work *Ahasuerus* as a pastiche of English deistic infidelity, Spinozistic pantheism, the atheism of d'Holbach, and the *sans-culottism* of Marat and Robespierre. The battle lines were drawn: the argument between Quinet and Brownson over the idea of Progress was between Voltairism on the one side and Catholicity on the other.[38]

Brownson, relying heavily upon Bergier's *Traité historique et dogmatique de la vraie réligion* . . . , traced French and English deism from their beginnings to their ultimate degeneration into "absolute pyrrhonism." These seventeenth- and eighteenth-century developments, far from being new, were merely repetitions of what had happened in the ancient world.[39] And here Brownson for the first time applied the theory of "cycles" to the history of the idea of Progress. Eighteenth-century deism, disposing of all exterior forms of Christianity, had claimed to preserve its essential spirit, its essential idea, which independent of churchly forms could, through the power inherent in humanity, " 'throw off the whole burden of the times, and reconstruct at a given moment, a new world upon a new ideal.' "[40] This sort of progressivist claim was not new to Brownson; it had been his own faith in the late 1830s.

The apparent conversion of Christianity to infidelity was, according to Brownson, "the key to the whole teaching of the Progressivist, the St. Simonian, Fourierist or Societary, Rationalistic, and Mythic schools of modern Europe and America."[41] For example, the word "spiritual" to Quinet meant the power of the invisible, of thought; Providence, to the French thinker, meant "nothing but the instincts or natural tendencies of humanity, or more simply human nature."[42] Obviously, neither of these definitions of centrally important terms could be accepted by a Christian. Yet, this "new Christianity" of the progressivists depended upon the "innate energy or irrepressible instincts of man," and was, indeed, merely the reflowering of Pelagianism. For, as Quinet argued it, God revealed Himself from age to age in the tendencies of the masses, and thus, God's will became the popular tendency of an age or country. Humanity and God had one and the same nature: *vox populi, vox Dei.*[43] "The dark background of being on which man is traced by an invisible pencil . . . as Hegel teaches, arrives at self-consciousness only in man. . . ." This theme of the "Movement Party" (Progressivists) summarized the goal of this party of the future which followed the Spirit of the Age: the social revolution of Humanity was necessary to Progress. Conversely, the Catholic Church in their eyes was the "Stationary Party"[44] which was "wedded to the dead past, a friend to abuses . . . and an enemy to liberty."

Brownson made a stern stand for the Church (which is responsible to God alone, and not to "self-styled representatives" of humanity); her teachings, not human instincts or tendencies, were the measure of right and wrong, of true liberty and lawless license. Far from being new men with new ideas, Quinet, Michelet, and the rest were simply respading old errors, and "with all your genius you cannot even invent a new blasphemy." The Church opposed, not progress, but these innovators' idea of progress which assumes that man without going out of himself can make himself more than he is, the imperfect is able to perfect itself, the possible to make itself real. . . . Progress there may be, but not without a power foreign to the subject of progress. The error of the movement party is not in demanding progress, but in demanding it of man alone. . . . The condition of progress is fixed, permanent, and immovable political and religious institutions. . . . It is only this madness which wars upon the established order, and seeks to destroy, for the sake of progress, the condition of all progress, that the Church opposes.[45]

Institutions, considered in themselves, were not progressive, Brownson maintained, and there was no such phenomenon as a self-perfecting institution. Without a superior aid outside itself, the imperfect could not become perfect. "Religious institutions may be improved or perfected miraculously by the supernatural providence of God," but never could improvement come in and of itself. History revealed that, though institutions decline, they are never progressive; there was no such thing as a spontaneous civilization, or of a savage people emerging from their savage state *instanter*. "The earliest period of all civil and political institutions is their purest and best period. The history of all states is a history of decline, corruption, deterioration of their institutions. The struggle of nations is always for their lost rights, lost privileges." Aside from those inspired by Christian influences, the best laws of modern nations were of ancient vintage; any seeming advance was merely in administration of these laws. Innovation without Christianity had proved to be decay, engineered by men who, in Sallust's phrase, were *rerum novarum cupidi*. There was no true progress, no true individual liberty without the Catholic Church.[46]

In the October, 1846, *Review* there were lingering echoes of the discussion[47] in two essays; the first was a reflection upon Fletcher Webster's speech on war and loyalty; the second, a review of the novel *Thornberry Abbey*.[48] In the former he reintroduces the notion of the "high destiny and grave responsibility to which [a] new people are called" and remarked in contrast upon the "tawdry," "turgid," "stale," "flaccid," "fulsome," and generally disgusting glorifications of the American nation which were so much a part of self-regarding and flatulent patriotic speeches. This patriotism "on tip-toe . . . eloquence on stilts" was the product of "shallow brains and gizzard hearts which are always prating of the American spirit, American genius . . . American greatness, and calling for

an American party."[49] Much of this false eloquence was framed
in denigration of any foreign state whose political institutions
differed from native ones. The true patriots, wrote Brownson, were
"those calm, quiet, self-possessed spirits," some of whom were young
men such as Fletcher Webster. These men rose above the tendency
of the age and country and manifested "some respect for the wisdom and virtue of their ancestors." Webster and the others gave
room for hope that "our noble experiment in behalf of popular institutions may not be destined to a speedy failure." The great danger
to such an experiment, the editor continued, was the "radical tendency . . . so wide, deep and active in the American people"; these
innovators venerated nothing, spurned the old, the fixed, and were
so willing to experiment with anything, that it seemed that "man
and Providence have thus far done nothing but commit one continuous series of blunders."[50] This radical tendency, born of the efforts
and thoughts of "the Garrisons, the Parkers, the Sumners, the O'Sul-
livans, the Channings, the Abby Folsoms, *et id omne genus*," was
dangerous in its appeal to young ignorance. "Change is not always
progress and . . . it is more creditable to be able to revere wisdom
than to contemn it."[51]

The review of *Thornberry Abbey* was really a discussion of the
current status of American literature which was "infidel" now, and
would not truly flower until America became Catholic,[52] since
modern civilization as a whole was the work of the Church, "and
is informed with the Catholic spirit, and will not assimilate to itself
what is not Catholic." Therefore, "no national literature not Catholic
can really flourish."

Brownson argued that the American national character was not
yet formed, and would not be formed till the mass of Americans
came into "harmony with Christian civilization." It was idle to seek
the roots of American character in Protestant forebears; such "national diversities and peculiarities [must] lose themselves in one
common national character, with common habits, views, tastes and
feelings"; with that development there would be present "the indispensable conditions for a national literature."[53] It was as yet too
early to expect a worthwhile domestic literature. Until then, "other
nations will supply us with books, and better books than we can
write for ourselves."[54]

The year 1847 saw little diminution of Brownson's probing of the varied facets of the American Idea. As is clear from the essays of 1846, he was growing more secure in his convictions that, first, progress was possible, but only progress properly understood; second, that the great threat to the American experiment was the radical tendency abroad in the land, and its concomitant lack of serious thinking about the American Idea and its essential bonds to the past; and third, the absolute necessity of the Catholic spirit, which had so informed all Western civilization, to the success of the American Idea. Indeed, it was becoming clearer that without Catholicity, in Brownson's mind, the American Experiment was doomed, and with it the American Mission.

The first issue of the 1847 *Review* is devoted in large part to two familiar names, Jules Michelet and Edgar Quinet.

Brownson began a review of Michelet's *The People* by praising the author who, though an able scholar, unfortunately theorized, poetized, and sentimentalized history.[55] There followed a parallel criticism to that which we have examined in the January, 1846, number of the *Review*: "It was not left to this age to be the first to preach the Gospel to the poor, or to discover the real worth of man as man. . . . Many is the fledgling philosopher or philanthropist who fancies the world is rapidly advancing, because he learned something to-day of which he was ignorant yesterday."[56] Brownson repeated the distinction he had made between philanthropy and charity, and wrote of the former that it disquieted the masses, helped to eliminate their struggle for advance, and thereby augmented their suffering. Brownson did not mean to downgrade the human, but he did demand recognition of the fact that "Christian asceticism is the only path to true good, individual or social."[57]

Reviewing G. T. Headley's *The One Progressive Principle*[58] in a brief notice at the end of the January number, Brownson called the author "a male sentimentalist," and Headley's " 'one progressive principle' . . . mere moonshine. . . . [Headley's] reading of history is all in his eye."

The principle of progress cannot be itself progressive, but must be immovable, and the author's slightest error is that of mistaking the effect for the cause. We [i.e., Brownson] go as far as any man in defence of liberty, but we are yet to be convinced that the progress of liberty is to be measured by the destruction of its guarantees. . . . What we want, whatever the form of government, are safeguards for liberty in the shape of checks on power. Absolute governments are always an evil, and the wisdom of the statesman consists in the adoption of methods for their limitation.[59]

After reviewing Emerson's *Poems*[60] in April, Brownson returned in July to his old foes, Quinet and Michelet. Obviously the problems they posed were important to him at this time, and, just as obviously, no judgment of Brownson's mind in the late 'forties can be complete without some knowledge of the issues at stake in the debate.

The chief book under discussion in this article was *The Jesuits*, a combined work of the Frenchmen.[61] Brownson admitted early that his opponents belonged to the party to which he had once given allegiance, the "movement party"—that is, "very nearly what is commonly meant in this country by the 'transcendental party'."[62] The movement party, like the Transcendentalists, labored to construct a universal Religion, "to labor for the Christian *idea*" as they saw it.[63] There was added to this the notion of Progress, since they held human nature to be continuously progressive, and involved in "a progress without term." The position assumed, it followed that religion, too, was never complete and must continually be developing from its original germ; when anything in it became outmoded, and consequently a detriment to progress, then that element had to be discarded. Yet this progress, including that of religion, was not the work of grace, but of nature, and man must develop his religion by the free action of his own intellect, without the interposition of any agent outside of himself. In short, whatever tended to make religion "inflexible, immovable, and immutable . . . is hostile to religion itself, anti-Christian, mischievous to man, and hateful to God."[64] This doctrine, Brownson thought, became that of the "Progressivists," who expected religion to be developed or "spun, spider-like, from [man's] own bowels," and was not so much a belief in the Commandments and Revelation as an adaptation to the times, a "sort of India-rubber religion" which was nearly but not quite as good as no religion at all.

Yet these oracles were silent when the goal of progress was demanded. To Brownson the central point of Michelet's and Quinet's argument with the Jesuits was the former's contention that there was no law imposed on man by outside authority—even by God—and that the doctrine of liberty of thought was rooted in this condition. Yet these professors who asserted liberty of thought had not further demanded a law which granted and guaranteed liberty of thought. The illogical procedure offended Brownson: "If all thought be free, I am as free to think against that freedom itself as you are to think in its favor."[65]

Modern Americans ("the Beechers, Bushnells, Kirks") appealed to American national spirit to inhibit the view opposed to this "progressivism"—that is, the growth of the Church. Religion thus needed to plead at the bar of politics or nationality when, according to the Puritan fathers, the "Church is free and sovereign and can never be compelled to answer at the bar of the State. . . . This is the Christian doctrine; it is the doctrine of common sense; it is, moreover, the *American doctrine*."[66]

The Jesuits were not so much against Progress as they were opposing the professors' "Progressism." The question was, which was the proper view of Progress? The view "of progress taken by the Professors is only a recent and a crude speculation, [and] is entertained only by the Professors and their party."[67] Although Quinet and Michelet had a certain kind of humanity, and did want a better order of things, their views were impractical, and, worse, they sought to have the end justify the means. "Ever are we riddles to ourselves, till we find in God the solution. . . . Man must be equal to the creation of man. . . . If [God] has not furnished us with the means of instruction and of grace, it is idle to seek for the melioration of society; and if he has, it is worse than idle to seek the end by any other means than those which he furnishes."[68]

A final 1847 article of importance to the purpose here appeared in October; it was a commentary on Count Joseph de Maistre's work on political constitutions.[69] Brownson had some doubts about what appeared to be the deistic implications of some of de Maistre's thought; he was uneasy, too, about de Maistre's use of de Lamennais' principle *consensus hominum* to prove the truth of Christianity. However, he praised the author who, together with de Lamennais before his heresy, was given credit for bringing order to the Voltarian chaos in France by undercutting the influence of the "progressists" there. De Maistre's present book had particular value, said Brownson, for those in the United States who followed Hobbes, Locke, Rousseau, and Paine, and who had forgotten "that Divine Providence had something to do with forming, preserving, amending, or overthrowing the constitutions of states."[70]

De Maistre's principle, stated in its simplest form, insisted that, where the existing order was monarchy, the principle bid citizens to support monarchy; where the order was republican, the republic must be supported, and so on. Now, since "in His Providence" God had established a republic in the United States, Americans could not resist it without disobedience to God, "from whom is all power, by whom kings reign and legislators decree just things." Clearly, then, republican institutions were to be defended on grounds of conscience rooted in an unchanging moral law, and not upon mere opinion or temporary intellectual conviction. If constitutions were in fact "generated, not made; [i.e.] . . . grow up by Divine Providence," then such political constitutions were mediately imposed by God Himself "as the expression of Divine Will."[71] Only thus could they be said to have legitimacy, for the generative principle of all political constitutions, properly understood,[72] was "Divine Providence, never the deliberate wisdom or will of man." This constitution of a nation was "a living spirit, a living power, a living providence, and resides wherever the nation is, and expresses itself in every national act." The American Constitution had "grown to be what it is through the providence of God."[73] Bancroft in his *History* had pointed out that neither royalty nor nobility had emigrated to America from England, and that "our government is simply the British House of Commons . . . divided for the sake of convenience into an upper and lower chamber, and with such few changes and modifications as were necessary to provide for an executive authority. The constitution was determined for us by the providence of God, which so ordered it that only the commons emigrated. . . ."[74]

The American Constitution determined by Providence could not be changed without destroying the nation; this fact, for example, explained for Brownson the failure of the republican form of government in Spanish America, since royalty and nobility had been part of their makeup from the beginning.[75] On the other hand, the United States "in declaring independence made no revolution; we only threw off what was foreign, while we retained what was indigenous. . . . The removal of the foreign or English authority only enabled the indigenous to manifest and exert itself in open day, in full . . . vigor."[76]

De Maistre's "conservative principle" was not unfriendly to social amelioration or to "administrative changes" that might become necessary, but the true reformer must act without destroying, and under "the supremacy of the law, and . . . its sacredness."

"Progressists" tended to sweep away the guarantees of such law, and Brownson warned against the tendency.

There is progress of individuals, but no progress of human nature . . . , of particular nations but none of the race. Nations are like individuals; they are born with their peculiar constitutions and capacities which determine all they can be. They grow up like individuals, attain their growth, their maturity, decline into old age, become enfeebled, and die, and pass away. It is the universal law, and there is no *elixir vitae* for nations any more than for individuals. . . . The limits of our national progress are fixed by inherent principles of our constitution, and it is madness to dream of passing beyond them.[77]

Brownson appeared slowly to be closing the door firmly on the American Idea, especially upon the Experiment and the Mission. If the cyclic tendency of his thinking on progress (under de Maistre's influence) was true in its effect, then unlimited progress was impossible. Indeed, he explicitly admitted that conclusion—degeneration awaited its denial. Moreover, the spreading of democratic principles over the earth—in short, the American Mission—would obviously now run counter to the expectations (indeed, the will) of Providence. The conservatism of Brownson's present position would continue to develop somewhat unevenly until some years later he would categorically deny the efficacy of the American Idea; the judgment would come in a review of a book by George Bancroft.

A strong, explicit denial of his early position on progress took up a major part of Article III of the January *Review* for 1848.[78] The idea of progress Brownson now associated with the "spirit or tendency of the age" which he found running counter to the standard of God and His Church; his loyalty to the latter demanded a "stern and uncompromising war" on the former, which was the standard of the heresiarch. The peculiar heresy of any nation (and it had happened in every nation) originated in an attempt to "conform the Church to [the particular nation's] dominant ideas and sentiments."[79]

The discussion was continued in April in an article entitled "Catholicity and Political Liberty,"[80] a subject which, as we have seen, interested Brownson very much during this period; his treatment of it reflected his changing attitude toward the American Idea. To him, at this point, the *form* of government in any given country depended "on the particular constitution of that country, and not on the immediate ordination of God"—a doctrine, according to

Brownson, which had been taught by "Aquinas, Bellarmine, Suarez, Concina, Billuart, Busembaum, Liguori," and others.[81] Indeed, this doctrine had been at the heart of the dispute between Bellarmine and James I of England; the monarch had contended for the Hobbesian or Antinomian principle that the power of individual kings is directly from God, is absolute and unlimited—that is, the divine right of kings. James's view was a departure from previous thought in England and had succeeded ultimately in destroying order when liberty was the object; liberty, when order was sought. Rousseau's teaching which made the obligation of law depend upon the general will had the same tendency, as had any doctrine placing obligation in the general *reason*.[82] In all cases, God has "*no* share . . . ; they have excluded him from the noblest of his works."

There followed his argument that the Catholic Church by her actions and views had preserved liberty, especially through her religious teaching; furthermore, "she operated on the political and social amelioration of Europe" through the celibacy of the clergy, which had prevented a caste system in the Church by maintaining equality,[83] and by the temporal power of the pope. Brownson contrasted the "regular and onward" progress of the Church in this matter with what seemed to him the "disastrous effects" of Protestantism on political liberty and civilization.[84]

As for America, the Constitution of the United States (the term was used in de Maistre's sense of "constitution") "is of all national constitutions the most like what the Church has always adopted in her own practice." Far from being an ogre for Americans, Catholicity provided a hope since it would preserve the Constitution and have "sufficient influence to preserve the people in order with little outward force."[85] For the vigorous sustenance of liberty depended not so much upon a written constitution, or upon material forms of government, but rather upon the good administration of the government. Assurance of this condition came only in religion, without which no government could save the governed from oppression. Liberty was impossible without religion; true religion was impossible without the Church.[86]

In his comments on "Recent European Events" in the July, 1848, number, Brownson reiterated his detestation for both kings at their worst and mobs at their best—both are despotic. The American people were neither superior to nor essentially different from Europeans in intelligence, morals, or religion; but the republican form of government, providentially provided as the American legal governmental form, would shield Americans from such European upheavals as the revolution in France against Louis Philippe. "We are, so to speak, natural born republicans . . ."; the French did not have such a republican "interior life."[87] Convinced that republicanism was the best form of government for Americans, Brownson argued that even with such a system good and wise government is not automatic. This fact explained why, for example, had Brownson lived in the fourteenth century, he could have supported feudalism *vs.* centralism; in the seventeenth, centralism *vs.* the democratic tendency; in his own time, republicanism.[88]

In the final issue for 1848, Brownson published a summing-up of his position in an article entitled "Conservatism and Radicalism."[89] In it he again discussed the problems of liberty and order, the need for religion as guarantee of liberty, the necessary distinctions to be made upon the "right to govern," the tendency of democracy (though not necessarily republicanism) to "despotism or autocracy," and the importance of Providence. Offering reasons why he believed his position on these matters to have been thoroughly consistent, he cited his past arguments as proof.[90]

To those who might argue that his "conservative position" went against the "progress of civilization," Brownson countered that these opponents made two invalid assumptions: 1. ". . . that the legitimate constitution of a State is, or may be, an abuse; and, 2. That the progress of civilization is denied, if the right to subvert the constitution is denied."[91] The first was a contradiction in terms (nothing legal can be an abuse); again, destruction of the constitution destroyed also the state, and invited despotism and anarchy. Either was fatal to civilization. Could one, then, advance civilization by subverting the state? Or was not "the progress of civilization . . . inconceivable without the progress of the state, and the progress of the state . . . inconceivable without the existence of the state"?[92]

Revolution solved nothing, as the French example showed; the so-called American Revolution had not been a revolution at all, since the colonies had been held by compact to the crown, and when George's tyranny had broken the compact, the colonies were absolved from allegiance. The reason was, then, that the colonies were "*ipso facto,* sovereign states, and the war . . . was simply a war in defence of their independence as such states. . . . There was no war on the constitution of the American states."[93] The residents of the United States were children "come to our majority"; the modern revolutionists were "parricides who knock the aged parent in the head, or cut his throat in order to possess themselves of the homestead."

Law is "will regulated by reason"; it is not arbitrary will. And the editor closed his efforts on the subject for the year 1848 with this statement of his "conservative" position:

Life has, and as long as the world stands will have, its trials; and, however impatient we may be, there is and will be much we can conquer only by learning to bear it. It is easy to stir up a revolution, to subvert a throne or a dynasty; but to re-establish order, to re-adjust the relations of man with man, of prince with subject, and subject with prince, so as to remove all evils and satisfy every wish—this is labor . . . work which no mortal man has ever yet been equal to. A man could lose paradise, bring sin, death, and all our woe into the world; only a God could repair the damage, and restore us to the heaven we had forfeited.[94]

Thus in a summary essay of his position in 1848 the pivotal idea of original sin received the strongest possible emphasis. What it was providing was a base for a new Eden of sorts and in more than figurative form. In any form, indeed, the notion of cycle cannot be far from the core even in irony. For Brownson, at least at this period in his life, the figurative had faded into the literal, and progress could be only circular. Consequently, early in 1849, Brownson was moved to write that "no man of sound sense and respectable scholarship" could accept the "modern doctrine of progress" since men were sinful creatures who have not on earth a lasting city; while it was true that clinging to superannuated forms, or to outmoded human institutions, was false wisdom, yet it was no more unwise than seeking "uncalled-for changes."[95] For this reason he opposed the "Young Ireland" movement, for example, because of its revolutionary and Jacobin character.[96] Brownson seems at this time to have been reading Edmund Burke, and he had been impressed, particularly by Burke's appeal to the Anglo-Saxon sense of justice and of reason.[97]

One of the major threats to what was now Brownson's conception of the American Experiment was socialism, itself a consequence of "modern *progressive,* philosophical, or radical democracy such as led to the French Revolution."[98] Indeed, it was "Progressists" (e.g., the Fourierists) who were to blame for the blood on Paris streets, and for the convulsions of the whole civilized world,[99] evils which stemmed directly from "Protestant and democratic premises held by the great body of our countrymen, and the . . . [so-called] enlightened portion of mankind."[100]

In America, Brownson suggested, the trend was from *political* democracy toward *social* democracy, and, ultimately, inevitably, centralism must be the result. Socialism, which lived in "Christian guise . . . in the language of the Gospel," had been introduced to America by William Ellery Channing,[101] though the first to unite Christianity and socialism was the Abbé de Lamennais. Brownson deplored his own role in propagating "the *Democracy* of Christianity,"[102] since the idea represented the principal evil of socialism which was really a heresy, a "counterfeit Catholicity."

As de Lamennais argued, Christianity did seek the good of man in this life; but Brownson further insisted that the change must come in and by Christianity, not through an agency outside itself, or independent of itself. To place the real good in the natural order alone, and then to assume that it could not be attained by individual effort, but only by collective action, was socialism's root error. For thus the individual was enslaved to nature and to society; these in turn depended upon wisdom, folly, passion, instinct, caprice, and the whim of other men. And true liberty was gone. Since Providence was alive, the Creator "[had proposed] the amelioration of the lot of man even . . . in this world. But how?"[103] Certainly it was no easement of his condition to close man off from his ultimate goal, especially by foreshortening his liberty in this world. Truly wise authority would concede the need of faith and of transcendent purpose.

In April, Brownson renewed the theme in an article entitled "Authority and Liberty"[104] wherein he consigned "Kant, Schelling, Hegel, Cousin, Leroux, Delammenais, Hermes, Schleiermacher, Carlyle, Emerson,[105] [and] Parker . . . to the Alexandrian [Syncretic] school," or Neoplatonism, which the editor pointed out was the root of all modern Continental or English "Platonism."[106] This Neoplatonism, which had received its strongest impetus through Erasmus ("the Voltaire of his time") and the humanists, had sown the seeds of practical infidelity which, combined with other causes, ultimately had produced the Reformation. The pantheistic trend of Neoplatonism was reproduced in "our modern syncretic, gentilist, rationalistic school," and socialism was "pantheism adapted to the apprehensions of the vulgar,—refined and voluptuous with the

Fourierists and Saint-Simonians, coarse and revolting with the Chartists and Red Republicans."[107] Thus did man's vaunted "progress" move in a circle—the nineteenth century was returning to the fourth, and the modern American recipients of the phenomenon were indebted to "Schlegel, Carlyle, Macaulay, Guizot, Bancroft, and *The Boston Quarterly Review*."[108] Summarily, Brownson's general rejection of modern Neoplatonism included these points: first, it treated authority and liberty as antipodal values; second, it reduced Christianity to mere rationalism, and revived Alexandrian gentilism; third, it denied moral accountability, and appeared, at least, to favor unbounded license; finally, it did not accept either divine sovereignty or the supremacy of the spiritual order.[109]

The pessimism carried over to the American Idea. In an article which reflected much of his earlier respect for Americans as a great people,[110] he yet had this to say of the American Idea: "That the American people have a destiny we do not doubt; that they have a great and glorious destiny we would fain hope; that they are on the road to such a destiny we have yet to be convinced. . . . The chances are against [their] attaining that destiny which seems to have been promised it."[111] Although America had started with many advantages, and far removed from Old World corruption, and though—as much as any people ever had—Americans had had the means of self-development in their own hands; yet they had not proven noticeably better than Europeans, however their external prosperity may have dazzled the eye. "Every people, consciously or unconsciously, struggles with all its power to realize the last consequences of the principles it adopts." If these principles were unsound, that people labored to destruction. Unless democratic philosophers would admit the truth of original sin, and the consequent need of supramundane authority and guidance, then the American Experiment was doomed to follow the path originally spaded out by Andrew Jackson. George Bancroft, who had falsified history "without misstating facts," and whose purpose was "the promulgating [of] his humanitarian theories of government and religion," might well have been the chronicler of the great American error.[112]

The final article of importance of 1849 was Brownson's essay on William Ellery Channing, published in October.[113] According to Brownson, Channing held that three interior elements of man (Love, Intellect, Power) were externalized in the Church, the University, and the State, respectively. Balance in human affairs came when all three were adequately harmonized; a philosophy of history is then possible which studies the "law of development" by which this harmony had been achieved, by man. To Brownson, a philosophy of history which was reduced to a science was impossible unless one could "measure the infinite freedom of the infinite and eternal God, and calculate the free agency of man, as elements in the production of historical events. . . ." Since such calculations were impossible, "history is simply a record of facts, and can be ascertained, without special Divine Inspiration, only in the study of the facts themselves."[114]

Channing greatly erred in ignoring all this, and tried to reconcile the irreconcilable; his eclecticism even attempted to balance "Christian Theism, German Pantheism, and French Socialism, or Progressism." Reasoning as though all these were fundamentally the same, Channing "wishes to harmonize [all] with the doctrine of progress furnished him by the dominant sentiment of the age, or modern *Welt-geist,* and which is his favorite doctrine, to which all in his system is subordinate."[115] But Christian theism and pantheism, Brownson insisted, were irreconcilable. The former postulated one God, perfect, self-existing, eternal, independent, and most simple, excluding multiplicity, variety, distinction; other existences (the universe, for example, visible or invisible) were only as created by Him out of nothing, or out of His own infinite fullness—"not *stuff* as Cousin maintains." Matter is not eternal, nor is God the *materia prima* of the universe.

Pantheism, on the other hand, denied a creative deity. Man and nature—as distinguished from God—were not real existences, but were of the infinite fullness of His own being. "The world of space and time is a mere illusion, for [to pantheists] there are and can be no separate existences coexisting, and no succession of events. All is eternal, immovable, silent."[116] This idea of non-creative deity which "denies the world of space and time, and therefore all progressibles," could not be reconciled, Brownson emphasized, "with the idea of universal and unlimited progress." This was Channing's problem; he attempted to solve it by equating "creative" with "uncreative," since creation is taken to mean evolution or development in variety. Then "in order to be able to conceive of God unfolding, and to reconcile the idea of uncreative Deity with the idea of progress, [Channing] imagines multiplicity and variety in God himself; that is, in the first cause. . . . ." Thus, according to Channing, God contained infinite variety, and He infinitely develops it. "Each evolution, since it is an evolution of God, is an image of God, . . . and . . . contains a variety in itself, which, in its turn, it must evolve. Its evolutions, again, each in its degree, contain a variety, which also must be evolved, that is, actualized. The successive or serial evolutions are what is meant by Progress." The danger here, according to Brownson, was that "the universe is the actualized God"; God is complete plurality, variety now *is* unity, and God and the universe may die together. Thus, by equating creation and evolution, Christian theism was lost, and pantheism was gained; "by placing multiplicity and variety in God . . . [Channing] dissolves his pantheism, and falls into pure atheism" which is the denial of unity and the assertion of multiplicity in the first cause. Atheism could not be reconciled with an idea of progress, for multiplicity is "subsequent to unity, and inconceivable without it. Hence, if placed in the first cause, represented as essential in the first link of the series, by excluding unity, they deny themselves, and therefore all existences, and then all progressibles."[117] Channing thus arrives at "nihility"; unless he could assert Christian theism, he could not assert progress, since he can conceive of progressibles "only inasmuch as he admits a *creative* God."

In Brownson's argument, then, Channing must, first, assert the Christian God, *or,* second, deny unity and assert variety in the origin of things as does the atheist, *or,* third, assert nihilism. If he asserted either the second or the third, he could not talk of progress. If he opted for the first, he might do so, for then he was positing "the universe with all its variety" and "supposes for it an adequate cause." This progress would be toward recovering a perfection lost, of "approaching a perfection eternally actual in God." The greatest mistakes, then, of modern progressists were the denial of the *Deus Creator,* "and in seeking a foundation for their doctrine in pantheism and atheism."[118]

A summary of Brownson's position worked out in the years 1845–1849 would appear to be a rejection in great part of his original conception of the American Idea. He was musing on long questions: original sin, a possible theory of history, an idea of cycle in human affairs, and the strength of Neoplatonism. During this period he examined critically such popular assumptions as the idea of Progress, the current optimism concerning the perfectibility of man, and the close relation presumed to exist between Protestant Christianity and democracy.[119] Each of these seemed central to the overall agreement upon the viability of the American Idea. In the course of Brownson's study during these years, he handled each of these assumptions roughly. By 1849 Brownson was willing to admit spiritual progress only; he now denied what he considered the pantheistic doctrine (tending to atheism) of "Progressism," with which he ranked socialism, that Christian heresy. Religion was necessary to virtue, virtue to democracy, and democracy was central to the American Idea in all its phases. Democracy was *not* to be equated with Christianity, and man, wounded by original sin, must be guided by grace. The organ of grace was the Church of Christ, the Catholic Church, and that Church was therefore necessary to the sustaining of popular liberty, without which there could be no true democracy.

Optimism was clouded only with respect to man in this world. Man could not better himself, Brownson was arguing, by revolution—the American Dream was actualized (if it *was* to be actualized) not by revolution but by a mere cutting of a political umbilical cord. The perfectibility of man in this world—given the assumption of original sin—was a chimera, and if the Experiment and Mission were limited to this objective, both were doomed. The religion of Democracy, which he noted a-building in the United States as part of the heritage of Andrew Jackson, was rejected, because it in turn had rejected the traditional Christian Church, which it ignorantly assumed to be Protestant. Since, among other weaknesses, Protestantism could interpose no vital block to the febrile rush for wealth and luxury in this country, it was moribund. Amelioration was still a proper aim for man, but it must be undertaken through the agencies of legitimate government developed according to the providential Constitution of the country, and not through the rapacity of revolution, either socialistic or Red Republican.

However critically, and from whichever of its many perspectives Orestes Brownson was examining the American Idea, it was never far from his thoughts in the years following his conversion in 1844.

NOTES

1. Rufus Griswold, cited in Schlesinger, *Brownson*, p. 194. It was this same Rufus W. Griswold who on March 27, 1846, wrote to Brownson from Charleston, s.c., requesting "a few facts connected

with your personal and literary life" to be used in Griswold's contemplated "A Survey of the Prose Literature of the United States," ultimately called *The Prose Writers of America*. It is from this work that the above quotation is taken. A like request had come to Brownson on March 31, 1845, from Wells and Co., publishers of the projected "The National Volume." The signature on this letter has been cut out; some other hand has added the initials "H.G." Both letters are in the Brownson Papers, AUND.

2. See *Ibid.*, pp. 193–195; H. F. Brownson, *Middle Life*, pp. 2–8.

3. From Brownson's first editorial published in *The Boston Reformer*. The material is in a scrap book containing the editorial ("In making my best bow as editor of the Boston Reformer, I must be allowed to say a few words in explanation, *etc.*"); Brownson Papers, AUND.

4. *BrQR*, II, 1 (1845), 78. This number began with a review of Theodore Jouffroy's *Cours de droit naturel*. Brownson was proud to claim that he had been the first to bring Jouffroy's work "to the notice of the American public by a favorable review of it inserted in the *Christian Examiner* for September 1837" (p. 54). See also Schlesinger, *Brownson*, p. 130.

5. *BrQR*, II, 2 (1845), 264–265. The phrasing reflects Brownson's general attitude at this time.

6. *BrQR*, II, 1 (1845), 94.

7. *Ibid.*, p. 77; italics are Brownson's.

8. *Ibid.*, p. 88. "Timocracy" is used probably in the Aristotelian rather than in the Platonic sense.

9. *Ibid.*, pp. 94–95. See also *BrQR*, VI, 1 (1849), 1–2.

10. *BrQR*, II, 2 (1845), 256.

11. Echoes of the debate can be found throughout other articles of the *Review* for this year. See, for example, *BrQR*, II, 3 (1845), 389–396; 402–407.

12. *Ibid.*, p. 396.

13. *Ibid.*, p. 397; emphasis is Brownson's.

14. *BrQR*, II, 3 (1845), 323–341. Note that in his examination of this idea, the editor again appears to have anticipated somewhat generally Max Weber's well-known study, although in Brownson's discussion of the Middle Ages the *et ego in Arcadia* theme ran rather heavily.

15. *Ibid.*, p. 327; italics are Brownson's. The inflamed rhetoric here is that of the passionate advocate, putting by for the stress of the moment what he must know were subtleties which, if they might not alter his final judgment, would very well lessen considerably the force of simplistic indictment. Brownson apparently thought the cause worth the candle. The error of judgment must be seen steadily and whole. A parallel simplicity of critical decision could ignore subtleties of *his* situation.

16. *Ibid.*, p. 330.

17. *BrQR*, II, 3 (1845), 406–407. See also an interesting essay on Schiller (*BrQR*, II, 3 [1845], 380–398). He commented on Rousseauistic

reformers and their dependence on nature (pp. 390–391); on rejection of authority (pp. 392–394); and on his opposition to the "dominant tendency" of the age (p. 395). "Who rejects the Church," wrote Orestes Brownson, "re-enacts the myth of Sisyphus" (p. 395).

18. *BrQR*, II, 4 (1845), 514–515.
19. *Ibid.*, p. 517.
20. *Ibid.*, pp. 520–521.
21. *Ibid.*, p. 521.
22. *Idem.*
23. One is reminded here of Madison's discussion of "faction" in No. X of the Federalist Papers; the connection with Calhoun's idea of concurrent majorities should also be noted. See Margaret Coit, *John C. Calhoun* (Boston, 1950), pp. 528ff.
24. Brownson gave three reasons for this position. See *BrQR*, II, 4 (1845), 523.
25. *Ibid.*, p. 525. Brownson's point: "master" was the word used for Jesus Christ by his own disciples.
26. *Ibid.*, p. 527. The word "statesman" appears to be used in this paragraph in a rather denotative sense—somewhat akin to the modern meaning of "political scientist" or "political commentator."
27. *BrQR*, III, 1 (1846), 40–61.
28. *Ibid.*, p. 42.
29. *Ibid.*, p. 49.
30. Philosophical or even theological motive aside, how far is Brownson here from the pith of the "Laboring Classes" essays?
31. Since, in fact, contemporary popular governments were dedicated to worldly ends.
32. *Ibid.*, p. 57.
33. *Idem.* The note of impending disaster is clear.
34. *Ibid.*, p. 59.
35. *Ibid.*, p. 60.
36. *Ibid.*, p. 61; italics are Brownson's. See Brownson's statement of the inevitability of America's becoming a Catholic country (*BrQR*, III, 1 [1846], 89).
37. Edgar Quinet, *The Roman Church and Modern Society*, trans. C. Edwards Lester (New York, 1845). Quinet had translated Herder's *Ideas of the Philosophy of the History of Humanity*; Jules Michelet had translated the *Scienza nuova* of Vico. For Bury's comments on Quinet and Michelet, see *Progress*, pp. 267–268; 314. For the article cited, see *BrQR*, III, 1 (1846), 107–127.
38. *Ibid.*, pp. 107–114.
39. *Ibid.*, pp. 114–116.
40. *Ibid.*, p. 117. The words are Quinet's as translated in the American edition which Brownson is reviewing.
41. *Ibid.*, pp. 118–119. Here, too, the editor continued, is the error of the "Young" groups: Young Italy, Switzerland, Spain, Ireland, America—all were "really infidel" at heart and in doctrine.

42. *Ibid.*, pp. 119–120.
43. *Ibid.*, p. 120. To Quinet, Jesus symbolized "the divinity of human nature, and the humanity of divine nature."
44. Emerson's term for the Movement Party was the "Party of Hope"; for the other, "The Party of Memory."
45. *Ibid.*, p. 124.
46. In denying Newman's theory of development, Brownson seems really to be denying his *own* theory of development which he had held prior to his conversion. For a discussion of the matter see H. F. Brownson, *Middle Life*, pp. 53–77; Maynard, *Brownson*, pp. 198–207. For bibliographical information see especially William George Ward's defense of Newman on the issue, Maynard, *Brownson*, pp. 433–443. Brownson's chief article is in *BrQR*, III, 3 (1846), 342–368. The point, of course, is that a viable theory of development in moral doctrine argues a continuing progress which Brownson in other fields was finding it increasingly difficult to accept. While it reiterates opposition to any theory of development, there is later comment by Brownson which is much more generous to an understanding of Newman and the Puseyites generally. See Brownson's review of Newman's *Loss and Gain*, *BrQR*, XI, 4 (1854), 525–526.
47. A problem arises in the April issue. Brownson said (*BrQR*, III, 3 [1846], 408) that of the five articles in the April number, two only were by him. Which were his, he did not point out. Therefore, I omit here the essay entitled "Schiller's Aesthetic Theory" (*BrQR*, III, 2 [1846], 262ff.), even though the ideas expressed therein might very well contribute to the discussion. The question is, is it Brownson's? Brownson did say (in the July article above) "on political and other matters not of faith, the editor is, however, to be held responsible for whatever may appear in his pages" (p. 408). But the Schiller essay appears to have been by another hand.
48. Webster was the eldest son of Daniel Webster. See *BrQR*, III, 4 (1846), 493–518; 534–544. The book mentioned above is *Thornberry Abbey: A Tale of the Times* (New York, 1846).
49. *BrQR*, III, 4 (1846), 494.
50. See the especially striking statement regarding this subject on p. 496.
51. *Ibid.*, p. 500.
52. *Ibid.*, p. 534.
53. *Ibid.*, p. 535.
54. *Ibid.*, p. 540. Cf. *BrQR*, IV, 3 (1847), 384–403.
55. Jules Michelet, *The People*, trans. G. H. Smith (New York, 1846). Brownson quotes Michelet's statement which is reminiscent of a remark of Walt Whitman's: "This book is more than a book; it is myself . . . it is I" (*BrQR*, IV, 1 [1847], 86). Edwin Fussell argues with what seems some diffidence that the title "Leaves of Grass" may have been suggested to Whitman by a passage in Brownson (cf. *Works*, III, 173). See Fussell, *"Leaves of Grass* and Brownson," *American Literature*, 31 (1959–1960), 77–78.

56. *Ibid.*, p. 96.
57. *Ibid.*, p. 99.
58. G.[?] T. Headley, *The One Progressive Principle* (New York, 1846). According to Arthur Ekirch, the name of this writer is Joel Tyler Headley; Brownson seems to have mistaken the first initial. There is little doubt that the two names refer to the same man. See Ekirch, *Progress*, pp. 192; 288.
59. These Jeffersonian principles, according to some, were "Conservative" (*BrQR*, IV, 1 [1847], 135).
60. R. W. Emerson, *Poems* (Boston, 1847); *BrQR*, IV, 2 (1847), 262–276. Especially noteworthy is the editor's comment (p. 263) that he cannot assign the highest merit to Emerson's poems since, as a Christian, Brownson cannot accept Emerson's beliefs. The tone and rhetoric of the statement seem to imply a profundity of feeling which, coupled with two other recent statements, might be considered keys to Brownson's spiritual struggles during this period. Cf. *BrQR*, IV, 1 (1847), 275–276; *ibid.*, III, 3 (1846), 276–277.
61. J. Michelet and E. Quinet, *The Jesuits* (Boston, 1846); *BrQR*, IV, 3 (1847), 305–334.
62. *Ibid.*, p. 306. For his comparison of the two parties see pp. 306–307. See also n. 44 *supra*.
63. *Ibid.*, p. 307.
64. *Ibid.*, p. 308.
65. *Ibid.*, p. 313. It was at this point that Brownson asserted his agreement with Edmund Burke's position on the French Revolution, a position obviously reversing Brownson's position in 1840.
66. *Ibid.*, p. 327; italics mine. Brownson argued that the American state had been founded on the argument over this principle, and the American Dream thus became religious in character (pp. 327–328). Apparently some Protestant teaching had not been all that much corrupted.
67. *Ibid.*, p. 329.
68. *Ibid.*, p. 332.
69. De Maistre's book was called *Essay on the Generative Principle of Political Constitutions* (Boston, 1847). Brownson's essay is *BrQR*, IV, 4 (1847), 458–485.
70. *Ibid.*, p. 468.
71. *Ibid.*, pp. 472–473.
72. "Constitution" is not to be taken here as meaning the written legal instrument which is at most a "memorandum of the real constitution" (*ibid.*, p. 473). "The constitution [of a nation] is the living soul of the nation, that by virtue of which it is a nation, and is able to live a national life, and perform national functions" (*ibid.*, p. 474).
73. *Ibid.*, p. 474. The importance of Brownson's earlier essay on Providence seems clear here and throughout the ensuing discussion.
74. *Idem*.
75. *Ibid.*, p. 475.

76. *Ibid.*, p. 476. Other examples were given of France, Athens, Rome, and England (pp. 477ff.).
77. *Ibid.*, p. 484.
78. *BrQR*, v, 1 (1848), 49ff.
79. Brownson cited the examples of Gnosticism, Manichaeism, Arianism, Protestantism, Lamennaisism—i.e., "The attempt to develop the Church in the sense of the dominant socialism of the day" (p. 51). Yet he spoke out against "exaggerated Conservatism" (p. 118).
80. *BrQR*, v, 2 (1848), 163–183.
81. *Ibid.*, p. 167.
82. *Ibid.*, pp. 168–173.
83. Brownson's authority here is, perhaps surprisingly, Guizot's *General History of the Civilization of Europe*, cited in *BrQR*, v, 2 (1848), 175.
84. *Ibid.*, pp. 177–181.
85. *Ibid.*, p. 182.
86. *Ibid.*, p. 183. Brownson admitted indebtedness here to a man who, during this period, had and would have some influence over his mind: the Abbé Jacques Balmes, especially in his work *Le Protestantisme comparé au Catholicisme dans ses rapports avec la civilisation européenne* (Paris, 1842–1844). This work was reviewed in the current (April) number of the *Review* (pp. 223–255), but not by Brownson. See also *BrQR*, vi, 4 (1849), 413–438.
87. *BrQR*, v, 3 (1848), 382.
88. *Ibid.*, pp. 386–396. "Sustain," wrote Brownson, "the existing constitution of the state, whether it conforms to our abstract notions or not; because in politics everything is to be taken in the concrete, nothing in the abstract" (p. 396). He warned, too, against the United States' allowing its government to become a "centralized democracy" (p. 410).
89. See *BrQR*, v, 4 (1848), 453ff.
90. *Ibid.*, pp. 470–475.
91. *Ibid.*, p. 476.
92. *Ibid.*, p. 477.
93. *Ibid.*, p. 478.
94. *Ibid.*, pp. 480–481.
95. *BrQR*, vi, 1 (1849), 8.
96. *Ibid.*, p. 60. For further views on the Irish situation, see *ibid.*, pp. 64–72.
97. *Ibid.*, p. 61. His earlier castigation of Burke has been noted.
98. *Ibid.*, p. 16; italics are Brownson's.
99. The material which follows is from Brownson's article "Socialism and the Church," *BrQR*, vi, 1 (1849), 91–127.
100. *Ibid.*, p. 93. Brownson here explicitly disavowed his "Laboring Classes" doctrines, but found them informing an article in the July, 1848, issue of the *North American Review*, entitled "The Distribution of Property." Since this latter *Review* was the "most conservative journal" in the United States, Brownson was clearly concerned with

the tendency toward doctrines against which he had been variously contending, at least since 1844 (cf. *ibid.*, pp. 94ff).

101. *Ibid.*, pp. 99–100.
102. *Ibid.*, p. 108.
103. *Ibid.*, p. 116. Again the idea of Providence was central. On this point see also *ibid.*, p. 127.
104. *BrQR*, VI, 2 (1849), 137–162. This article is a review of J[ames] D. Nourse's *Remarks on the Past, and its Legacies to American Society* (Louisville, 1847). On Nourse, see Ekirch, *Progress*, pp. 103–104.
105. With regard to Neoplatonist influence upon Emerson at least, Brownson anticipated the judgment of Frederic Carpenter in Chapter III of his work *Emerson and Asia*. To Carpenter the Neoplatonists were the real "teachers of Emerson."
106. *BrQR*, VI, 2 (1849), 140.
107. *Ibid.*, p. 145.
108. *Ibid.*, p. 137.
109. *Ibid.*, p. 161.
110. Cf. n. 27 of this chapter. The current article is in *BrQR*, VI, 2 (1849), 176–195.
111. *Ibid.*, pp. 178–179.
112. *Ibid.*, pp. 191–192. For Channing's contribution to all this see *BrQR*, VI, 2 (1849), 209–239.
113. *BrQR*, VI, 4 (1849), 438–475.
114. *Ibid.*, p. 443–444.
115. *Ibid.*, p. 467.
116. *Idem.*
117. *Ibid.*, p. 469.
118. *Ibid.*, p. 470.
119. Reiteration seems necessary, for the overtone of this word here and elsewhere (certainly for the rest of this chapter) is subject to the vagaries of Brownson's seemingly idiosyncratic usage. Generally, when the word was used approvingly, he meant it in the sense of "constitutional republic"; when pejoratively, it had a Jacobin cast.

6

BROWNSON'S QUARTERLY REVIEW, 1850-1854

THE YEARS TO BE COVERED in this chapter represent Brownson's last in Boston. In 1849 Archbishop John Hughes had encouraged Brownson to move to New York.[1] Undoubtedly, increasing disillusion with the irritating censorship of Bishop Fitzpatrick and discontent with the general situation in Boston aided the editor's ultimate decision to move. Yet much, perhaps too much, has been made of Brownson's random comment in a letter in 1849. "Since," writes his biographer, "Fitzpatrick's authority extended only to theology, Brownson's *renewed* interest in social affairs meant, as he told a friend, that he was 'writing from himself rather than according to order'."[2]

Now, as has been pointed out earlier, Brownson had by no means scanted at least the *bases* of social questions as they affected America particularly. What may be misleading is the impression apparently fostered in Schlesinger's pages that some sort of revolution took place in Brownson's writing prior to the move to New York, and that his social views either changed or were to change at the root instead of, perhaps, in their emphasis. For example, as we have tried to point out, and as we shall see further, Brownson never denied the necessary balance of liberty and order. If he insisted more upon the one at one time than at another, the emphasis was merely what a journalist striving to be both profound and timely could hardly have avoided. Orestes Brownson never completely denied the efficacy of either liberty or order; he consistently argued for their necessary interaction. A few critics seem to be too ready to dismiss this point, and to share the regret of some contemporaries that the editor never returned to the "Laboring Classes" era of his life. It may be that, in general, these "Laboring Classes" essays, through which he has received at least marginal acceptance, were not so much indicative of his early thought as they seem. If that is true, Brownson was much more consistent than has been assumed heretofore, though, of course, no claim can be made for complete consistency. And this consistency seems especially true of his treatment of the American Idea.[3]

Moreover, quite as much as any thoughtful man, Brownson was severely cross-cut by the inner demands for truth, and he had to do both his thinking and his living out loud. Badgered as he was both within and without the Church, and certainly not without reason, his views are in many ways remarkably consistent—unless one means by consistency a dogged persistence to a position which even under stress of thought and experience and the pain of living never changes. Brownson was not such a vegetable, nor indeed were Whitman and Emerson, who saw hobgoblins here, and knew that pigeon-holes were for hacks and not for men. Rufus Griswold, it seems, did not.

In an article entitled "An A priori Autobiography" written for the January, 1850, number of *Brownson's Quarterly Review*,[4] Brownson, who took credit for introducing Leroux to the American public, analyzed the French philosopher's influence upon himself especially from January, 1842, until July, 1844. The chief lesson consisted in the assertion of "an ontological basis for Christianity"— that is, that Christian mysteries were objective (i.e., ontological) facts, and not subjective (i.e., psychological) wishes. But, pushing the lesson too far, or, perhaps, not far enough, Brownson claimed that at that time he had asserted a "natural ontology," instead of seeing these mysteries in "the supernatural order, the peculiarly Christian ontology."[5] This error thus "vitiated" whatever he had learned from Leroux, including the latter's enthusiasm for Progress. Brownson here admitted "that mankind are progressive . . . but . . . they are also retrogressive, and . . . if in one time and place they advance, they in another decline and suffer deterioration. Their history, universal history, must take note of this fact, and record the decline and fall of individual nations, as well as their rise and progress."[6] If, as the contemporary James Freeman Clarke was to put it, "no man has ever equalled Mr. Brownson in the ability with which he has refuted his own arguments,"[7] it does seem true that Brownson was constantly re-examining both his current and his former views and analyzing both for their differences. If that is dishonest, then Brownson was dishonest.

Tucked away in the "Literary Notes" at the end of the April issue was a brief review of James Russell Lowell's poems.[8] Here Lowell was dismissed upon the same general base that Emerson had been: he had written "exquisite poetry" and might be a great poet "if he were not a great philanthropist." The philanthropist was to Brownson

of all men . . . the most intolerable. Poor Dr. Channing has much to answer for. His everlasting preachments about the "dignity of human nature," has corrupted our literature, as it has our morals; and if philanthropy, which receives such an impetus from him, continues to rage much longer in this Commonwealth, it will be necessary for every honest man and peaceable man to emigrate from it.[9]

Philanthropy, once the central stone of Brownson's social platform of amelioration and progress, had become a term for half-humorous reference.

In October, Brownson returned to his full-scale study of the basis of civil society with a review of three works by Vincenzo Gioberti, the Italian philosopher.[10] According to Brownson, Gioberti, who held that civil society was of "sacerdotal origin" and that civil power derived from God through the priestly caste, tended in some views to "modern liberalism and socialism." Thus Brownson felt that Gioberti's support of recent Italian revolutions aided the *risorgimento,* helped to exile Jesuits, Count Rossi, and Pius IX, and enabled Mazzini to set up the "infamous Roman republic."[11]

Emphasizing that the point of view of his criticism of Gioberti was "practical" rather than philosophical, Brownson contended that the current rigid disjunction between the ecclesiastical and temporal orders was a schism which, when "taken in its principle," had become the source of all the spiritual or temporal disorders of modern society. This split between Church and State had secularized the state, permitted philosophy to reject theology, science, and religion. Art tended to breed unbelief, and there was no peace either for an individual or for society when both were torn by two irreconcilable forces. Gioberti, who assumed this schism, believed its principal cause to be the loss by the sacerdotal society of its moral and intellectual superiority over lay society. The former's refusal to recognize the fact toughened the carapace of error. The remedy proposed by Gioberti was the reunion of the two cultures—that is, "of the Christian spirit and the spirit of Italo-Greek gentilism."[12] The editor rejected this solution on the ground that it merely substituted means for ends: the proposal was directed at the "earthly felicity" of man, not at his eternal salvation. However opposed to socialism Gioberti might be in doctrine, he was aligned with it in the "practical tendency" of his proposal, for he appeared to forget that supernatural grace alone saved men from destruction and that the minister of grace is the sacerdotal society. In Brownson's opinion, Gioberti's view that the natural chiefs of society, the *optimates*, should rule under a kind of hierarchical principle was suspiciously Saint-Simonian in character. The latter group believed that from the time of the Roman Empire's demise till the reign of Pope Leo x the *optimates* were the Catholic clergy; since that time the lay society had surpassed the clerical, and achieved practical leadership of society. Brownson denied that the *optimates* were now laymen; he denied further that they were superior to the clergy, except in mathematics and some physical sciences—that is, in "secondary matters."[13] Gioberti, wrote his critic, for all his apparent ultramontanism was really united with de Lamennais (especially in the Italian's argument for Progress)[14] and with that "inverterate pantheist" Thomas Carlyle who also made of the *optimates* accidents of time and place, totally outside any idea of Providence.

"The *optimates*," noted Brownson in his own definition, "are always those who are legitimately invested with authority, and are such solely because so invested. The right gives the capacity to govern, not the capacity the right."[15] Although the pope did not exercise the power he once had, he still possessed the *right* to exercise that power; "progress" must take that fact into account. Civil society was the creature of the priesthood, and it was through that priesthood (the true notion of *optimates*) that Almighty God "invests civil society with its authority to govern."[16] Insofar as civil society receded from this governing power, it retreated to barbarism, as Brownson saw it, for the principles of civilization were from not the natural but the supernatural order, and "the elements of barbarism are inherent in human nature, reproduced in every new-born individual, and retained in the bosom of every human being as long as he remains in the flesh."[17] However Gioberti's philosophy may be praised, therefore, Brownson could not accept the ramifications he had found in the Italian's view of civil society, especially in his idea of the purpose of that society. Indeed, Gioberti had not truly projected his philosophical principles,[18] and had compounded his error by mistaking a legitimate means (the amelioration of society) as an ultimate end.

At the close of the October number, Brownson reviewed briefly Tayler Lewis' *Nature, Progress, Ideas*.[19] He praised the author, a professor of Greek at Union College, as one of the ablest Presbyterians in America. Yet it was Lewis' Protestantism which forced him "to stop short in following out the principles he adopts to their legitimate consequences." As Brownson viewed the matter, Lewis was quite aware that the tendencies and dangerous speculations of the age struck at the very roots of Christianity, and even of natural religion, philosophy, political government, and of society itself.

[Lewis'] strictures on the modern notions of the "philosophy of history" are profound and just; his vindication of Providence against the rationalistic and pantheistic doctrines of the hour, which resolve Providence into necessity, and all history into the struggle and development of eternal ideas, excluding from all share in it both God and man, is creditable to his good sense, and to his desire to retain some vestiges, at least, of Christian truth; and his refutation of the modern doctrines of progress and socialism leaves little to be desired, considered in itself. . . .[20]

Yet all this was vitiated by Lewis' refusal to recognize that the errors he attacked were the logical development of the Protestantism he espoused, and to see that, logically, only a Catholic could hold the ground he had adopted. To Brownson, "No man who holds that the Protestant movement was a divine movement can consistently object to the philosophy of history as held by Michelet . . . ," for, again logically, whoever held the doctrine of private judgment, and the justification of the Protestant Reformation, could not simultaneously maintain "the Divine origin of power, the sacredness of law, and the inviolability of government."[21] Such a man thus made not war upon but common cause with "modern humanism and naturalism." Therefore, Lewis was forced to use the humanist argument against Catholics, and a Catholic argument against humanists. Thus, by laying himself open to logical rebuke, Lewis did little service to the cause of truth, whatever be the merit of his arguments.

Early in the following year Brownson attacked the American press, and its censor, "the mob." Especial members of the latter's cast were "the scum of foreign demagogues cast upon our shores by the revolutionary tides of Europe since 1831."[22] American public support for the European revolutions of 1848 was the result, Brownson held, of the disproportionate influence of these "foreign mobocrats" upon American public opinion. In the course of the discussion he pointed out again the republican character of the American Experiment (insisting that it was providentially designed), and contrasted it with the essentially Jacobin character of the European revolutions, which differed from the American in beginnings, ends, and means. The American Republic was "legal" in origin; "loyal and conservative" in character; the European democracies were in all their phases "mere wild anarchy." The American Experiment was in danger of confusing the two disparate systems because of the power of the popular press.[23]

In a companion piece,[24] Brownson isolated two errors which the American Experiment should shun: first, the tendency, under guise of liberty, to anarchy; and again, the tendency, under guise of authority, "to civil despotism or *Statolatry,* or the worship of the state . . . elevating the state above the Church, and putting it in the place of God."[25] This article was followed by one entitled "The Decline of Protestantism,"[26] wherein, having already pointed out that the two tendencies originate in Protestantism, Brownson wrote that Protestantism, having lost its vitality, allowed only two alternatives: Catholicity, or absolute infidelity leading to "nullism." The editor then cited Carlyle (that "genuine Protestant") who called Modern Protestantism "a sham."

In the "Literary Notices and Criticisms" section of the April, 1851, edition there is early evidence of Brownson's disenchantment with the physical sciences, evidence few critics of Brownson have apparently observed, and which is directly relevant to his current notion of Progress.[27] Reviewing S. E. Coues's *Outlines of a System of Mechanical Philosophy; Being a Research into the Laws of Force,*[28] Brownson had some contemptuous things to say of the physical sciences. He had respect for Coues as a profound and original thinker, and admitted that his own knowledge of the subject matter was too meager to do justice to whatever value the book might represent. Coues, at any rate, seemed not to have approved of Isaac Newton, and this, too, Brownson highly approved. To him, Newton was "a humbug"; indeed, both Newton and Francis Bacon, "the [so-called] two great lights of the modern world," were "humbugs." Brownson was certain of Bacon's humbuggery since he claims to have studied the pertinent material; until he had read Coues, he had not been so certain of Newton. Brownson at this point admitted that he had "no great proficiency in the study of the physical sciences"; years before he had studied them with great interest at first but "found them so unsettled, so uncertain, and changing so often, that he gave them up in despair. . . . [Although] we admit the moderns have extended their observations, and have collected a mass of facts which *may* have been unknown to the ancients, we do not believe that in *science* proper we are a single step in advance of Aristotle." He granted that he accepted the heliocentric rather than the geocentric theory, but insisted (in 1851) upon its theoretic character. "The only progress we moderns make is in returning to forgotten, or in rediscovering lost truths."[29]

In October, there appeared one of those major essays on social theory which give insight into the development of Brownson's mind on the whole question of progress and its meaning to the social order, and to political problems of liberty.

In a review of Saint-Bonnet's work on "Social Restoration"[30] Brownson repeated some of those ideas already familiar to any faithful reader of the *Review*. Among these the central notion was that original sin had been the root cause of civilization's trouble; the spirit of revolution, its proximate cause. This rebellious spirit stemmed from the mid-fifteenth century—the time of the fall of Constantinople, and of the Renaissance. And, given the premises of the revolutionists, Brownson conceded, the intervening time *had* been progressive,[31] for the revolutionary principles had been reduced to practice. But, in reality, the assumed progress had merely been a kind of neopaganism with effects in every field of human activity: politics, morals, philosophy, art, the market place. While the wheels were turning forward, the vehicle, removed from any real ground, as Brownson saw it, was being borne back ceaselessly into the past. The "lost Eden" was to be regained by compartmenting the secular and the spiritual, in order to make of man eventually "an inhabitant of this world, and a creature of mere animal wants and instincts."[32] "Progress," according to Brownson, had resulted in "the dissolution of society itself," to the point where present momentum was forcing to the fore "Communistic and Socialistic theories." The only alternative was a return to Catholicity.[33] Socialism, which contravened "all the laws of Providence," was simply the result of paganism; Catholicity could be the only civilizer, and thus its vital presence was the real necessity to re-establish society and proper political order. Heathenism, a forebear of socialism, assumed that man was sufficient to complete and develop himself by his own efforts, and this was what the age called Progress: man was joint creator, or, in part at least, the first cause of himself.

Progress in this heathen sense is, as somebody has said, the Evangel of the nineteenth century. We find it asserted everywhere, in theology, ethics, politics, metaphysics, and in universal cosmology. All modern science, in so far as it deigns to recognize a creative God at all, recognizes Him as creating only the germs of things, which are completed by their own internal law or force.[34]

This "all pervading" doctrine of progress seems by now Brownson's chief enemy, for it was the thread which ran truly through the fabric of modern heathenism. Therefore, in opposition to it, the editor outlined a doctrine which he took to be the true doctrine of progress, a kind of "double-cycle" theory. The first cycle was "the procession, by way of creation not emanation of existence from God as their first and efficient cause"; the second was the return of these existences "without being absorbed into God, as Indian pantheism teaches, to him as their final cause or last end."[35]

Both these cycles were present in both the natural order and the supernatural order. Progress, understood in the second cycle, was moral progress rather than physical, "a progress in *doing*, not a progress in *being* . . . not in making ourselves, nor in completing ourselves physically, but in fulfilling the end for which God has made us—in a word, a progress in moral perfection. . . . This progress is very admirable, and we cannot insist too strenuously on it, or have too much of it."[36] On the other hand, there was no progress whatsoever, if by progress one maintains any possible agency by the "progressing subject." God is the sole Creator in both natural and supernatural orders. "Creation ad extra, or placing existences in space and time, may or may not be progressive, according to the will of the Creator; all we mean to deny is, that it is progressive in any sense by the agency, will or concurrence of the creature."[37] Modern heathenism which asserted progress in this first cycle thus revealed the "real error of the age . . . in attempting to do God's work, and in neglecting its own." Man was not his own first cause, in part or in whole, nor was he even joint creator—"God is our sole final cause only in that He is our sole first cause."[38] After examining objections to his point,[49] Brownson concluded that socialists, for example, did not assert that man is born perfect in the first cycle, "but . . . that he is born perfect as to the second cycle, that is, without sin, pure, holy, in no need of pardon or redemption"—in short, they denied the concept of original sin.[40]

Society was necessary to whatever moral progress (aided by the Holy Ghost and grace) that man could make; only individuals progress, the race could not. Now this society and whatever was essential to it—e.g., order—must be instituted before the race could begin to continue itself. Since man, then, started from the highest level, the "aristocracy" was originally a priesthood, and "was given in the beginning, was originally in Adam, and during the whole continuance of the primitive or patriarchal order, [was] in the patriarch, in the *pater-familias,* who was both priest and king."[41]

Adam contained at least in potential the clergy, the king, the nobility; whatever virtue they had was the only virtue with which mankind started. That is to say,

the aristocracy have always subsisted in the race, and never been evolved from the people, or obtained as the result of the . . . progress of individuals. . . . The aristocracy, in our sense of the word, subsist from the beginning; therefore, from the beginning society exists, is constituted; and therefore from the beginning there subsist all the necessary conditions of individual growth . . . for the individual to fulfill his destiny, that is return to God as his final cause. [Men] have nothing to do with founding society, or founding an aristocracy to found it. God has done all that for us.[42]

In what sense of the word did Brownson use "aristocracy"? He meant, he wrote, an aristocracy "of office, of position, education, science and manners . . . which does not make itself" but which God makes, mediately or immediately for religious, moral, or social purposes. "Aristocracy is an office, a trust, and they who hold it are responsible for the manner in which they discharge its duties." When the word became expressive of a mere social rank, and that alone, then the original vitality was lost, and the concept eventually fell into disrepute.

According to Brownson, the errors of Gioberti, de Lamennais, Saint-Bonnet, and Ventura lay in their attempts to defend religion and society with the weapons of the opponents of religion and society. That is, they considered Catholicity in relation to society and civilization rather than in its proper role in the supernatural order.

Their idea of amelioration was enveloped in the natural order, the order of temporal wealth, which was a snare and a delusion. One could not "adapt" the Church to earthly wants; nor could one reform society through redistribution of wealth or property, since the seed of evil "is in the individual human heart," and must be combated by Catholic faith, sacraments, and discipline. In this way alone could anything be done "to remove even national evils, and secure temporal well-being. Here is the conclusion of the whole matter."[43]

Finally, Catholicity was absolutely necessary as the founder and preserver of society, and the only real defender of liberty. The real accent should be first upon the supernatural, then upon the natural; too often God and heaven were considered from the point of view of man and society:

in the [Church] is the . . . *première mise de fonds* of liberty, the blood that forms the true aristocracy; nay, the true aristocracy itself, that institutes, preserves, or restores society. She through her clergy can preserve the old civilized state, restore the State when fallen into the condition of modern European nations, and civilize the most barbarous and savage tribes, by insisting, *and because insisting*, only on the things which pertain to the salvation of the individual soul, if she be obeyed and her instructions followed.[44]

During the winter of 1851–1852 Brownson had given a course of lectures embodying his current ideas on Progress, and upon the indispensable necessity of the Church to true civilization.[45] The Honorable Hugh A. Garland of St. Louis had been invited to rebut Brownson, and to prove the "compatibility of Protestantism with civilization and good government." The lectures were printed, and, in the April, 1852, number of the *Review*, Brownson reviewed the lectures.[46]

According to Brownson, Garland "properly" denied the idea that man began in a savage state; but "[Garland therefore] denies and refutes, whether he intends to do so or not, the whole modern doctrine of the progress of the species, or the perfectibility of human nature."[47] Moreover, Garland asserted a spiritual order over the temporal, but did not seem to recognize a truly supernatural order. That is, the highest spiritual faculties of the soul still remained within the natural order, and Garland, in Brownson's view, assumed that without revelation and grace these faculties could reach truth. This was a garden-variety Transcendentalism or rationalism, and its exposition opened the grave for Garland's logic. Such putative truth could not rise above the natural order, or be the agent of the performance of that which was above nature. Religion was thus compressed within the natural order.

In his own lectures Brownson "pressed home . . . one great fact," i.e., original sin. For with this, and with no supernatural means such as grace to break its hold, no true civilization could exist. By civilization he meant "the supremacy of reason, or the freedom of man's higher faculties; and barbarism is . . . the predominance of appetite and passion, or of man's lower nature."[48] Only Catholicity, considered both as teacher and repairer, was the sole agent of that supernatural power needed to subject the lower nature. This theme carried the major force in Brownson's own lectures.

Although Garland disputed the general argument, Brownson believed that he never met Brownson's objection that man could not raise himself by his own waistband; indeed, that man tended to barbarism without supernatural aid. No true liberty was possible without grace, and Garland had no answer for that argument; he had merely assumed the natural origin of civilization, and the capacity of nature to sustain proper civilization. In so doing, he overlooked the impossibility of nature alone even to keep the natural law.

Brownson rejected Garland's thesis that the evils of society could be blamed upon the heathen priesthood and the succeeding Catholic priesthood,[49] and repeated his now familiar idea that the Protestant view of the subjection of the Church to the State is fatal to both religion and civilization. Catholicity, conversely, held that State and Church are distinctly subsisting powers, yet not that they were equal in either rank or authority. For the supremacy of the spiritual was always asserted: it was the obligation of the temporal power "to rule in secular affairs in obedience to the law of God as defined by the spiritual authority instituted by Almighty God, and supernaturally assisted and protected for that purpose."[50] Brownson closed with a hint of his recognition that Garland's problem had been at one time his own for, as he put it, Garland's church "is in the future, and so is his civilized order. He takes refuge in hope, and sings,

'There's a good time coming, boys'

but when or how he confesses himself ignorant, as must every Protestant."[51]

There remain but two important articles for the year 1852. One of these was a spirited defense of the common law; the other, a vigorous and certainly specific rejection of the American Idea as embodied in the fourth volume of George Bancroft's *History of the United States*. In general these two would sum up all that Brownson had to say on the general subject we are examining here, for the editor had little beyond occasional references to add between 1853 and 1855.

The article on the common law was ostensibly a review of *The Works of Daniel Webster*.[52] Webster, contended the editor, though an excellent man in many respects, held Jacobinical principles, even if he never pursued these to logical conclusions. Those conclusions would have been socialistic (e.g., "the sovereignty of the people"), and could truly be maintained only by an atheist.

Brownson thought that the curious bifurcation in Webster's thought was caused, on the one hand, by his acceptance of common-law principles "in accordance with the teachings of our holy religion which forms the basis of that [common law]"; and, on the other, by his discipleship to Hampden, Sydney, Locke, and Rousseau— affinities he shared with "the elder Adams . . . and the whole Federal[ist] party." This latter attachment to Locke and the others really had defeated the Federalists, Brownson believed, even with their high personal qualities; their practical wisdom had faded "before their less scrupulous, but more logical and self-consistent rivals, headed by Thomas Jefferson."[53] For the Federalists had been "*via media* men," set between two antagonistic principles.

The chief mistake which these men—including Webster—had made had been the attribution of America's freedom and prosperity to her political institutions, instead of, properly, to the common law "inherited from England . . . before the Reformation."

The common law, the American rule of justice, "regulates the relations not only between individual and individual, but to some extent between the citizen and the state." No constitution or positive law could actually *be* law if it was contrary to justice; no constitution or positive law might be upheld which offended against the common law which was "the law of the land." Any such offensive principle was "*ipso facto* null and void, and may be declared so and set aside by the Common Law courts."[54]

Now it seemed to Brownson that the revolutionary or Jacobin spirit might not so much aim at overthrowing the government; much more insidious was its threat to the common law which would leave "no restraint on lawless power, and no standard of justice but the will or caprice of the majority for the time being."[55] This spirit he found abroad in Europe, and to a lesser degree in America. What had to be defended was the "sacredness of the law," a law which reflected a perduring moral order in the universe.

Constitutional law, indeed, was but the "application of the Common Law to the constitutionality of legislative enactments . . . ," for the common law in its principles and definitions Brownson considered as "both logically and historically anterior" to political constitutions. Brownson called it the "higher law," therefore, for the legislature in its enactments; additionally, it was the clearest expression men had of that "Divine law from which all human laws derive their legality."[56] Obviously, then, no law "repugnant to any one of its *essential* principles, is or can be law for an American citizen."[57]

As the "fundamental constitution" of the country, anterior and superior to political constitutions, which might be the source of American political rights, common law discovered, according to Brownson, those natural rights which were independent of and prior to political rights. It had as its "distinguishing excellence" the fact that it was *"lex non scripta"*—i.e., "a living tradition in the reason . . . conscience . . . sentiments . . . and customs of the people, and therefore in some sense independent of mere political organizations."[58] The comparative "sobriety and reserve" in both English and American Revolutions could be traced to the acknowledgment of this fact.

On the Continent, the civil law, developed from Roman law, was a body of written law which conceived of the sovereign as the "fountain of justice"; the state, therefore, had the initiative granted it by the fact of concrete written law. Thus, when trouble came, written law might easily be suspended. When that occurred, there resulted virtual lawlessness, or anarchy—the assumption that law was dead.

Brownson emphasized that the common law could never be considered dead. An unwritten code, traditional and habitual, it was above mere political power which it tended to restrain within proper bounds; thus, since it was not identified with mere political power, it could not be overthrown with that power, and could continue to lend its support to liberty and the social order "so long as the people remain in any sense a living people." The difference in the histories of England and France in this matter Brownson saw as evidence in point.[59]

The Roman Law extends only to cases foreseen and provided for, the common law to all cases not taken out of its jurisdiction; the former is of gentile origin, simply modified by the Christian emperors so as not to exclude Christian faith and worship; the latter is of Christian origin, and grew up among the Anglo-Saxons as they were converted from paganism and entered under the guidance of the church upon the career of Christian civilizations. The common law starts from the principle that society and the state are for man, and it seeks primarily the protection of private rights. . . . The Roman law starts from the heathen principle that man is for society, and society for the state, and it seeks primarily the protection of public rights, or the rights of the prince. The former abhors despotism, the latter abhors anarchy; the one makes the state absolute, supreme, omnipresent, the other presupposes a power above the state, limits the political power of the state, and asserts a law to which the state itself owes obedience, which subsists, and can, when need is, operate without the express sanction of the political sovereign.[60]

The common law which recognized the people as distinct from and surviving the state could support an "orderly republic"; "a nation trained under the Roman Law system can never be other than monarchial in effect, whatever it may be in name and pretension, or at farthest, a close aristocracy."[61] Again, the common law, which could not be introduced "into a nation whose character is already formed," was by no means inevitably stable. It could be lost, and when it was, it was lost forever. Americans who had received the common law from England—though it had been "slightly marred" after the Reformation—should strive to transmit it to their posterity. Next to Christianity itself, no greater legacy was possible.[62]

American society was deteriorating, concluded Brownson, and "the democratic order is exceedingly unfavorable to either intellectual or moral greatness. If it has a tendency to bring up a degree or two the very low, which may be questioned, it has a still stronger tendency to bring all down to a low and common level. . . . [This] is a fact so plain that even the blind may see it."[63] There was danger that through negligence and ineptitude Americans would lose the common law.

Brownson's respect for the past, his dislike for innovation, his distress at American deterioration, might all be cited as evidence for his increasing "conservative" trend. His praise for Burke could also be adduced. It might be remarked that the editor insisted upon the traditional cast of the common law, its inheritance by America as essential to the American way, and its necessity for the American future. The distinctions drawn between Roman law and common law, and between French and English law, pointed up his final rejection of French political and philosophical influence under which he had himself moved in those years prior to his conversion.[64] Moreover, the connection of "Common Law" (which, at times, Brownson seemed to confuse with the more general concept of "natural law") with a transcendent purpose reinforced his conviction of Providence. Finally, it should be noted that for all his interest in "order," it is, as we have seen, the common law which "abhors despotism," and which would protect private rights against the prince, and guard against "statolatry."

In his review of Bancroft,[65] Brownson specifically rejected his older concept of the American Idea. For this reason, the essay is of especial interest here.

Although he had considerable respect for Bancroft, he could not, he now thought, rate him in the first rank as an historian, since Bancroft was really not an historian at all. He "uses history for the purpose of setting forth, illustrating, confirming, and disseminating, his [own] speculative theories on God, man, and society. The history he writes is not written for an historical end, and the facts he relates are grouped and colored in subserviency to his unhistorical purposes." Now history, Brownson argued, was not a speculative science, but one which dealt exclusively with facts, with a record of events as they passed in sequence. Whatever theory the historian used to arrange and explain these facts must be truly an historical theory, not a merely speculative one:

that is, it must be a theory for the explanation of the purely historical, not the metaphysical, origin, causes, relations, and meaning of facts. It must be itself within the order of facts, and like all inductive theories, a mere generalization or classification of facts in their own order. That all historical facts have a speculative origin, causes, relations,—a meaning in the world which transcends the world of space and time,—is of course true; but in this sense they are eternal, have no succession, and therefore, no history. In this sense they transcend the province of the historian, as such, and pertain solely to that of the metaphysician or theologian.[66]

According to Brownson, the modern school of history, especially in France and Germany, overlooked this distinction between the provinces of history and theology, and used history to "prove" its adherents' preformed theories of God, man, and society. Any facts contrary to the theory are either muted, denied, or rejected as irrelevant. "Herder, Kant, Hegel, Guizet, Cousin, Michelet, . . . Carlyle and Macaulay are instances in point. . . . None of these gives us genuine history, or even their own views of history; they merely give us speculations on what is not history, and what according to those speculations ought to be history." These men were the "so-called philosophical historians," and to their company belonged George Bancroft:

Herder finds in all history only his Ideas of human progress; Kant . . . his categories; Hegel finds the significance and end of all history, the operations of Divine Providence, of all mankind, and of all nature to have been the establishment of the Prussian monarchy; Mr. Bancroft finds that the original purpose of creation, of God and the universe, is fulfilled in the establishment of American democracy.[67]

There remained a transcendental plan to history, Brownson conceded, but that plan was God's, not man's, and we might learn it only through revelation. Bossuet, aware of divine revelation and speaking as a bishop, could give to history "something of the character of a speculative science, or furnish a philosophy of history . . .: a divine, not a human philosophy."[68] It was impossible from historical or even psychological facts to obtain a philosophy by induction, for induction could never deliver causes or principles: the "Baconian universe . . . is a universe of effects without causes,—a manifest contradiction in terms."

Only from the viewpoint of divine intelligence could there be a logic in history; from the human viewpoint, Brownson asked, who was to assess adequately such variables as "the natural and supernatural providence of God and the free-will of man [which latter is] in a fallen and abnormal state, as well as in a supernatural state, to which [man] is elevated by the grace of Christ"?[69] All these had their effect upon "logical" sequences of history, and no man could evaluate their influences.

Moreover, with freedom in the antecedent, the conclusion cannot be logically deduced; for logic can deduce only *necessary* conclusions. To the historian history is never a series of logical sequences, for if it were it would not be history, as there would then be no chronological sequence, or succession in time. To [the historian] much must always appear anomalous, arbitrary, inexplicable, the result of chance; although in . . . fact there is no chance, and though there is freedom, there is nothing arbitrary, or without a sufficient reason. All the so-called philosophies of history, or attempts to reduce history to the form of a speculative human science, proceed on a pantheistic assumption,—are founded on the denial of creation and providence, the free-will of God, and consequently the free-will and moral accountability of man. They all assume virtually that the universe is purely phenomenal, and is to be regarded only as the necessary expression of an inherent principle of Life, which evolves, moves, and agitates the whole by an intrinsic law of necessity. They all assume and inculcate the doctrine of absolute and universal fatalism, which binds alike in the same chain of invincible necessity, God, man, and nature.[70]

Theology was necessary, then, to the true historian, but Brownson emphasized that theology originated with God, not man, and could not be subservient to history. A "theology" concocted for purposes of historical explanation should not be dignified as history; untrained readers might mistake "speculative notions" or "philosophical crotchets" for historical facts. And the method of precisely this sort of fabrication was that of George Bancroft who, as a "progressive democrat," believed that democracy was not alone the best, but indeed the only, form of legitimate government.

The popular will is for him the supreme law, and the popular instincts and tendencies are the infallible criterion of truth, beauty, and goodness. The people are to him the infallible church, and humanity is his God. There is . . . no God for man but the God in humanity, who speaks only in and through popular instincts and tendencies. Hence the author defines elsewhere democracy to be "eternal justice ruling through the people." The race is progressive, and the progress of society is constantly towards the realization of democracy as thus defined. Here, in a word, is the general theory which he writes his History of the United States to establish and disseminate.[71]

Brownson admitted that his criticism would not be "minute" but general, and proceeded to divide his commentary into four parts: *a*) the history of the colonization of Carolina; *b*) Bancroft on Salem witchcraft; *c*) Bancroft's account of Quakerism; *d*) Bancroft on the " 'progressive' " principle of American democracy.[72]

In his discussion of the last point, Bancroft had insisted, according to Brownson, that the American revolution was only a relatively modern link in a continuous chain of revolutions designed to topple progressively the barons, the church, and the king, and to leave the commons to rule themselves. Bancroft had argued further that these facts proved the "continuous progress" of society, and that the real American patriot would support the ideal of "progressive or social democracy" which Bancroft "wishes to see established throughout the world, if need be by Red Republican revolutions, and all the blood, and carnage, and horrors of both civil and international war."[73]

Bancroft supported his thesis with his view of the "solidarity of the human race, as taught," interpolated Brownson, "by that arch-socialist, Pierre Leroux."[74] The reviewer then equated the doctrine with those of the Hungarian Louis Kossuth, and the Italian Joseph Mazzini—"the old Jacobinical doctrine of 'the fraternity of nations,' on which was founded the pretended right of revolutionists in all countries to conspire together, and to rush to the assistance of each other in any particular country where their aid may be necessary to overthrow the existing government."[75]

Brownson rejected Bancroft's praise for Lord Baltimore's contributions to religious liberty;[76] he denied, too, Bancroft's view of Christianity which, the reviewer claimed, assumed that man was God, for "the office of Christianity is not to reveal the will of God, to make redemption for sin, to give spiritual life to men, and elevate them to God . . . as their ultimate end, but to embody the aspirations and to guide the advancement of the race!"[77]

Finally, Brownson accused Bancroft of advocating the liberty of heresy and unbelief under the mantle of religious liberty in order to seduce Catholics from their allegiance to their Church and to ease the path of the real enemies of religious liberty, the "European Red Republicans and English Protestants."[78]

This essay is pivotal to an understanding of what Brownson was really rejecting; it indicated well just how far he had come from the days of the *Boston Quarterly Review*. For here he now denied by implication that America could have truly represented a "dream" in the sense of the Progressists, that is, the culmination of the long progress of mankind. He ridiculed the "experiment," certainly in the sense that Bancroft had thought of it, by denying that eternal justice utilized the people *en masse* as agent for its will. And the American Mission—what he had once called the grand destiny of the American people—had now been reduced to a nullity by Brownson's rejection of revolutionary parties scheming in the manner of a Comintern to overturn governments in lands beyond their own borders.

Brownson saw all these phases now through a different glass, and darkly. America's contribution to humanity had been, he now saw, to help to re-establish the freedom which the common law had granted prior to the unjust assumption of power by English kings; the American democratic experiment represented a progress only in that it blended the best of past monarchical, oligarchical, and representative governments; the danger was that the experiment, its principles and purposes misunderstood, could be manipulated to the point where all freedom would be lost. Brownson feared, in brief, revolution, and he saw as paradigm to the future in America the bloody revolutions in Europe. These he clearly recognized as the children of the darker side of the French Revolution—the practical results of the theorizing in the French *salons*. Ideas did have consequences: religion could not be allowed to be reduced to pantheism, and ultimately rendered impotent; government must not become a "mobocracy" which would call for the antidote of an omnicompetent state, with consequent loss of all freedom; the theory of progress could not be permitted to mesmerize its followers into a long red and black night of horrors. Original sin must be faced as a fact: every generation was "equidistant from eternity," and those, like so many of his contemporaries, who denied its abstract life were blind to the practical consequences of that denial. It was on this ground that Orestes Brownson stood in October of 1852.

The year 1853 saw a consolidation of these views in Brownson's mind, but with apparently little addition or deepening. It is true that in his review of Bancroft's fifth volume of the *History* Brownson's tone was more irenic, and his manner much more friendly.[79] Yet this was true only because the editor felt that Bancroft had committed here "comparatively few of the faults we have previously pointed out in Mr. Bancroft's work." There is hope expressed that if the improvement continues at comparable rate we "shall begin to be proud of our countryman."

There were two brief reviews in the July number which reflected Brownson's concern with socialism proper, and of his conviction that it could be opposed only by Catholicity. In the first of these, a review of *Considerations on Some Recent Social Theories,*[80] a book written by a Protestant, Brownson emphasized the difficulties of a Protestant in condemning socialism: "In order to be a Protestant, he must concede the premises of his [socialist] opponent"; and he must continue by "sacrificing logic to common sense, as they [the socialists] can oppose him only by sacrificing common sense to logic." Thus, it was only the Catholic who could adequately defend against the socialist through both logic and common sense, and successfully oppose radicalism; it was "only he who can defend authority without defending despotism, or liberty without defending anarchy."[81]

This brief review was followed by another, that of Richard H. Clarke's *Socialism in America*,[82] originally an address before the Philodemic Society of Georgetown, a Jesuit college in the District of Columbia. Brownson supported Clarke's view that socialistic tendencies were stronger in the United States than even "intelligent and patriotic" men were willing to believe or imagine. These tendencies, according to the editor, were furthered by "the prevailing Calvinism and Puritanism of a large portion of our people,"[83] and he instanced the Maine Liquor Law movement and Abolitionism; "women's-rights-ism" Brownson found reminiscent of "what Calvin attempted at Geneva, and the Puritans in the early colonial days." Such movements were "decidedly socialistic," since they sacrificed the individual to society, "the liberty of the individual to the despotism of the state."

The leading political doctrine of the day, democracy itself as now generally understood, is only the political phase of Calvinism, and it wants little of being pure socialism, for it excludes God, and renders society supreme. In fact socialism is nothing but Protestantism gone to seed, and no man can be a consistent Protestant without holding all the principles necessary to serve as the logical basis of socialism.[84]

Only a Catholic, therefore, could properly and successfully attack "the socialistic tendencies of the country."[85]

In the fourth article of the *Review* for January, 1854, Brownson returned to the discussion of the Catholic basis of civilization. The trend of the argument here was that whatever remained preserved of Catholic tradition was the only guarantor of a healthy society even in Protestant nations.[86] In the same place, Brownson cited with great admiration the "profound" *Essay on Catholicity, Liberalism and Socialism* of Donoso Cortés,[87] and remarked that even Catholic nations had forgotten their heritage and seemed to rely, in opposition to Providence, upon Protestantism, not as a religion, but as an agent of civilization and a worldly prosperity imbued with all the false principles of the age.[88] This was, of course, a fatal road to follow, however unpalatable it may seem to have been for Brownson to point it out continually.

A few pages on, Brownson came to what was again an implicit denial of the idea of the American Mission. Writing of conditions in Italy, the editor conceded that the Italian government could not be remade after the American model. The habits, manners, customs, tastes, and the exterior and interior life of Italians—their whole genius and energy—were, he thought, opposed to democratic institutions.[89] "No," he concluded, "you cannot benefit Italy by attempting to Anglicize or Americanize her institutions."

In "The Mercersburg Hypothesis," an article in April of 1854,[90] Brownson distinguished three types of Protestants from the "vulgar" or common Protestants: first, the rationalist type which denied all religion "distinguished from simple human philosophy" (e.g., Unitarians, German Neologists, and American Transcendentalists). These rejected Christianity really, and fell below pagan philosophers. The second group was that which had a "Romanizing" tendency (e.g., Puseyites); the third class accepted the Catholic Church down to the sixteenth century and felt that Protestantism was merely its logical development (e.g., the Mercersburg theologians). It was this third group which Brownson attempted to refute in a most friendly fashion.[91]

In the course of the refutation, the editor attacked, in a way familiar to a careful reader, the whole idea of development and progress of the human race. Man did not evolve; that theory confused first and final causes; it was, at bottom, pantheistic. This theory of human progress was connected by the Mercersburg people with a theory of development or evolution of Christianity; to them Christianity was something to be developed, perfected; it was not "as a law to be accepted and obeyed." Since this opinion involved the "assumption of legislative power by the creature," the seminal principle of atheism was thus encountered. Brownson was now willing to concede that development and progress might take place in man's individual *knowledge* of Christianity, but denied that the same could be true in the religion itself.[92] Further, since the thought of the Mercersburg group differed fundamentally with Catholicity (even in the sixteenth century), Brownson denied that they were logical heirs of that prior period. That was to say that only the present Catholic Church could be that heir. The editor then identified "the grand error of nearly all the later German and French philosophy," which was also the error of Mercersburg:

[By] referring creation to God as being and intelligence, rather than to God as will, or free activity, they [the philosophers and Brownson's Mercersburg opponents] naturally regard—nay, are compelled to regard—human life as an evolution of the human being and as a development of human intelligence. It is always a becoming, *das Werden,* and consequently ceases in so far as it ceases to be progressive. The end of human living is therefore progress, or the continuous development of intelligence and growth or evolution of being. . . . Nature is not completed in the original act of creation but tends always to complete itself.[93]

Thus man's legitimate activity was presumed to be in developing and augmenting his nature, rather than in the exercise of activity in fulfillment of a moral law.

Brownson's answer was by now a familiar one: Nature was not *becoming,* but completed; religion "objectively considered is finished"; Christianity had been perfected by God; the "doctrine of development is no better than a blasphemous dream."[94] Progress, therefore, in the sense the Mercersburg faction had considered, was in fact impossible, and, as life in Christianity was, in Brownson's mind, analogous to the life of God's visible creation, there could not be progress in nature either. This "blasphemous dream" had its effects in society: revolution, carnage, anarchy. And these results hardly represented the old dream of social amelioration.

In July, there appeared to be a subtle shift in Brownson's thinking on the subject of Native Americanism. The change, however, may be more apparent than real. In his earlier discussion of the Native American Party he had excoriated its patrons, its members, and its ideals. But it must also be remembered that he had warned the Irish over and over again to assimilate themselves into American life, to guard against the "ghetto," to become, in short, Americanized. Indeed, he had become rather unpopular with the Irish and their journals on this account. But, again, the reader must look to Brownson's change of emphasis rather than easily assume his ability to turn his coat. Otherwise, it is easy to misundertstand the mind of this man. And he must remember that Brownson could admit a mistake.

In the article entitled "Native Americanism"[95] Brownson insisted that there was such a thing as "American nationality," which was predominantly of English origin and descent. These people were the "original germ" of the American people, the source of nationality, the founders of American institutions, and the bearers of "the grand and fertilizing current of American life." It was their spirit which must eventually animate other races which would come here. This spirit was considered a modification of the Anglo-Saxon or Anglo-Norman spirit, and, however enriched by tributary streams, it had its own essential character. It was too simple, therefore, contended Brownson, to confuse a proper native feeling with an anti-Catholic bias.[96] Some such alliance could certainly be admitted. But one must admit, too, that there was native American Catholic support for the Party; indeed, its first journal "was conducted by Catholics, descended on one side at least from an old American Catholic family."[97] It must be remembered further, the editor went on, that any nation had "the natural right to preserve itself, and that which constitutes it. What it is,—its national spirit, genius, usages, manners, customs. . . . Therefore [it] has a natural right to guard against any influx of foreigners, which, in its judgment, is incompatible with the maintenance of identity."[98] For foreigners to claim a "natural right" to be placed on equal footing was to assert "that abominable doctrine [i.e., Leroux's] of the solidarity of peoples maintained by the infamous revolutionists of Europe, and which is incompatible, not only with all regular government, but with all national independence."

Although there was strong residual native feeling in the United States against the Irish, Brownson yet considered the most dangerous immigrants to be those non-Catholic immigrants from Europe's continent who were imbued with "the infidel and anarchical principles of mad European revolutionists." To prevent *their* naturalization, loyal Catholic immigrants, however loyal, should not, he believed, press for that privilege.[99] For the radical tendencies of the bulk of these central and southern Europeans ran counter to the "stanch, uncompromising" republican native spirit which was peculiarly and happily adapted to a rule of law. The founders of this country "attempted no Utopia"; their objective had been to guard against despotism on the one side, and license on the other. They did not confuse proper authority with despotism, nor true liberty with radicalism, an anarchic movement which was "we may almost say introduced [here] by Protestant Irishmen from the North of Ireland" who themselves had been influenced by French Jacobinism. Since the Catholic religion, taken in itself, was neither despotic nor radical but genuinely conservative, Brownson contended that the future would see it as a force for preservation, an indispensable element to American life. The Native American Party, now goaded by irresponsible foreigners, had become "really a foreign party" and true Americans would disavow it. Yet it was for Catholics to stand by their preservative principles, to develop a deep and widely informed knowledge of the problem, and to strive for mutual understanding and forbearance.

In October, Brownson returned to the discussion with an article entitled "The Know-Nothings." While in large part it is a restatement and attempted clarification of the earlier effort, its author makes quite clear the emphasis of his concern for "our American republicanism such as it was in the minds of our fathers."[100] Native Protestants fear Catholicity on secular grounds for three reasons: first, as a foreign product and therefore one opposed to American nationality; second, as anti-liberal, and therefore opposed to American republicanism; third, as anti-industrial "and repugnant to the material growth and prosperity of nations."[101]

Now, all these objections had to be met; to oppose them properly, the distinction between "Old America" and "Young America" must be borne in mind. The former stood for "constitutional republicanism," not democratic republicanism; it held to the principles of the founding fathers; it placed political sovereignty in the people collectively, as a civil society which, while acting according to constitutional rules, subjected them to the "empire of the laws." To "Old America" the state was the state, not a mere association, and though the sphere of government was limited, and its use of power not at all arbitrary, that power must be imperative within its proper limits, and must have the right to concomitant force to execute its legal commands. These views represented "the true, genuine, original, political America."[102]

"Young America," so-called, was a "bastard America," since it was not legitimate, that is, not warranted by the Constitution and other institutions of this country; it was of foreign rather than native origin. "Young America" was the radical, ultra-democratic America, which many foreigners had confused with the real America. "Young America" equated native institutions with "European democracy, with French Jacobinism, and the universal Red Republicanism or revolutionism of the Old World."[103]

The pressing imperative for Catholics, particularly immigrants, was to recognize the difference and subsequently defend "the old genuine Republican America." Especially in ignorance of the essential distinction were the Irish radicals who in their support of "Young America" were misleading native Americans about the true character of Catholicism. Brownson's concluding assertions were that he himself had held this view of the two Americas since 1841, and that his experience of the ensuing years had only clarified its truth, even though, somewhat ruefully, he admitted that he had earned for himself the title " 'the best abused man' in all America" for his opposition to "Young America."[104]

It seems true, then, that by the time Orestes Brownson was leaving Boston for New York he had not stopped insisting on the points which had been cardinal to his thought for many years. He continued to maintain the necessity of society to civilization, the necessity of government to society, and the necessity of authority to government. He continued to hold, however, that in every state personal liberty and governmental authority must be balanced, and this he found to be the result, though not exclusively, of a republican form of government, properly understood. While he was still emphasizing that the form of government might well and properly differ in different places, the republican form was for the United States its original constitution, understood in de Maistre's sense still, and had been developed under the English gift of the traditional common law. The distinction he drew between "Young" and "Old" America was clearly the one he had been drawing for years between the democratic and republican forms of government. "Young America" represented all those Jacobin elements which were revolutionary in origin and anarchic in character; "Old America," that which had stemmed from the original American base, represented the true American government, and was essentially conservative, preservative. But the balance he demanded between liberty and authority must be insisted upon here, and the fact that he felt that this equipoise could be properly accomplished through Catholic principles since these both recognized the existence of original sin, and provided the providential means to combat it.

The perfectibility of man was a chimera precisely because of original sin, and any optimism stemming from its assumption as a grounding for social amelioration was fatuous in the extreme. For as Protestantism receded farther from its source, and continued to insist upon private judgment, it tended to sectarianism, and descended to natural religion which, in turn, became pantheism, and finally atheism. This condition could not but contribute to social anarchy, since the truth about man was an imperative which, unrecognized, could destroy civilized society. Authority, pushed out the door, would come in the window perhaps in the form of socialism, that Christian heresy, and state power would ultimately crush individual liberty.

Progress, the evangel of the nineteenth century, was a delusion; it was founded upon such grounds as the humbuggery of the physical sciences, led by Newton and Bacon, and upon the "solidarity of the race," a gift of Leroux, the "arch-socialist." If Christianity and democracy were to be twin rulers, they could not be Protestant Christianity or Jacobin democracy.

For Brownson now, the American Idea, in decline since 1844, was practically dead. The founding fathers planned "no Utopia" in this country; the "lost Eden" could not be regained by making of man a creature of mere mean animal wants and instincts. Bancroft's theory of history was unacceptable: a miracle was emphatically *not* the current end of a progress, either providentially inspired or stemming from some unnamable force in nature. A "philosophy of history" such as this was untenable; only theologians could view history in that way, and even they must begin with God, not end with His false likeness. Indeed, if there was hope for the American experiment, it would come from a currently unacknowledged quarter: "our sole reliance for the preservation of American liberty and American institutions. . . . The American experiment in self-government, is on the Catholic Church which . . . so far from being opposed to republicanism . . . is absolutely essential to its wholesome working and successful maintenance."[105] Brownson suggested, though he did not insist, that European Catholics refrain from becoming naturalized Americans,[106] so that immigrant revolutionaries from Europe could be controlled. This, too— this negation of the old dream—was now to Brownson a necessary tack of the experiment.

What of the American Mission—the spreading of self-government, of democracy throughout the world? What Brownson had written in 1854 in the case of Italy could stand for other countries: every country had its own constitution; that constitution may not be tampered with; democracy would not prosper where it was not providentially designed. In any case, the *form* of government was not the important point. The balance of liberty and authority was the paramount issue, and might be achieved under any legitimate form of government. In the final judgment, one could set up a democratic state elsewhere only by revolution, and that above everything else, now it seemed, was anathema in political life.

Thus the last Boston issue of *Brownson's Quarterly Review* was written and published. Whatever its new home would see in changes in its editor and his thought prior to the Civil War, he had spoken his farewell in the uncompromising terms which Boston had once admired but now could not understand.

NOTES

1. Schlesinger, *Brownson,* pp. 218–219.
2. *Ibid.,* p. 209. The Brownson quotation is from Brownson's letter to the Rev. J. W. Cummings on June 23, 1849. See H. F. Brownson, *Middle Life,* p. 195. If Fitzpatrick's authority extended only to theology (and it did), how was Brownson inhibited by censorship in his writing about "social affairs"? Moreover, to write of a "renewed interest" makes too little of the record of *continued* interest reflected in articles in the *Review* as has been noted in the previous chapter. But see Schlesinger, *Brownson,* pp. 279–281.
3. "Yes," Brownson once wrote, "I deny that I have *changed,* though I own that I seem to myself to have *advanced.*" Cited in Schlesinger, *Brownson,* p. 281 n. 9.
4. *BrQR,* VII, 1 (1850), 1–38.
5. *Ibid.,* pp. 2–3. The object, Brownson now believed, determined the subject; "otherwise, knowledge is impossible, and all real certainty out of the question." Religion, therefore, existed not in emotions, or sentiment, or any combination—this was the kind of subjectivism (or, to use Brownson's term, "psychologism") which vitiated Transcendentalism. See *BrQR,* VII, 2 (1850), 159–190, especially 163–177.
6. *BrQR,* VII, 1 (1850), 6.
7. Cited in *BrQR,* VII, 3 (1850), 299.
8. J. R. Lowell, *Poems* (Boston, 1848); see *BrQR,* VII, 2 (1850), 170–271.
9. *Ibid.,* p. 271.
10. *BrQR,* VII, 4 (1850), 409–448. The three works are *Del primato morale e civile degli Italiani* (Lausanne, 1846); *Introduzione allo*

studio della filosofia (Brussels, 1844); *Del bello e del buono*
(Lausanne, 1846). There is no space here to discuss Brownson's
"ontologism" and Gioberti's influence upon his thought in this regard. It must suffice to state generally that the influence appears
to have been great: Brownson took the key phrase *Ens creat ex-
istentias* from the Italian. For published discussions of the problem,
see Schlesinger, *Brownson*, pp. 219–220; 229–230; Maynard, *Brownson*, pp. 268–269; 396–397; and *passim*. The only full-scale study
of Brownson's philosophy is Sidney Raemers, *America's Foremost
Philosopher* (Washington, 1931). For a discussion of Brownson's
own contemporary statements on the point here, see H. F. Brownson,
Middle Life, pp. 215–217; 220–223.

11. *BrQR*, VII, 4 (1850), 410–411.
12. *Ibid.*, p. 413.
13. *Ibid.*, p. 416.
14. *Ibid.*, p. 419.
15. *Ibid.*, p. 420.
16. *Ibid.*, p. 421. Brownson argued that he had held this view even
    as a Protestant in 1843, and evidenced his articles in the *United
    States Magazine and Democratic Review*.
17. *BrQR*, VII, 4 (1850), 422. The implications of this to the Idea
    of Progress seem too obvious for comment. For Brownson's com-
    ments on the *jus divinum* and its relation to positive law, see *BrQR*,
    VIII, 3 (1851), 364–370.
18. *Ibid.*, pp. 434–448.
19. Tayler Lewis, *Nature, Progress, Ideas* (Schenectady, 1850); *BrQR*,
    VII, 4 (1850), 532–534. Brownson spells the author's given name
    as "Taylor." For comment on Lewis and his importance to the
    discussion of Progress in America, see Ekirch, *Progress*, pp. 124–125;
    174–176; 193. Cf. Joseph L. Blau, "Tayler Lewis, True Conserva-
    tive," *Journal of the History of Ideas*, 13 (1952), 218–233.
20. *BrQR*, VII, 4 (1850), 533.
21. *Idem.*
22. *BrQR*, VIII, 1 (1851), 29–67; the quotation here is on p. 31. Brown-
    son specifically excepted the Irish from the "scum," and the native-
    born Americans from the "mob"; the article is entitled "The Hun-
    garian Rebellion."
23. *Ibid.*, pp. 31–33.
24. *Ibid.*, pp. 80–97.
25. *Ibid.*, p. 93.
26. *Ibid.*, pp. 98–114.
27. *BrQR*, VIII, 2 (1851), 269–270.
28. (Boston, 1851); *ibid.*, p. 270.
29. *Idem.* Any theory of Progress (that is to say, all contemporary
    theories of progress) was built upon optimism stemming from the
    rise of rationalistic science. Brownson's naïveté here was obviously
    a drawback in his apprehension of either the real contributions of
    science or the debt which material progress owed it. However, his

ignorance, according to biographers, had by 1863 given way to keen observation, spurred on by Darwin. Especially had he, says Schlesinger, a "sharp perception of the limitations of science—rare in a day which tended to confound Newton with God . . ." (*Brownson*, p. 263). See *ibid.*, pp. 262–266.

30. B. Saint-Bonnet, *De la restauration française* (Paris, 1851). *BrQR*, VIII, 4 (1851), 452–492.

31. *Ibid.*, p. 453.

32. *Ibid.*, p. 454. There is further foreshadowing of the thesis of Max Weber on p. 455.

33. *Ibid.*, p. 456. Brownson admitted indebtedness to Saint-Bonnet here, and had praise for Proudhon ("clear head, iron nerves, and invincible dialectic") who had not shirked the consequences of thinking through the logical extension of principles. Proudhon, "a great man, and for the moment one of the most useful men of society," had given the age its formula ("LA PROPRIÉTÉ, C'EST LE VOL"), and revealed thus the age to itself—i.e., that nothing remains but socialism or Catholicity (*idem*).

34. *Ibid.*, p. 458. Brownson here claimed that John Henry Newman fused to the spiritual order what the Progressists had applied to the temporal order—he had attempted with most worthy motives to harmonize unchangeable Christian doctrine "with the modern heathen doctrine of progress" (*ibid.*, p. 459). See also pp. 462–463.

35. *Ibid.*, p. 461. The Thomistic overtone of this seems clear.

36. *Idem.*

37. *Idem.* According to Brownson, Newman's error lay here, for he "undeniably transports human activity into the first cycle, the peculiar province of God," and makes man joint Creator with the Holy Ghost of Christian doctrine" (p. 463).

38. *Ibid.*, p. 464.

39. *Ibid.*, pp. 464–470.

40. *Ibid.*, p. 470.

41. *Ibid.*, p. 479.

42. *Ibid.*, pp. 479–480.

43. *Ibid.*, p. 490.

44. *Ibid.*, p. 491.

45. For details see H. F. Brownson, *Middle Life*, pp. 347–349, and *BrQR*, IX, 2 (1852), 263.

46. *Ibid.*, pp. 263–278. The review is entitled "Protestantism and Government." See also Hugh A. Garland, *A Course of Five Lectures . . . on Protestantism and Government* (St. Louis, 1852).

47. *Ibid.*, p. 266.

48. *Ibid.*, p. 270.

49. *Ibid.*, p. 272.

50. *Ibid.*, p. 278.

51. *Idem.*

52. (Boston, 1851); *BrQR*, IX, 3 (1852), 341–382.

53. *Ibid.*, p. 345.

54. *Ibid.*, p. 350. This, said Brownson, was precisely Webster's own argument in the Dartmouth College Case (*ibid.*, pp. 354–355).
55. *Ibid.*, p. 351.
56. *Ibid.*, p. 355.
57. *Ibid.*, pp. 355–356; italics mine.
58. *Ibid.*, p. 360.
59. *Ibid.*, p. 358.
60. *Ibid.*, pp. 359–360. Brownson was characteristic in argument: order balances liberty.
61. *Ibid.*, p. 360.
62. *Idem.* Brownson had great praise for Edmund Burke both here and elsewhere in this article (e.g., p. 343). Taken "all in all," Burke is "the most eminent among the distinguished statesmen who have written or spoken in our language" (*ibid.*, p. 377). But Brownson gave little concrete evidence that he had studied Burke at any very great length. There is evidence here, however, that Brownson may have read Bossuet carefully (*idem*).
63. *Ibid.*, p. 380.
64. See, for example, his current opinion of Cousin, *ibid.*, p. 415.
65. George Bancroft, *History of the United States* (Boston, 1852), Vol. IV. *BrQR*, IX, 4 (1852), 421–459.
66. *Ibid.*, p. 422. On this whole subject, see Ryan, "Historiography," pp. 10–17; 122–130.
67. *Ibid.*, p. 423.
68. *Ibid.*, p. 424.
69. *Idem.*
70. *Ibid.*, pp. 424–425.
71. *Ibid.*, p. 428. This statement was preceded by a sharp attack upon Bancroft himself which concluded with the accusation that the historian's only defense could be the principle that the end justifies the means. The acerbity of Brownson's comments was hardly eased by the relatively muted praise which had preceded them.
72. *Ibid.*, pp. 428–431.
73. *Ibid.*, p. 432. These words, of course, are Brownson's, not Bancroft's.
74. *Ibid.*, p. 439.
75. *Idem.* There followed the suggestion (evidenced only by strong hearsay to Brownson) that Bancroft once had belonged to the revolutionary "Illuminati, or Carbonari . . . engaged in a revolution in Naples." Brownson's earlier interest in the "Carbonari" has been noted in Chapter 1.
76. *Ibid.*, pp. 453–459. Religious liberty stemmed from God, not from Lord Baltimore, who came "fifteen hundred years too late." Baltimore represented no progress in this matter: "[The Church] does not acquire wisdom and sanctity with the progress of the ages; she was born perfect in both" (*ibid.*, p. 455).
77. *Ibid.*, p. 451.
78. *Ibid.*, pp. 458–459.
79. *BrQR*, X, 2 (1853), 280.

80. *BrQR*, x, 3 (1853), 414. The book appears to have been anonymous: it was printed in 1853 by Little, Brown and Company, Boston.
81. *Idem.*
82. Richard H. Clark, *Socialism in America* (Washington, 1852).
83. *BrQR*, x, 3 (1853), 415.
84. *Idem.*
85. See *BrQR*, x, 1 (1853), 26–62; 87–110; *ibid.*, x, 2 (1853), 185–218; *ibid.*, x, 3 (1853), 281–314; 332–365 (with prominent mention of Donoso Cortés); *ibid.*, x, 4 (1853), 529–542.
86. *BrQR*, xi, 1 (1854), 87–106.
87. Juan Donoso Cortés, *Ensayo sobre el Catholicismo, el Liberalismo, y el Socialismo, considerados en sus principios fundamentales* (Madrid, 1851). Donoso Cortés, marqués de Valdegamos, was called to Brownson's attention by Montalembert in a letter dated "Easter Sunday, 1850" (H. F. Brownson, *Middle Life*, p. 229). Well-known in Europe among Catholic intellectuals, Donoso Cortés, at this time the Spanish Ambassador to Paris, was one of a group planning a European Catholic quarterly review. Others were Montalembert himself, Louis Veuillot, and de la Tour. See *ibid.*, pp. 326; 405. For an opinion on Donoso Cortés' importance see Béla Menczer, *Catholic Political Thought, 1789–1848* (London, 1952), pp. 157–160; 185. Also see the unsigned review of Menczer's book, *The Month*, N.S. 8 (August 1952), 123.
88. *BrQR*, xi, 1 (1854), 98–100. Brownson here indicated that the apologetical cast of his *Review* since 1844 has been under the guidance of principles "prescribed" by Church authorities (p. 100). But see *BrQR*, xiii, 2 (1855), 183–209.
89. *BrQR*, xi, 1 (1854), 126–127.
90. *BrQR*, xi, 2 (1854), 253–265. The relevant article under review had appeared in the *Mercersburg Quarterly Review* for January 1854; that *Review* was published at Chambersburg, Pennsylvania.
91. He had high praise for Dr. John W. Nevin and Dr. Philip Schaff.
92. *Ibid.*, p. 257; for the argument see pp. 257–261.
93. *Ibid.*, p. 263.
94. *Ibid.*, p. 264.
95. *BrQR*, xi, 3 (1854), 328–354.
96. Remarked Brownson, "We ourselves, when first a Catholic, committed that mistake" partially, at least, "through our own imprudence" (*ibid.*, p. 339).
97. *Idem.*
98. *Ibid.*, p. 340. See also *ibid.*, xi, 4 (1854), 454–455.
99. *BrQR*, xi, 3 (1854), 343. This suggestion would be made again. See *ibid.*, xi, 4 (1854), 456; 459. The "non-Catholics from the Continental States of Europe" are "Germans, Hungarians, and Italians" (*ibid.*, xi, 3 [1854], 343).
100. *BrQR*, xi, 4 (1854), 458.
101. *Ibid.*, p. 469.
102. *Ibid.*, p. 479. For a parallel statement of this same point, see Hugh

Seton-Watson, "Neither War nor Peace—A Survey of Our Times," *U.S. News and World Report* (August 29, 1960), pp. 67–68.
103. *BrQR*, xi, 4 (1854), 481.
104. *Ibid.*, p. 483. See also *BrQR*, xii, 1 (1855), 114–135.
105. *BrQR*, xi, 4 (1854), 457.
106. He did insist, however, that naturalization was not a *right* but a privilege.

7

BROWNSON'S QUARTERLY
REVIEW, 1855-1859

IN A REVIEW of Heinrich Ritter's *The History of Ancient Philoso-phy*,[1] Brownson began the year 1855 by denying in a familiar way the possibility of a history "of [the] steady progress of Philosophical thought." Progress there had not really been, since man's tendency "has been to depart from and lose sight of the primitive tradition made by God to man," and because the unaided reason could not advance its sum of knowledge through either the reflective or the intuitive modes in which the reason operated.[2] Man originally possessed all the philosophical truths, and whatever progress in philosophical knowledge had been made had been really a recovery rather than an advance.

This, then, was still Brownson's basic position, and it was now being articulated beyond the scope of Bishop Fitzpatrick's possible censorship.[3] This notion of progress which had preoccupied much of Brownson's thought during the most productive period of his life was still central to his thought, and in 1855 he would return to it again and again. Indeed, in the same issue, he reviewed George Bancroft's sixth volume of his *History*.[4] Brownson agreed with the historian that the "American Revolution" was precisely named only in that it reflected an attempt to restore essential rights—that is, to restore legitimacy. The reviewer then took up the substance of Bancroft's recent lecture, his "very remarkable Address on Progress."[5] He had respect for Bancroft's point of view which was not "higher" than that in which both he and Brownson had been educated. Brownson was particularly happy with the historian's current awareness that there was "something more in the controversy between the Athanasians and the Arians . . . than a simple dispute

179

about a simple diphthong," and that Bancroft further recognized "that the God of consciousness, of humanity, of history, as well as of theology, is triune."[6] Thus there is the implication that Bancroft could hardly hold any longer the doctrine of the Progressists which was pantheistic (tending to atheism); for that matter, the principal difficulties which Brownson had had with the progressist cast of Bancroft's earlier volumes had "nearly all disappeared from the present [volume]." Clearly, Bancroft appeared to be revising his views on the American Idea, and Brownson plainly stated his trust that when the *History* was fully completed, "and has received its last revision," it would be a monument to the genius of its author, and of America.[7]

In April, the editor returned to the notion of progress once more, this time observing it in its relation to Protestantism. A Protestant minister, the Rev. Rufus W. Clark, had commented that one significant difference between Catholics and Protestants was that the latter excelled in "thrift, prosperity, and general happiness"—that is, in those " 'elements of civilization and social happiness, to say nothing of the religious and spiritual bearings of the two systems.' "[8] Brownson's rejoinder is again evocative in part of the burden of the later Weber–Tawney studies: Protestantism, having lost sight of the "spirituality of the Gospel," had secularized and materialized Christianity; its emphasis now appeared to be generally upon the

low and utilitarian . . . , its glory in the production and multiplication of material goods. It is a mercantile age, a shopkeeping world. . . . Intellect is utilized . . . and the heart is neglected, the soul is left to starve; wealth is made a god, industry a religion, commerce a worship, men and nations are measured by the material standard, and trade is regarded as the first of missionaries to the heathen. . . . In our own country thrift is the first of virtues, and poverty is a crime, and everywhere punished as a crime. . . . Nobody is well employed, in the estimation of our Protestant age, unless employed in making revolutions, finding out new markets for trade, new articles of commerce . . . [or] industry . . . , that is unless employed in making or helping others to make money. Such is the world in which Protestantism predominates. Now this materialism of the age has passed into the religion of Protestants. Protestantism—and this is its boast—is not a stationary religion, but a progressive religion, feeling always the impulse of the age, and yielding to its spirit.[9]

Indeed, concluded Brownson, Protestantism had "progressed" into its own death. For "the American mind is beginning to open to something better and nobler than it has hitherto had. . . ."[10]

This reiteration of accent upon Brownson's denial of the idea of progress, with regard both to Protestantism specifically and to history generally, makes all the more surprising the material in the article following the one just discussed. Entitled "Liberalism and Socialism,"[11] the essay represents as startling a change as does any essay of 1841 in the *Boston Quarterly Review*. Indeed, there may well be room for argument that this essay rejects much of what Brownson had been saying during the ten years of his conversion, and that it is a landmark of his return to earlier principles. Brownson himself seemed aware of this critical possibility, and made a patent attempt to explain that, as Lord Morley later said of Edmund Burke, he had shifted not so much his ground as his front. Whether one can accept Brownson's explanation of a changed emphasis depends largely, it seems, on whether or not one considers his previous position on socialism as a conviction heightened by rhetoric, an *ex parte* argument designed to underscore the more negative aspects of the idea without any explicit denial of the values to be found in it. This appears to have been Brownson's own view, and it was pointed up by an argument he had used before, at the launching of *Brownson's Quarterly Review* in 1844. As has been indicated, at that time Brownson had insisted that the purpose of the *Boston Quarterly Review* had been to stir up discussion, to "throw out" ideas for the contemplation of his readers. The new review, on the other hand, was to be a definite statement of his views, since he felt in 1844 that his aim should be to give positive instruction rather than merely to excite inquiry and debate.[12] In the article under present discussion, Brownson explained his changed emphasis by indicating that to have emphasized the good in either liberalism or socialism in 1848, for example, "would have tended to give the people a false direction." He could not then stop to "analyze and distinguish" since his purpose had been "to expose the dangerous errors and tendencies of the revolutionary systems and movements." But in 1855, "when the danger comes from the opposite quarter, [i.e.,] autocracy, we are free to labor for the conversion of those whom these false systems have misled, by distinguishing and accepting the truth or half-truth which they misapprehend and misapply. There is a time for all things, and our motto should be, Every thing in its time."[13]

Whatever one may think of the argument, and one cannot forget the heat of Brownson's comments upon socialism and Pierre Leroux—upon the former as "Protestantism gone to seed" and upon the latter as the "arch-socialist"—it seems to have satisfied Brownson's strongly logical cast of mind. He may have been mistaken, but, unless some proof can be offered, he was not dishonest. Careful readers of the *Review* may well have been startled, however; it is not difficult, given the perspective of more than a century, to understand why.[14]

The article praised both Donoso Cortés, a foe of socialism, and Pierre Leroux, "the great man of the modern socialistic school."[15] Indeed, the praise seems extravagant: the books under review "are on the subject treated the two profoundest works to be found in the whole range of modern literature." Donoso Cortés, who had a "higher order of genius" than Leroux, wrote to instruct his readers upon the dangers of socialism, and, assuming that Proudhon was the best representative of the socialists, especially of the socialists' contradictions and negations. Donoso Cortés kept closely to a refutation of Proudhon, a task he carried off brilliantly.[16] But since Leroux had "some religious instincts . . . , [he] attempts to give the positive or affirmative side of Socialism."[17] Briefly put, Brownson himself intended to show what the socialists have that is true, even though "humanitarian or pantheistic Socialism," as Donoso Cortés pointed out, must be refuted as a body of doctrine, and one which is "so rife in our time."[18]

Socialism recommended itself to its followers through what truth it had; truth of any kind was good, for error (like evil) was privative, that is to say, was a defect of truth (or, with evil, a defect of good). To win the attention of the socialists, a beginning must be made by recognizing the good in the system before the evil is pointed out. Otherwise, the generous and noble individuals—and there were some—who espoused it could never be converted. "Much . . . of what is most living, least grovelling, least servile, most manly, and most elevated, outside of the Church, is found to-day in their ranks."[19] While it was true that socialism ends in gentilism, yet the creed could have originated only in a "community which had once been Christian," and the socialists' seminal doctrine of philanthropy is the only form which the love of mankind can take outside the Church.[20] Though Brownson still condemned the liberal and socialistic revolutions of the past seventy years, his contention now was that they had had a philanthropic origin"—that is, they had wanted through state agency to effect in the world what the Church had shown she could achieve through Christian charity. The movement "overflowed with generous sentiments" which had been mismanaged by its leaders.

In what appears a surprising shift, Brownson now insisted that there had been warm and benevolent aspects to the French Revolution, attitudes which were primed to reform the very real abuses existing prior to the Revolution; to say that abuses after the Revolution were worse, should not obscure the presence of those aspects which were "traces of . . . Divine similitude; . . . though it may be generally more in accordance with the fact to say, *Vox populi, vox diaboli*, than *vox populi, vox Dei*, yet there is a sense in which it will not do to deny that 'the voice of the people is the voice of God'."[21] The attempt to redress the existent evils prior to the French Revolution had been a "sacred duty imposed alike by charity and philanthropy . . . though of course not by unlawful means, certainly not by revolution, which could only make matters worse." Conservatives should use their indignation less against the idea of revolution than against the conditions which breed it, or religion would be rendered "odious" to mankind suffering those abuses. A philanthropy based upon the old "equal rights" doctrine "after all faintly mirrors the Christian doctrine of the unity and solidarity of the race." There had been truth in the Jacobinical doctrine of "fraternity."[22] And then in a seeming reversion to his pre-1840 doctrine, Brownson bluntly wrote that "Man equals man the world over."[23]

The editor contended that the champion of equal rights was not Calvin, as Bancroft had argued, but Catholicity.[24] The Calvinistic doctrine of total depravity could not explain the equal rights of man; this doctrine of equality might stand only upon the Catholic teaching that there was an "inherent freedom, dignity, and nobility of human nature in every man, which requires the assertion of the unity of the race. . . . God made Man in his own image and likeness, and therefore Man in his very nature must copy, imitate, or mirror his Maker."[25]

This doctrine of solidarity and communion of the race, which Leroux found fundamental to Christianity and a basis of socialism, should be at least carefully studied; it was "through that doctrine, as set forth by Leroux . . . that by the grace of God we were led to the Catholic Church, and . . . the same was true of several of our friends, one at least of whom is now a most worthy member of the Catholic priesthood, and one of the most indefatigable and successful Catholic missionaries in the country."[26] That doctrine could only be completed in Catholicity, and, while Leroux's principles were "substantially true," they needed such completion.

At this juncture in the discussion Brownson listed what he believed to have been the main points of his letter to Dr. Channing (1842), and concluded that "the life of any one man is the joint product of him and every other man," and that, therefore, there is a "solidarity of the life of all men." As every generation overlapped its successor, and the new generation "communes" with its predecessor, that solidarity was "not only a solidarity of all men in space, but of all men in time, linking together, in one indissoluble life, the first man with the last, and the last man with the first."[27] Although this doctrine[28] had been taken from Leroux, Brownson applied it differently; Leroux had denied "the personality of God, the personal immortality of the soul," and "the Incarnation in the individual man, Jesus, instead of the race." Yet he had failed not so much in asserting communion and solidarity, but in giving them greater significance than the Christian mysteries such as the Incarnation, Holy Communion, the apostolic succession, and so on. The fact was that natural truths symbolize Catholic dogma, rather than the reverse. Moreover, Brownson saw no opposition between the theory of the natural communion of the human race and the principles of the sacraments. While the former did not necessarily introduce men to the latter, yet anything which hindered man's natural communion with God, or Man, or Nature, struck at God's will and humanity's interest. Anything which aided that communion, then, became a great and solemn duty. Insofar as liberalism and socialism contributed to communion, they were good; to the degree they hindered it, they were not. Thus, for example, their historical end was just, even obligatory; their means were to be condemned.

Brownson felt that he "cannot absolutely deny" the right of the people of one country—under the solidarity theory—to go to the aid of another particular people, struggling for their rights. The argument held irrespective of the governments involved.[29] The principle here was a true one, but it could have only a "rare application," and that not through whim or caprice, but by "an authority competent to decide." Otherwise, legitimate governments might be placed unfairly in jeopardy, and "order . . . is as sacred as liberty."[30]

The chief error of the liberals and socialists, according to Brownson, resided in their attempt to effect a good end through the agency of "the state," a procedure contrary to true liberty. Philanthropy had to be transmuted into its real substance, Christian charity, and the end sought must be furthered in Catholicity. Brownson re-affirmed his interest in "free principles," and closed by writing that "we are still in some sense a man of our age."[31]

This essay is followed by Brownson's review of Isaac Hecker's *Questions of the Soul*.[32] The editor wrote that Hecker "has done what we ourselves have often attempted to do, and would have done had Almighty God given us the genius and ability to do it. We can now throw the manuscript of our own partially completed work on the same subject into the fire."[33] The gravamen of further comment was that Catholicity in America had been defensive, and had yet to learn how to present itself to the "real American character." The problem was complicated because that "character" was still undeveloped, and had had, therefore, not yet received a true expression.[34] The "real American heart" was under the surface, and if he would grasp it, the observer must study

what we are becoming, rather than what we are. Like children we live in the future, not in the present or the past, and look forward not back-ward. We have hope but no memory.[35] As a people, we feel that we have no past, and we despise the present. We feel ourselves bound by no traditions, whether of truth or error; we have faith only in what is to come. The great words we sometimes use are spoken prophetically, and express what we feel we are to be, not what we feel we are. . . .[36]

However vague the phrasing may be here, the reader will recognize for the first time since 1840 the full return of the American Dream.

Americans as yet had no fixed form of belief, although they were not an infidel people. Rather, they were on a kind of neutral ground. Surprisingly, they espoused a "religious indifference," while, at the same time, they possessed a strong religious nature. "We are best represented by those who have outgrown all the forms of dogmatic Protestantism, and are looking, like Emerson and Parker, for something beyond the Reformation, and have glimpses of a truth, a beauty, a perfection above it, to which they long to attain; but feel that they have not as yet attained and know not how to attain." Few in number, these people, Brownson felt, were "the real American people . . . and theirs are the only words that as yet fetch an echo from the American heart."[37]

Brownson maintained that the Protestant sects had dissolved or were disintegrating under the caustics of American life; there was, he thought, an "agency" at work in the country which eroded sectarian religious belief and "would transform Catholicity in the same way, were it not divine truth, protected by the hand of God himself." Therefore, to ascertain the real American character, one must look to those who have cast off the sects without becoming materialists, or irreligious, and whose number, though small, is growing. "In these is our hope, for he who can speak to the minds and hearts of these speaks to the real American mind and heart."[38] To reach these people, Catholics needed to minister to "the innate cravings of the soul," and reach "the heart and the intellect through the heart," not slighting the "mystic element of the soul," that element "perhaps stronger than any other in our American nature."[39] All this Hecker had attempted in his book, and had done it well.

Brownson's final appeal was to "Young America," by which he apparently meant the same group which had borne the brunt of his harsh criticism less than a year before:

Young America, we know, is not just now in good repute, but we know that there are thousands of warm and generous hearts among our educated young men, crying out for the great and kindling truths[40] of [Hecker's] book. . . . They have each a mission. Our glorious republic too has a mission, a great work in Divine Providence, the sublime work of realizing the idea of Christian society, and of setting the example of a truly great, noble, Catholic people. . . .[41]

Thus, Brownson, passing quickly from the echoes he has evoked of the American Dream, quite flatly asserted, for the first time in many years, the reality of the American Mission. But there was a difference. Where heretofore the Mission had been the spread of liberty and equality through a democracy properly understood, now the Mission was the spread of a Christian (i.e., a Catholic) society. And yet, remembering his essays of rather recent origin, the reader can recall that democracy[42] was rooted in Catholic principle, and that, therefore, the difference may not be so great as at first appears. True liberty was still the end. If so, then the American Experiment, too, was resurrected, for, as has been shown, that was to have been the working-out of the idea that free men could govern themselves. And, thus, barring the changes noted, Brownson seemed definitely to be reverting to his own younger hopes.

Brownson's praise for the "benevolent" aspects of the French

Revolution was restated in the October, 1855, edition of the *Review*. Actually developing their theories from "Catholic conceptions," the revolutionists had retained "a very distinct and vivid reminiscence" of these conceptions, and had made their major error not in so doing, but in misapplying them, and in utilizing improper means to their attainment. Yet, "they were great truths founded in eternal justice, and are dear to the better interests of all human hearts."[43]

In the article which immediately followed, Brownson repeated in comparatively mild terms his opposition to European revolutionary movements; these, he wrote, really imposed restrictions upon true liberty which itself presupposed a sovereignty of the spiritual order which alone could harmonize the just demands of both authority and liberty. Yet such an order was rejected both by modern monarchists—that is, in Brownson's lexicon, the proponents of excessive authority—and by modern democrats (revolutionists), the defenders of excessive liberty. The first group placed the king, the second, "the people" above all law, and, in either case, "political atheism results."[44] This fact was understood by few; even Catholics were not properly aware of it. The separation of philosophy from theology after Descartes had contributed nothing to the "progress" of discovery of truth.

In the purely material order, there have no doubt been discoveries . . . of greater or less value to our simple animal life, and this we may very well assert without supposing any corresponding discoveries in the intellectual and moral order. . . . Out of [the material] order it has, unassisted, accomplished less than nothing . . . [and] has reduced man to a pig or a digestive tube open at both ends.[45]

In 1855, Brownson seemed alert to the need of converting as well as convincing his opponents, and offered this reason for what appears to be a major change in his thinking. He himself did not so regard the alteration, but characterized it as a mere change in emphasis. His primary point was again that a balance must be kept between the demands of order and of liberty, and that emphasis had now to be placed upon the latter in order to redress the balance. Even if Brownson's estimate is accepted, it must still be noted that the change in emphasis appears once more to have resurrected the American Idea, somewhat transmuted now, especially in the Experiment and Mission phases, by his Catholic faith. It should be noted, also, that Brownson seems to have forgotten—or at least did not discuss—the effect of this American Mission upon the idea of political constitution which he had borrowed from de Maistre, and which he had held and accented for so many years. Finally, his "change of emphasis" did not yet include his rejection of the idea of progress as that concept was developed by what he had been wont to call the "Progressists." The concession he made, the admission of material progress, is one he had been making for some time; but, in his view, it had not progressed in any essential sense; Brownson still had little patience with the theory as a whole.

The connection Brownson had found to his old view of the American Idea, and its transmutation through the agency of the Catholic Church, were two subjects which continued to occupy his attention during 1856. In the first article of the *Review* for that year, the editor, arguing that the Church was "an organism, living and operating from her own central life, derived from the indwelling Holy Ghost,"[46] asserted further that in the Church, and only therein, could be found the solution to the old philosophical problem of unity and multiplicity. Modern philosophy tended to be either atheistic or pantheistic, depending upon whether it accented multiplicity or unity to the sacrifice of the other concept.[47] In America, the tendency was toward atheism; the American mind weakened a valid concept of unity when the concept was confused with totality or the aggregate. "The God it asserts is not the living God, but an induction from particulars, the last generalization of observable phenomena. . . . [Thus] multiplicity precedes unity, and the universe is prior to its creator. Its unity is the sum total, composite in its nature, therefore divisible, and therefore no true unity at all."[48] Thus American Protestants could grasp the "substantial unity" of the Church since, for Protestants, the individual believer preceded the Church, and she derived her life from Christ through believers, rather than believers' gaining theirs from Christ through her.

The Church, the editor proceeded, had never had anywhere in history at any time such a providentially designed theater for her social and civil order (her "civility—*civiltà*") as in America. For the founders of this country, through Providence, "retained from the old civilization of Europe only those principles which harmonized with Catholicity; and added to them only those principles which the Popes had for ages been urging in vain upon European statesmen."[49] Thus, in America, the individual was both a man and a citizen whose civil duties and personal rights "are harmonized as they are under the natural law, which the Church presupposes, accepts, and confirms." There was, therefore, a harmony between natural and supernatural, reason and grace, the civil society and the Church. Once the conversion of individuals took place, America would become "an eminently Catholic nation, with a true and lofty Catholic civilization," and, perhaps, even "a new and higher development of Catholic civilization itself. . . ."[50] The American Catholic laity could become the most "free and intelligent" laity the world had ever seen.

In the same issue Brownson, commenting upon a review of Frédéric Ozanam's work in *Le Correspondant*, apparently reversed himself with regard to the acceptability of a philosophy of history. Indeed, he called for a history of the Protestant movement done from the "rationalist" point of view,[51] since his age had no Bossuet who could refer it "to the providential plan of the universe." The method suggested must, of course, be done "with due subordination to the supernatural purpose of God."[52]

The comments which M. Foisset, the author of the article in *Le Correspondant*, had made concerning Ozanam's theory of progress[53] seemed not to have been lost on Brownson, and may have contributed to his renewed view of the possibility of "rationalistic" history. In any event, the opening article in the April, 1856, issue was a review of the Abbé Poisson's *Essai sur les causes du succès du Protestantisme au seizième siècle.* [54] In this article Brownson argued that the principal cause of sixteenth-century Protestant success had been the upheaval caused by social and other transformations as Europe shifted from medieval feudalism to modern monarchy. Brownson traced these changes step by step from the fifth century to the sixteenth; the change since then was characterized as one from monarchy "to Republicanism or Democracy." With respect to this change, the editor wrote that "European society is and has been subject, since the Christian era, to the law of change. Many would say, *perhaps not without some truth, to the law of progress.*"[55] The Church, or rather churchmen slow in perception of change, had clung tediously to outmoded customs and manners so that opponents, confusing the churchmen with the Church, had relegated the latter to a limbo of history. Yet, Brownson continued, the Church herself had never lost sight of principles, nor become enamored of revolution.[56] Indeed, feudalism, which certainly had its evils, had contained "the great principles of civil liberty and personal independence; our own genuine American system, which unhappily so many are laboring to convert into that of the ancient pagan republicanism, is, if we did but know it, only a development of Feudalism, by which every man is authorized to be a proprietor, and every proprietor is a baron or feudal lord."[57]

Brownson's point was that the Church had been identified with feudalism when in fact she had given that system only its viable principles; later, she had been identified with monarchy when she attempted only to preserve order; she was now looked upon as antipathetic to republicanism when actually she was defending against license. Yet, Brownson insisted, Catholics must become aware of change, even of progress, and avoid "binding ourselves to an order of things that has passed, or is passing away, and to prepare ourselves for the future which is advancing. We must accept, both for the sake of religion and of society, the new order as it comes up and establishes itself."[58] While the editor could not defend lawless revolution any more now than in 1848, yet he demanded recognition that the "democratic transformation of Christendom is sure to be effected. . . . Every Catholic, taken in the concrete, has a twofold character; one derived from the Church, the other from society; and [therefore] changes as changes the society in which he lives." In the United States the democratic order had been established, and ought to be sustained if the Church was left free. In religion authority had a special place, "but in all else we must cherish the Spirit of freedom. We owe this even to our religion. . . ."[59]

In recognizing the process of change from feudalism to republicanism Brownson seemed to accept some kind of law of progress; however, he further suggested that what was good in the varied governmental forms which the process germinated had been produced by principle based upon an unchangeable natural law protected by the Church. Here he seemed to cling to permanence rather than to progress.

In two articles, one in April and one in July, Brownson further investigated the implications of the American Idea as he now conceived of it. In the first,[60] he argued with some force that the principle of religious liberty—as opposed to religious tolerance—had been brought to America and fostered, not by Lord Baltimore, but by the Puritans. Religious liberty, by which Brownson meant the supranational independence of religion from the state, was thus a part of the original American experience. This condition was continued by the practice and intention of the founding fathers when they wrote the Constitution. America, therefore, recognized the autonomy of religion. Sectarian Protestantism had become so devitalized that there was now a tendency to think in terms of religious "tolerance," in the sense of indifference to religion. The situation could lead only to the ascendancy of secularism, and to the denial of an essential part of the American Experiment. The hope for America, therefore, must be the Catholic Church, a fact which was, he thought, becoming clearer to discerning Protestants.[61]

The second article[62] was entitled "The Church and the Republic"; it contained the substance of two lectures given by Brownson at the Broadway Tabernacle in New York in February and April, 1856. Both lectures were inaccurately reported both by the *New York Times* and by the *Freeman's Journal,* and though the material was admittedly familiar to Brownson's readers, he inserted it into the *Review* because he felt that it was "adapted to the times, and meets, in a popular manner, the principal objections just now urged with the most vehemence against the Church."[63] The lectures undertook to prove that religion was necessary to the American Experiment; that there was no true religion without the Catholic Church; and that, far from being hostile to Catholicity, the American Republic could not exist without it.

None of the material was new, as Brownson forewarned. The accent upon the American Dream and Mission, however, is worth notice, particularly in the light of what was to be the leading article of the next (October) issue of the *Review*. Making a familiar distinction between democracy in Europe and in the United States, Brownson suggested that, "The first realization of the Christian Republic seems in Divine Providence to have been reserved for our New World. . . . The founders brought with them the element of liberty . . . principles of personal freedom . . . which had been introduced in European society, after the downfall of Pagan Rome, by Christianity and the Barbarian conquerors, and incorporated into English Common Law."[64] That liberty could never be maintained without discipline: "And how, without disinterestedness, without sacrifice are we to sustain our republic; and realize the great and glorious mission which it has pleased Almighty God to assign to the American people?"[65]

This comment was prelude to a full-scale discussion of the concept in the subsequent number of the *Review*. It is not without significance that this article, entitled "Mission of America," should be developed as a review of Bishop Martin John Spalding's *Miscellanea*.[66] Spalding's attitude delighted the editor, since both agreed that the Church was no threat to American liberty, and that, although the dominant sentiment of the United States "is non-Catholic, . . . the political and civil order is in accordance with Catholicity."[67]

Both the author and the reviewer warned against the excessive government which they had detected in a part of a feeble minority "of Catholic immigrants who merely give to the Know-Nothings a spurious cause." They should join with native American Catholics—who were as American as their Protestant counterparts—and make themselves part of "the great current of American nationality"; by so doing, they might reap benefits of a political and social order which, although it "gives and secures freedom to all to aspire," would never grant success to the torpid, the sluggard. "Catholics who are self-reliant and energetic, who enter into the spirit of a country, and conform to the inherent laws of American society may succeed. . . . But such as are frightened at that spirit, who throw up their hands in holy horror . . . denounce it, and stoutly resist it, will count for little in the commonwealth, and be generally regarded with suspicion or contempt."[68]

Self-reliance was not, as the Protestants argued, a virtue in the spiritual order, but it might very well be one in the temporal. God demanded that, with due propriety to a scale of values, men develop their natural faculties to the fullest in order to build the highest possible order of civilization. Grace did not destroy nature "nor change the national type of character." Rather, it elevated and purified nature and underscored the best in the national character, for "no national character stands more in need of Catholicity than the American . . . and never since America's founding . . . has the Church found a national character so well fitted to give to true civilization its highest and noblest expression."[69] America was the country toward which Catholics throughout the world should turn their hopes. For "America, we need not say, is the future of the world."[70]

For Brownson now, progress seemed again to be the law of society; modern civilization, especially European civilization, was "doomed," and would be supplanted, as it had itself replaced Graeco-Roman civilization. The seat of the new order could only be here in America. Although the Germanic tribes "prepared the way for modern civilization and the progress of society by the aid of the Christian Church," yet they retained what they found worthy in the outmoded system: Roman jurisprudence, its fiscal system, ideas, manners, and usages. Unfortunately, among the latter were kept some unhappy elements which had vitiated what was now the old system: ". . . Modern civilization, though a progress, a great progress on the ancient, is imperfect, and far below that order of civil society which accords with the Christian ideal. It is too imperfect, too pagan, and too little Christian, too incompatible with Christianized humanity, to be the last term of human progress."

The only hope was a "higher and more Christian order." Such an order was impossible in a Europe divided into the party of authority and the party of revolution, since "each alike is opposed to the progress of civilization."[71] Only in the United States was there available those elements and conditions "of this advanced civilization," of this new order of life. Only in this country was there present the "promise of the future"; only here are we "free to make the proper distinctions, to reject what is bad in medieval civilization," to balance liberty and order, "and to accept and harmonize with the Church the good these movements of the age indicate, but are incompetent to realize."[72]

Most of the old pagan elements in society which had corrupted European civilization were left behind by our fathers "by singular good Providence" when they came here. Brownson believed that the Roman jurisprudence they had brought had been modified and improved through the English common law and the influence of Christianity; their political system was that taught and developed by popes, councils, and doctors during the Middle Ages; their view of natural justice and equity, which had been recognized in Europe, but left without adequate guarantee, was brought to American shores. These men "had collected and embodied in themselves the fruits of the past labors of mankind, especially of the Christian Church in regard to politics and jurisprudence. . . . They were, in regard to civilization, the advanced guard of the human race in their times. . . ."[73]

None of this had been lost in colonial times; indeed, advances were made by the time of the Constitutional Convention. It must be remembered, wrote Brownson in his complete reacceptance of the terms of the American Dream, that the circumstances of the country and of the times were favorable to the founding of an advanced civilization. The land was new and unsettled, and the colonists, whose virtues of self-reliance, boldness, energy, and perseverance were providentially necessary, faced only the major encumbrance of the primitive forest, since, the mother country behind them, they could have a free and full development along fresh and original lines. They could "mould their institutions in accordance with reason and nature, the wisdom of experience, and the dictates of common sense. Hence they cast deep the foundations of an original and advanced civilization." Geographically fortunate, they could support themselves economically, and thus ultimately be free from foreign interference to the point of ultimate independence. "No nation will voluntarily go to war with us, and we have only to pursue a calm, dignified, and just policy towards other nations, to remain virtually at peace with the whole world."[74]

The population, too, was providentially fitted for this country's "Mission." The races which predominated in America—the Teutonic, Iberian, and Celtic—were the strongest races in Europe; America was relatively free from "the inferior races of Asia and Africa." Rapidly there was forming here a homogeneous people

with an original national character, superior, perhaps, to any which the world has hitherto seen. . . . Our national character has a noble foundation in freedom. . . . As a people we have very generally the conviction that Divine Providence has given us an important mission, and has chosen us to work out for the world a higher order of civilization than has hitherto obtained. We look upon ourselves as a providential people . . . with a great destiny . . . glorious to ourselves and beneficent to the world. . . . We believe ourselves the people of the future and that belief itself will do much to make us so.[75]

This American Mission, *this* sort of " 'Manifest Destiny' " of America, was recognized by other countries, some with hope, some with fear. But it was not the "manifest destiny" of cheap journalists, scribblers, or filibustering quacks. Perhaps Americans would expand over the whole American continent; that was a small affair, and no worthy mission in the grand sense.

The manifest destiny of this country is something far higher, nobler, and more spiritual,—the realization, we should say, of the Christian Ideals of Society for both the Old World and the New. Many things below this, and in themselves far enough from being in harmony with it, Divine Providence may permit, and compel to serve it, but these should never be the term of our ambition; they should never be encouraged by us,—

should be carefully eschewed, or at best tolerated only as unavoidable evils for the time being.

This manifest destiny of our country, showing that Providence has great designs in our regard, that he has given us the most glorious mission ever given to any people, should attach us to our country, kindle . . . a true and holy patriotism, and make us proud to be Americans.[76]

It was true that a discrepancy existed between this ideal and the real situation in current American life. Private and public life abounded in every manner of corruption and, as the *Review* had pointed out, these faults could very easily stultify promise and wise effort. Yet these vices were not inherent in Americans as a people, and were actually abuses of "sound principles and grand qualities." The people had lost their faith in Protestantism, and had been thrown back upon nature, with the aid of Christianity. The truth was that Protestantism was inherently opposed to the American order—for example, it insisted upon the idea of total depravity—and yet had not been able to "suppress our American civilization"; in fact, Protestantism had given way before it.[77]

Thus, many Protestants were looking for a "Church of the Future" to counteract the danger of the situation. Their churches would have to recognize "the natural law upon which our American order is founded"; further, they must refuse to recognize the Protestant doctrine of total depravity; they could not deny nature in favor of grace, nor reason in favor of faith; they must labor to "fulfill . . . purify, elevate, direct, and invigorate" nature. The true church was already here—the Catholic Church which "comes to give us precisely the help we need, and as our country is the future hope of the world, so is Catholicity the future hope of our country; and it is through Catholicity bringing the supernatural to the aid of the natural, that the present evils which afflict us are to be removed, and the country is to be enabled to perform its civilizing mission for the world."[78]

Brownson was careful to establish that there need be no "new development of Christian doctrine," nor any change in Church teaching.

We believe in progress *by* Christianity, not in it; by the Catholic Church, not in it; and the new order of civilization we speak of is not a new Christianity, *but a new progress in society,*[79] which places it as civilized society in more perfect harmony with Christianity, with Catholicity or the Church. . . . All that is needed . . . is to bring the sentiments, manners, and morals of the people into harmony with American institutions, or the American political and social order.[80]

Therefore, through Catholicity, there could be achieved "a new and higher civilization than the world has hitherto known"; in this achievement, Catholicity would "make ours the land of the future."[81]

But this grand design would not be achieved without free human agents; the efficacy of the Church's work in fulfilling her mission "depends on the fidelity or non-fidelity of Catholics themselves," because, granted the assumptions set forth above, only Catholics could duly grasp the proportion of the immediate task and the grandeur of the prospect. Consequently, "we Catholics must become a reading and a thinking people, developing in the highest degree our moral and intellectual faculties, taking broad and comprehensive views of men and things, and applying them with freedom and conscientiousness to all the great questions of the age or the country as they rise."[82]

What was needed, wrote the editor of the *Review*, were vital, dynamic men, not "safe" men; "we do not want to keep things quiet. . . . We want progress . . . to advance the cause of truth and civilization. As Catholics we must go forward, or cease to hold our own in the country."[83] Even with the best effort evil could not be entirely eradicated, since the effects of original sin would somehow always be present. But if those effects could be kept within "the bosom of the individual"—that is, could be prevented from breaking out into society and become part of its "institutions, public manners, or social usages"[84]—then much would be gained.

What was unnecessary was the "false liberalism" of Kossuth and Mazzini; no persuasive argument could be made for the violent revolutionary power to introduce this socially ordered condition where its pre-conditions did not exist;[85] they did obtain in germ in the United States and here was the theater of action. Yet, in conclusion, Brownson reaffirmed the *general* application of his ideas, and, in the process, restated his revived belief in the American Idea:

The field is as broad as your activity, the work as high as your ambition, as great as your thought. You may, if you will, add a nation, a nation destined to rule the future, to your Church, and to the world a new civilization. You may bring faith to the doubting, hope to the desponding, and peace to the troubled,—send freedom to the down-trodden millions of the Old World, redeem long-oppressed continents, and fill with joy the broken-hearted friends of the human race. Let each one work in his own sphere, according to his ability and opportunity, but always with a view to the greater glory of God, and with a firm reliance on Him for support and ultimate success.[86]

Thus, by 1856, the American Idea had returned with honor to the pages of Brownson's *Review*. However similar it may seem superficially to what he had preached prior to 1840, it was now considerably altered at the base. Optimism, for example, was again present, but an optimism which recognized the perdurability of the effects of original sin, and which argued its case not in denial of these, but in defiance of them. Progress became again the watchword, but whatever might have been the lingering influences of the old days, progress now was by God's design *through* and *by* the Catholic Church. The link between democratic (i.e., republican) ideals and Christian teaching was re-echoed, but it was not Protestant Christianity, or a Christian "Church of the Future," but the necessary ligature provided by the Catholic Church. And, finally, the "perfectibility of man" had become the attempt to build a Christian society increasingly adapted to the demands of natural law. The American Dream was a dream of a Christian (i.e, Catholic) social order: the American Mission became the spread of Catholicism throughout the world.

It seems, finally, that in his attempt to bring together the two worlds of American life and the life of the Church, Brownson had returned to the prevailing concept of America as the God-anointed country. Once, he felt, his country really knew the Church as she was, then those elements of natural life which America possessed, and which she had gained from a tradition both Catholic and European, would join with the same characteristics still part of Catholicity, fuse, and proceed to expand society to its greatest limits. Such now was his faith, and, beyond, his hope.

Whatever effect all this may have had upon America, the editor of *Brownson's Quarterly Review* was no voice in a void. In the opening article of the *Review* for 1857, Brownson himself quoted an anonymous antagonist in the highly respected *Universalist Quarterly Review*: " 'Few American readers need to be told who or what is O. A. Brownson. Perhaps no man in this country has, by the simple effort of the pen, made himself more conspicuous'." The comment went on to cite Brownson's many readers (" 'intelligent men of all sects and parties' ") and the power of his expression

(" 'Extraordinary ingenuity of his logic, the vigor of his thought, the clearness and directness of his style' ").[87] Brownson, for his own part, then proceeded to defend the position he had taken on the need for the Church to the sustenance of the republic. That need, essentially, was "to restrain authority from becoming social despotism, and individual freedom from becoming anarchy." The anonymous opponent of the *Universalist Review* conceded this point; the question then was, would that Church be representative of religion as an organization, or as a mere organism? In short, was religion to be a "power" or an "ideal"?

By the latter was meant "a simple opinion"; by the former, "a *power* resting on a basis independent of the nation and the individual . . . strong enough to restrain either from encroaching on the rights of the other."[88] If one assumed religion as an *idea,* then it was involved with private conviction and could not be independent; it had to become a predicate of either the state or the individual, and thus render itself powerless to arbitrate conflicting claims. Some religious organization therefore was necessary, one which was "above the natural law [in order] to secure the ends of the natural law, and as the Catholic Church is the only organization of the sort . . . since the abolition of Judaism, we may conclude . . . that she is necessary to the preservation of the republic. . . ."[89] Since Protestantism was dying, the question divided between supernatural religion (as represented by the Catholic Church) and "the simple law or religion of nature."

In the same number of his *Review* Brownson defended his own hopeful view of "the predispositions of his country men" against Bishop John Hughes of New York;[90] and in a brief review, he praised the Viscount Chateaubriand's *The Genius of Christianity,* newly reprinted in Baltimore in 1856.[91] This work, according to the editor, "has certainly done good, and we owe, personally, a debt of gratitude to the author; for this very work many years ago [i.e., in the early 1830s], falling into our hands while we were an avowed unbeliever, had the effect to remove the hostility we felt to the Christian religion, and to make us able to study its evidences without prejudice."[92]

In April Brownson resumed his debate with representative Protestant organs, this time with a critic in the *Methodist Quarterly Review.*[93] He asserted that the "pretence" of the Reformers was not "progress," nor was it the discovery or development of "new ideas in faith"; what they sought was a return to what they considered the pristine purity of primitive Christianity. Brownson continued:

After all, this talk about the emancipation of the mind, and the progress of philosophy, science,[94] government, etc. is mere rhetoric founded on the cant of the day. It is, moreover, with Protestants, of recent origin. Nothing was heard of it in my boyhood, and I believe no small share of the shame or the credit of introducing it to my countrymen belongs to my own labors in my Protestant nonage. I took this ground, not because I believed it the ground actually taken by the Reformers, but because I saw no other ground on which their movement could be defended, and because I wished to establish a principle on which I could defend my own departures from so-called orthodox Protestantism. Yet the theory has no foundation in the facts of the case. What is new is not always true, and changes are not always improvements.[95]

The Reformation, therefore, had actually retarded progress.[96]

One of those surprises so common to Brownson's method came in October, 1857. The editor reviewed Isaac Hecker's *Aspirations of Nature*,[97] and in the course of the essay, seemed to deny the propositions which he himself had set forth in the "Mission of America" essay a scant year before. Since the background of this review together with a discussion of the contents of both Hecker's book and Brownson's essay are admirably set forth by Hecker's able biographer,[98] there seems little need for any extended recapitulation here. Briefly, then, Brownson maintained that Hecker had two main purposes in writing the book: to prove 1. that religion was the goal of the natural aspiration of all men; 2. that the Catholic Church alone could satisfy those aspirations. Hecker asserted in the course of his argument that the majority of Americans have cast off Protestantism, and as "earnest seekers" relied now upon simple nature; Brownson disagreed, but insisted that the irreligious majority (for he agreed thus far) was rather indifferent than earnest, and was insanely devoted to mundane pursuits.[99] Once awakened from their torpor, Brownson went on, they tended to join Protestant sects; Andrew Jackson and Henry Clay were cited as examples. In short, said the *Review*, "the American mind properly so-called, whatever we may say of it or hope from it, is as yet thoroughly Protestant."[100] Hecker seemed to address Americans as though they were all once Transcendentalists, but the latter were practically extinct now;[101] Hecker further underrated the effects of original sin, and overrated what could be done solely by reason and nature.[102]

Moreover, Catholicity could not be "Americanized," that is to say, the dogmas of faith could not be accommodated to national will or taste. Hecker might not have intended such an implication, but, wrote Brownson, the implication was there (as, he admitted, it might be in his own past writing).[103] Proper respect must be accorded the Catholic prelacy by the laity, and, above all here, there had to be obedience to constituted authority. "What we call our Americanism does very well in the political order,—at least so our countrymen hold,—but it can not be transferred to the Church without heresy and schism."[104] There *is* a "work of magnitude" and "a glorious field of activity" in the conversion of Protestants in America, but the conversion of bad Catholics was the major problem. The solution of this difficulty would itself aid as a solvent of the other. For:

There is scarcely a trait in the American character as practically developed that is not more or less hostile to Catholicity. Our people are imbued with a spirit of independence, an aversion to authority,[105] a pride, an overweening conceit, as well as with a prejudice, that makes them revolt at the bare mention of the Church. . . . The American people, like every other people, have, no doubt, their peculiarities, their idiosyncrasies, but their conversion will never be effected by seeking in these [Hecker's views] our *point d'appui*.[106]

Brownson closed by re-emphasizing the scope of the monumental task, warning of the dangers involved, exculpating Hecker from any fault, and praising his friend's capacity for hope. Brownson's own hope he characterized as "spasmodic, . . . but it is always better to take counsel of our hopes than of our fears . . . which . . . may spring from ill-health, under the depression of which we are forced to write."[107]

While it is true that this review might well have been more severe without the prior intervention of Hecker's friend George M. Deshon,[108] there is also considerable evidence that the essay is at least partially a product of mood as well as it is reflective of the darker side of Brownson's conviction. As has been shown, in his letter to Hecker of September 29, 1857, Brownson praised the American spirit of submission to legitimate authority, and spoke of his difference with Hecker not in terms of ultimate success, but as a difference of hope in immediate success. Again, he wrote in the same place that he was more discouraged "than ever before in my life," not so much about the issues involved in the controversy, as about personal business matters. What weight should be given these admissions is, of course, debatable, but they cannot be completely put aside. Finally, there is evidence that Brownson eventually regretted this article, although one must admit that this feeling might have been due essentially to the hurt it may have done to Hecker's cause in Rome.[109] In the two years which follow there is evidence that Brownson still was confused occasionally by the implications of the American Idea, and it might be well to include here, although it is slightly out of chronology, a statement of his own which points up the difficulty of a writer placed in the position in which he constantly found himself:

Every periodical must, if it intends to have a living interest, treat the questions of the day as they rise, and as these questions are perpetually changing their aspects, the periodical must continually change the aspects under which it treats them. The Editor has before his mind at each successive moment all he has previously said; and writes with the presumption that it is also before the mind of his readers.[110]

Brownson's argument with the *Universalist Quarterly Review* was renewed in January of 1858. His opponent was still unconvinced that Christianity could not be a power unless it was objectified in a church, and in a system of doctrine. Brownson now argued that his antagonist's position would logically lead to a nation of Deists, which, he wrote, "has never existed. Men will have more or less than Deism, and when they cannot have Catholicity they will have daemonism."[111] Still preoccupied with the breakdown of true religious spirit in America, he warned in a later number of the *Review* of the dangers of "this age of Mormonism and lightning telegraphs," and encouraged able young American Catholics:

We have talent and genius enough in our ranks, if excited to activity, to revolutionize the whole literary world. There are thousands of richly-endowed minds and noble hearts among us, that are preying upon themselves, and consuming their own energy in doing nothing, because they find no outlet, no work. We live in a fast age, and we must keep up with it, nay, we must run ahead of it, not stand aghast at it, or remaining fixed, cry out at the top of our lungs to it, "Stop, stop, good Age, run not so swiftly by us." It is for the Catholic genius to throw itself into the current, and direct its course.[112]

Yet activity was not to be such that the earlier concept of the American Mission could not be reactivated. In a return to the principles of Count Joseph de Maistre, Brownson reiterated an old doctrine:

. . . we are among those who believe constitutions, if real, are generated, not made. Providence gives to each people that is a people, the constitution the best adapted to its genius and wants, and true political wisdom consists in adhering to it, and governing in accordance with it. Republicanism is the best form of government for us, and we ought therefore to accept it, and shape our institutions, as far as subjected to human prudence and freedom, so as to preserve and develop it; but the very reasons which induce us to maintain it for ourselves, should forbid us to attempt to force it upon others, or to persuade other nations to adopt it. . . .[113]

As the American Experiment neared the great crisis of the Civil War, Orestes Brownson opened his *Review* in 1859 with a very able summary of his own criticisms of Cousin, Leroux, and Gioberti as philosophers.[114] In general the article continued to reject what its author considered modern subjectivism, whether it be in philosophy wherein it tends to solipsism, or in religion wherein the tendency was to pantheism or atheism. Deism, which "disjoins Providence from Creation," was also rejected and its influence deplored.

In April, Brownson again insisted that he did "not distrust the people or seek to limit their power."[115] It was the old distinction: the people "when in convention assembled" were sovereign in a proximate way; the people considered simply as population—"the essence of democracy"—were not sovereign at all. The editor was still "attached to our American institutions as they were left us by our fathers" but opposed the "substitution of Jacobinical democracy for true American republicanism."[116] These statements were followed by a full-scale discussion of Progress as the implications of that subject appeared to the editor in 1859. Entitled "Père Félix on Progress,"[117] the article was a kind of review of Brownson's own thinking, a rejection (through his criticism of Félix) of some of his own past attitudes, and a call to Catholics to make sharp distinctions in controversy over the places of the supernatural and the natural in any discussion of "the spirit of the age."

The modern age, contended Brownson, had, in the natural order, all the advantages of the past; in the supernatural order, the same held true. Thus modern men should at least equal the achievements of past ages, "if not even surpass them." If his contemporaries fell below the achievements of the past, they did so because they allowed the reputations and the weight of past authority to crush initiative and confidence. The Idea of Progress itself could be understood (and debated) not so much on logical grounds but upon the ground of "the sentiments and affections with which it is associated in the minds of its adherents."[118] Thus Félix, for example, had missed the truth beyond the fact which the doctrine of progress actually contained.

Admitting the importance of that doctrine to his own development,[119] he labeled Progress the "great word" of the nineteenth century, as "Liberty" had been for the eighteenth, and "Reform" for the sixteenth. Although all these catchwords had been abused in their time, there was a good in all of them which must be recognized. Félix recognized this truth and attempted "to distinguish between the true doctrine of progress by Christianity, and the false doctrine of progress by the inherent law of growth or natural development asserted by the age outside of the Church."[120] Now, to "restrict all progress to this interior Christian perfection is to sport with the age, is to play tricks on words, and to give the age a series of homilies on the Four Cardinal Virtues, and the Seven Deadly Sins, when and where it looked for a Christian, philosophical, and practical discussion of the popular doctrine of progress."[121] There had been progress in modern society—"outside of the interior of the individual or the spiritual life"—in the "science of politics, in the physical sciences,[122] in industry, and commerce," in law, social advancement, the benevolence of humanity and in "exploring, reducing, and utilizing the forces of nature." There had been progress in effecting a recognition of the rights of man. In brief, "these are facts which nobody can deny."[123]

Further, the idea of progress antedated the pantheism or socialism of some of its followers who had risen to leadership when Christianity had seemed to refuse scope to the idea of progress; therefore, one could not refute such people merely by denying "their pantheism, naturalism, or theologianism. . . . The party of Progress today want freedom to labor for progress, and to effect it as a practical fact, but the mass of them never heard of Hegel, Leroux, Enfantin, or the pantheistic nonsense Père Félix . . . refutes. . . ."[124]

The current party of Progress "includes the greater part of the civilized world. Since we face a practical not an abstract question we must show that the Church favors progress [as she does] in both the supernatural and the natural orders"; in the latter, of course, she merely reserved the right to dissent when there was any infringement of "revealed truth and the moral law."[125] For the Church aided natural society by "creating and sustaining the virtues which secure heaven, and in promoting supernatural welfare, she indirectly promotes man's natural interest." Progress in a supernatural virtue was indeed indispensable but there need also be progress in natural society. Catholics could and must labor for such progress, "not precisely as members of a supernatural society, but . . . as members of natural society"; they must work for progress

in science, art, literature, government legislation, political and civil liberty, agriculture, industry, and commerce, so as to make society as perfect as, with the imperfection of humanity, it may be. The age attaches, no doubt, too much importance to what is called the progress of society . . . of civilization. . . . We must take our age as we find it, and accept it as far as we lawfully can, respect even its prejudices, where they are not sinful, in the hope of winning its regard for that higher progress proposed by the Church and possible only in her communion.[126]

In July, Brownson came again to the case of de Lamennais, this time in response to a communication from a "highly esteemed correspondent" who felt that Brownson, like de Lamennais, was not keeping a strict harmony with the terms of the encyclical *Mirari* of Pope Gregory XVI, issued on August 15, 1832.[127] In the course of his own defense, the editor also defended de Lamennais up to a point. The opponents of the Frenchman, Brownson explained, never really understood him, and, while de Lamennais' philosophical system was unsound, his doctrine that "Christianity is the only doctrine there is, or ever has been, and that it is the universal belief of the race," was a kind of "internal tradition." All error "has, in a certain sense, its origin in the truth which it misconceives, misinterprets, or misapplies."[128]

Brownson maintained that de Lamennais was gravely wrong in identifying Christianity with "the general or universal reason," for thus the common consent of mankind became authority for doctrine and faith. Such a judgment could not, in the final analysis, be substituted "for the positive teaching authority of the Church."[129] Nettled and harassed as he had been on every side, de Lamennais came to believe "that there is no infallible guide for mortals, and no church but the people"—which, Brownson contended, was a "conclusion of despair, not of reason." His error could not be condoned; indeed, de Lamennais would never have made it had he been properly understood originally. What he had really wanted was a regeneration of true Catholicity in the nominally Catholic populations. And that end, wrote Orestes Brownson, was precisely one which he, in his own writing, had demanded in America. If it could be achieved in the New World, American society would then be more in accordance with Catholic principles than any society had ever been. Europe could give America nothing except the faith. It could teach Americans little about political and social organization, for people in the New World were some centuries ahead of Europeans in those matters. Further, Brownson saw no need of what he regarded as the spurious "Catholic culture" of Europe. America had no place for either the Caesarism on the right or the Ultraliberalism of the left.[130] Both had developed out of false notions of liberty; either would be fatal to the American Experiment. What was mandatory was a balance, a proper equipoise between extremes: "we pray our readers not to forget when reading what we say of liberty, what we have said of authority, and when reading what we have said of authority not to forget what we have said of liberty, for the one is qualified by the other."[131]

During the years 1855–1859, then, we have noted that the idea of Progress, one of the original pillars of the American Idea, was still being critically examined by Brownson. At the beginning of the period examined in this chapter, he denied the possibility of progress in philosophical knowledge, since he argued that the unaided reason could not add to the primitive tradition which God had originally given to man. Protestantism, which had secularized and materialized Christianity, could hardly represent progress; Brownson argued that, as a result of the Reformation, "wealth is made a god, industry is a religion . . . , poverty is a crime." This statement of ideas which would be central to the work of later scholars such as Max Weber and R. H. Tawney was, of course, nothing new to Brownson; as we have seen, he had examined them several times before.

If his ideas on progress seemed to have changed little in early 1855, his essay "Liberalism and Socialism," which he published in April of the same year, reflected another of those curious turns of emphasis which seemed almost a part of Brownsonian method. In his anxiety now to combat the "autocracy" which he thought ascendant in Europe, he praised the good in socialism which, though it ended logically in gentilism, really had its origin in the Christian community. Revolutions were still condemned, yet conservatives were urged by the *Review* to help remove the conditions which bred revolution before they launched attacks upon revolutionaries. Brownson now found some class affinity between the Jacobinical doctrine of "fraternity," the Progressist's idea of "philanthropy," and the Christian notion of charity. Reiterating his own adaptation of Leroux's ideas of "Communion" and the solidarity of the race, Brownson now defended the possibility of social amelioration which would come, not through the agency of the state, but through Catholicity.

The centrality of Catholicity was emphasized again in Brownson's review of Hecker's *Questions of the Soul*. The American Idea—that old faith—was again revived, although the spread of Christian society rather than democracy was now to be the American Mission. Contemporary statements of the American Mission—e.g., "manifest destiny"—were to Brownson mere chronicles of vapid irrelevance. The temporary lapse of his optimism which had occurred in October, 1857, may have been, as Brownson explained it, caused essentially by his disagreement with Hecker about timing. Both Hecker and Brownson seem agreed on the end to be pursued.

In 1859, Brownson was preaching "progress" again—but a limited progress, and one which was certainly not reflective of the hope he had held in 1838. By the time the *Review* closed for the year 1859, Brownson was again quoting de Lamennais and arguing for his own transmuted American Idea: America needed a regeneration of true Catholicity to achieve an American society which would be in accord with true Catholic principles. If such a regeneration was forthcoming, the American Idea was possible, even probable; without it, the American Idea was stillborn.

In this essay Brownson had emphasized the distinction to be made between the Church and European society, and his hope for the Church in the new soil of the new continent, free from European influences. The Church could blossom in America and achieve her greatest triumph: Americans were not beholden to a European past; their institutions were naturally geared to her supernatural principles: the opportunity for the Church was extraordinary. The Mission of America—now its Catholic role in reforming civilization and society throughout the world—was the final affirmation of Orestes Brownson in 1859, the year which welcomed Darwin's *On the Origin of Species*, and which was itself the immediate prelude in time to the raw crisis of the American Experiment. The Civil War would test thoroughly the assumptions of the American Idea, and the post-war world would become in many ways a laboratory for post-Darwinian study. The facts of the Gilded Age would present serious obstacles to those who had believed, perhaps naïvely, that the new Eden, like the old, was to be a paradise and not a jungle.

NOTES

1. Heinrich Ritter, *The History of Ancient Philosophy* (Oxford, 1838).
2. *BrQR*, XII, 1 (1855), 22–24.
3. The point here is that Fitzpatrick's putative influence in Boston, if it had ever indeed extended to Brownson's view of the Idea of Progress (among other things), had, perhaps, the resonance of tin.
4. *Ibid.*, pp. 135–144. The volume referred to is *History of the United States from the Discovery of the American Continent* (Boston, 1854).
5. For a commentary upon this address and its importance in America to the history of the Idea of Progress see Ekirch, *Progress*, pp. 262–263. For an interesting contemporary comment on both Bancroft's lecture and Brownson's review of it, see the letter, Hecker to Brownson, December 21, 1854, Hecker Papers, Archives of the Paulist Fathers, New York (cited hereafter as APF).
6. *BrQR*, XII, 1 (1855), 136.
7. *Ibid.*, p. 137. Brownson had only mixed praise for and sharp criticism of John Gilmary Shea and Thomas D'Arcy McGee as historians (see *ibid.*, pp. 137–142).
8. Quoted from Clark's book *Romanism in America* (Boston, 1855). The material here is cited by Brownson, *BrQR*, XII, 2 (1855), 153.
9. *Ibid.*, pp. 156–157.
10. *Ibid.*, p. 182.
11. The books reviewed are Juan Donoso Cortés, *Ensayo sobre el Catholicismo, el Liberalismo, y el Socialismo considerados en sus principios fundamentales* (Madrid, 1851); Pierre Leroux, *De l'humanité de son principe, et de son avenir, où se trouve exposée la vraie définition de la religion, et où l'on explique le sens, la suite, el l'enchaînement du Mosaisme et du Christianisme* (Paris, 1840). See *BrQR*, XII, 2 (1855), 183–209.
12. *BrQR*, I, 1 (1844), 5–6.
13. All the citations in this paragraph after note 12 are from *BrQR*, XII, 2 (1855), 190. Compare these comments with his defense of Montalembert (*BrQR*, XII, 3 [1855], 316–317) and his distinction between the need of defending either liberty or order when either is attacked (*ibid.*, pp. 317–322).
14. See Chapter 5.

15. *BrQR*, XII, 2 (1855), 183. Brownson admitted that his praise for Leroux might be excessive because of his emotional debt to the Frenchman who "revolutionized our own mind both in regard to Philosophy and religion, and by the grace of God became the occasion of our conversion to Catholicity" (*ibid.*, p. 184).

16. Brownson's respect for Donoso Cortés did not mask his lack of enthusiasm for monarchy (*ibid.*, p. 186). He summarized Donoso Cortés' position: all things have their ideas or archetypes in divine essence; human society, therefore, originated in divine society, in the Trinity; the characteristic of this divine society was "unity, diversity, and diversity in unity," and, since this was the original type of all society, all human society must reflect it, as all creation reflected the Creator (*ibid.*, pp. 187–188).

17. *Ibid.*, p. 186.

18. *Ibid.*, p. 189.

19. *Ibid.*, p. 191.

20. The reader will recall that it was partially because of their "philanthropy" that Brownson had rejected the Transcendentalists; its presence infected the poetry of both Emerson and Lowell.

21. *Ibid.*, p. 192. Note how the argument of human society reflecting divine society had influenced Brownson here. The influence seems, of course, to be that of Donoso Cortés. It is almost inconceivable that Brownson would make such an admission, not so much, indeed, since 1844, but since 1840.

22. *Ibid.*, p. 193. Even such limited praise for the French Revolution must have made Brownson's readers glance up quickly to insure visual reality. Brownson went on to say that he had little sympathy "with the ordinary shallow and selfish declamations of conservatives against revolutionary movements" (*ibid.*, p. 193).

23. These were doctrines which had caused his editorial fulmination a short year before. Here he cited Robert Burns' "A man's a man for a' that" (*ibid.*, p. 195). Originally, the phrase was "Man measures man the world over" (see Chapter 2 at n. 53 [p. 41]).

24. See the argument, *ibid.*, pp. 196–199.

25. *Ibid.*, p. 199.

26. The reference was to Isaac Hecker, whose book *Questions of the Soul* Brownson would review in a subsequent article in this number.

27. *Ibid.*, p. 204. Malone has found this whole argument (a kind of secular statement of the "Communion of Saints") somewhat unsatisfactory, especially from the viewpoint of Brownson's apologetical method (see Malone, *The True Church*, pp. 67–69).

28. *Ibid.*, pp. 202–204.

29. *Ibid.*, p. 206. This opinion seems a direct reversal of his vehement statements to the contrary in prior years. One must note, however, the *caveat* cited, and the ones which follow. In any case, the American Mission is again possible.

30. *Ibid.*, p. 207.

31. *Ibid.*, p. 208.

32. *BrQR*, xii, 2 (1855), 209–227. See also *ibid.*, xiii, 1 (1856), pp. 81–102. See I. T. Hecker, *Questions of the Soul* (New York, 1855).
33. *BrQR*, xii, 2 (1855), 211. As far as I can ascertain, this is the only reference ever made to such a manuscript. Yet the point is that Brownson and Hecker may very well have been close together on the ideas which follow—at least in 1855. On this point see Holden, *Yankee Paul*, pp. 192–194; 202–203.
34. Brownson quoted from his own *BQR* articles on this point. See *ibid.*, p. 211.
35. This was another adumbration of Emerson's "party of hope" and "party of memory," and of Brownson's own earlier phrases, the "movement party" and the "stationary party."
36. *Ibid.*, pp. 211–212.
37. *Ibid.*, p. 212.
38. *Ibid.*, p. 213.
39. *Ibid.*, p. 214.
40. Phrases such as this—especially the provocative word "kindling"—were staples in Brownson's writing up to 1840; they had disappeared thereafter.
41. *Ibid.*, p. 227. See *BrQR*, xii, 3 (1855), 409.
42. The word "democracy" again seemed to mean to Brownson what he currently called "revolutionism." That is, he equated it with what he considered its present radical or "Jacobin" manifestation in Europe. But the old democratic ideal was not rejected, and it is in that sense that the word is used here. The distinction, in reiteration, is very important. See *BrQR*, xii, 3 (1855), 316–322.
43. *BrQR*, xii, 4 (1855), 489.
44. *Ibid.*, p. 501. Note the prediction of an impending "catastrophe" resulting from this condition (*ibid.*, p. 502).
45. *Ibid.*, pp. 519–520.
46. *BrQR*, xiii, 1 (1856), 1.
47. It may not be out of place to remind the reader of the difficulties of Henry Adams with this problem. See Henry Adams, *The Education of Henry Adams* (New York, 1931), pp. 379–391.
48. *BrQR*, xiii, 1 (1856), 1.
49. *Ibid.*, p. 17.
50. *Ibid.*, pp. 17–18. It should be noted that with all of Brownson's change of emphasis—his "liberal" rather than "conservative" views in 1856—he still could refer to John C. Calhoun as "one of our greatest and most enlightened statesmen" (*ibid.*, p. 119).
51. That is, "to take broad and comprehensive views of the human and social elements which have been at work . . . so that we may see events in their various relations, and arrange them according to some really scientific principle." Catholics having the key to the "inner sense of historical facts" could do this; others could not (*ibid.*, p. 133). This represented, apparently, a shift in thinking since he had ridiculed Bancroft's *History* in 1853. Then no such "rationalist" history had been possible; now it was—but Catholics

alone could do it. For "it is mainly through history that we can reach the cultivated class of our time" (*idem*).

52. *Ibid.*, p. 127.

53. *Idem.* Brownson does not further identify M. Foisset. It seems never to have been remarked before, but it is interesting that Ozanam may have had some influence upon Brownson, especially in the latter's present conviction that America provided a superior opportunity for the full play of Catholic principles. See Brownson's review of Lacordaire's edition of *Oeuvres complètes de A. F. Ozanam* in *BrQR*, XIII, 4 (1856), 462–485. Also see *BrQR*, XII, 3 (1855), 313.

54. This work was published in Paris in 1839. *BrQR*, XIII, 2 (1856), 137–173.

55. *Ibid.*, p. 159; italics mine.

56. The principle of the inviolability of property rights was cited as one example. And this principle was "recognized everywhere by our American jurisprudence. Here was a principle which the Church was the first to introduce into society, and it is the basis of all civil liberty" (*ibid.*, p. 168).

57. *Ibid.*, p. 169.

58. *Ibid.*, p. 171.

59. *Ibid.*, pp. 172–173. Cf. the views expressed in this article with those in *BrQR*, XIII, 3 (1856), 400–402.

60. *BrQR*, XIII, 2 (1856), 252–267.

61. *Ibid.*, p. 266.

62. *BrQR*, XIII, 3 (1856), 273–307.

63. Brownson explains the situation regarding the inaccuracies. See *ibid.*, note, pp. 273–274.

64. *Ibid.*, pp. 280–281. There is again in this essay that emphatic and staple distinction between liberty and authority and their necessary balance which is so easily lost when procrustean attempts are made to categorize his thought as "liberal" or "conservative" (*ibid.*, pp. 281–292).

65. *Ibid.*, p. 291.

66. M. J. Spalding, *Miscellanea: Comprising Reviews Lectures and Essays on Historical, Theological, and Miscellaneous Subjects* (Louisville, 1855). See *BrQR*, XIII, 4 (1856), 409–444. The word "review" was used in the text here in the sense in which Brownson always used it in his journals—i.e., as a departure-point for his own comments. It should also be noted here that Brownson called Isaac Hecker the "godfather" of this article, and indicated that the latter "inspired" it (Brownson to Hecker, September 29, 1857, Hecker Papers, APF). Nevertheless, a reader must note, *mutatis mutandis*, the closeness of its arguments to the American Idea of Brownson's youth.

67. *Ibid.*, p. 412.

68. *Ibid.*, p. 415. On the following page Brownson exhorted Catholics to match the efforts of their Protestant countrymen in "labor, trade,

law, medicine and every honest calling." *Laborare est orare*, he said in effect, and, as man had dominion by God's law over lower creation, Catholics were free to engage "in the chase after this dominion" without detriment to either faith or piety. Voluntary poverty may be meritorious; poverty resulting from quietism, indolence, improvidence, or intemperance is not. Whether he was thinking of the Irish he did not say.

69. *Ibid.*, p. 417.

70. *Ibid.*, p. 419. Here the secular American Dream appears to have been baptized. And the Arcadian picture is not to be spoiled by presence of groups such as the Know-Nothings: the American people "in their national capacity" had never rejected Catholicity (*ibid.*, p. 418).

71. *Ibid.*, p. 420. The Church, indeed, was still in old Europe, but the Church addressed itself to conscience and free will; it could not save men or "even civilize them against their will" (*ibid.*, p. 421). Brownson noted, too, that condemnation of radicals, socialists, and revolutionaries was an easy matter; what should be done was to examine those true and just things which they shared with humanity.

72. *Ibid.*, p. 422.

73. *Ibid.*, p. 423.

74. *Ibid.*, p. 424.

75. *Ibid.*, p. 425. Brownson carefully emphasized that native belief in the glorious American Mission was without illegitimate or ignoble ambition or design.

76. *Ibid.*, p. 426. Catholics especially should be "genuine American patriots" and aid in the spread of "that free, pure, lofty, and virile civilization which the Church loves" but could never introduce, opposed as it had been historically by the superstitions of ancient Rome and by the barbarian invaders of the empire.

77. Brownson's reasons for what may seem an exceedingly bold statement are developed on pages 426–430. They should be read in their entirety. This brief statement may be partially indicative: American Protestants had founded the American order not upon Protestantism "but on the natural law, natural justice and equity as explained by the Church, long prior to the Protestant movement of Luther and his associates, and they our ancestors only followed out those great principles of natural right, justice, and equality, which Catholic councils, doctors, and jurisconsults during fifteen hundred years had labored to render popular" (*ibid.*, p. 428). Thus our ancestors were "bravely inconsequent and 'builded better than they knew' " (*idem*). The Protestant doctrine of acts done in a state of nature as sin; the denial of nature to make way for grace, and of reason to make way for faith; the Protestant insistence upon religion as a subjective fact and its consequent insistence upon private judgment or private illumination; the Protestant tendency to sectarianism and the implications of that tendency—all these had led the people logically, ulti-

mately, and "practically to place their politics above their religion," and to trust to natural instincts to the degree that they rejected Protestantism. This situation endangered the American Experiment, and led the discerning Protestant to look for a "Church of the Future." The employment of Emersonian rhetoric is, one may judge, a minor, if unintended, irony.

78. *Ibid.*, pp. 430–431.
79. Italics added.
80. *Ibid.*, p. 431.
81. *Ibid.*, pp. 432–433.
82. *Ibid.*, p. 436.
83. *Ibid.*, p. 438.
84. Brownson did not explain how this was to be done. Obviously the oversight (or impossibility) was not the weakest of objections which could have been raised against him.
85. *Ibid.*, p. 441. But Brownson still insisted that the social order was not for America alone, but for the world. How it would be introduced elsewhere he did not make clear; the implication was that the world would (providentially) follow American example willingly. "The American Mission is not restricted in its intent . . . or results to a narrow and exclusive nationality. The legitimacy of American nationality is in the fact that it is not exclusive, that it is founded on the principles of natural justice and equity, and is as broad as the human race. . . . Is not the American mission in the interests of all Catholics and of all men?" (*ibid.*, p. 442). This argument had domestic point also: it was designed to bring all Americans together, and hasten, as it were, the action of the "melting pot" (see *ibid.*, pp. 442–444).
86. *Ibid.*, p. 444.
87. Cited in *BrQR*, xiv, 1 (1857), 2.
88. *Ibid.*, p. 9. Cf. *BrQR*, xiv, 2 (1857), 192–224.
89. *BrQR*, xiv, 1 (1857), 25. Brownson pointed out that not all Americans need be Catholic, though he would hope for that; all that was necessary was that the Church *be* here the "predominating influence on the ruling mind and heart of the country" (*ibid.*, p. 28). Cf. *BrQR*, xiv, 3 (1857), 327–348.
90. *BrQR*, xiv, 1 (1857), 114–141. Hughes thought Brownson too sanguine upon the subject of the readiness of Americans for conversion. The prelate also believed that the real influence of Catholicism upon American life would probably be delayed until the majority of American Catholics were native-born.
91. *Ibid.*, p. 144. Chateaubriand's volume was first published in Paris in 1802 as *Le génie du Christianisme*. The edition to which Brownson here referred was the translation and annotation of Charles I. White, entitled *The Genius of Christianity, or the Spirit and Beauty of the Christian Religion*.
92. *BrQR*, xiv, 1 (1857), 144. The fact that Chateaubriand and Ozanam were at least quondam intellectual acquaintances may be of small

moment; the fact that each in his way had some influence on Brownson's thought may not.

93. Brownson cited the article "Spiritual Despotism" in *Methodist Quarterly Review* (New York) for January 1857.

94. Brownson often meant "philosophy" when he used the word "science." However, in context here, he apparently meant physical science.

95. *BrQR*, XIV, 2 (1857), 199.

96. See Brownson's argument on this point, which—perhaps surprisingly—has elements of his old cyclic view of history. Ozanam's apparent influence may be seen in the editor's historical arguments assuming that "the starting-point of modern Europe is, the date of the destruction of the Roman power by the Germanic conquerors, say at the beginning of the sixth century" (*ibid.*, pp. 200–201).

97. Isaac T. Hecker, *Aspirations of Nature* (New York, 1857). The idea may not be new, or original, but the development Brownson gave it should be studied (*ibid.*, pp. 200–209).

98. Holden, *Yankee Paul*, pp. 320–327.

99. *BrQR*, XIV, 4 (1857), 467.

100. *Idem.*

101. According to the editor, Transcendentalism had found "little response from the national heart, and was . . . an exotic transplanted to our American garden from Germany" (*ibid.*, p. 468).

102. "If men by reason and nature alone erect the noble institutions of human society, what becomes of all our talk about the services rendered by Catholicity to modern civilization?" (*ibid.*, p. 477).

103. *Ibid.*, p. 492.

104. *Ibid.*, p. 494; see also p. 497.

105. This opinion seems contradicted in the sentiments expressed by Brownson in his letter to Hecker, September 29, 1857. See also the letter Brownson sent to Hecker upon the latter's departure for Rome, and dated August 5, 1857. See Holden, *Yankee Paul*, pp. 324–325. The letters are in the Hecker Papers, APF.

106. *BrQR*, XIV, 4 (1857), 496–497.

107. *Ibid.*, p. 503.

108. Holden, *Yankee Paul*, pp. 321–322. For a brief biographical sketch of Deshon, see *ibid.*, p. 181.

109. *Ibid.*, p. 326.

110. *BrQR*, XVI, 3 (1859), 395.

111. *BrQR*, XV, 1 (1858), 126. The word-play covered a most serious concern.

112. *BrQR*, XV, 4 (1858), 513. See also Brownson's plea for a forthright literary style, *BrQR*, XV, 4 (1858), 545.

113. *Ibid.*, p. 523.

114. *BrQR*, XVI, 1 (1859), 58–90.

115. *BrQR*, XVI, 4 (1859), 225.

116. *Ibid.*, pp. 225–226.

117. The volume under review is Félix's *Le progrès par le Christianisme* (Paris, 1858). Cf. *BrQR*, XVI, 2 (1859), 262–280.
118. *Ibid.*, p. 270. This fault of attacking by logic "what is not purely logical in its nature or origin" was the general fault of "Catholic controversialists." It was also—though the editor did not seem to recognize it—one of Brownson's chief faults as a controversialist.
119. "We feel that we have some right to be heard on the modern doctrine of progress, for we once held it, and were, if not among its ablest, at least among its most earnest and resolute defenders" (*ibid.*, p. 272).
120. *Ibid.*, p. 274.
121. *Ibid.*, p. 275.
122. Perhaps this occasion was the first time that Brownson had admitted this.
123. *Ibid.*, p. 276. It might be argued, said Brownson (and he had done so in the past), that the bad features of this "progress" outweighed the good, and that therefore the general effect was deterioration. But "we have never been disposed to deny that there has been a real progress in the respects named" (*idem*).
124. *Ibid.*, pp. 276–277. Brownson here downgraded what he himself had employed as a method.
125. *Ibid.*, pp. 277–279.
126. *Ibid.*, p. 280.
127. *BrQR*, XVI, 3 (1859), 372–395.
128. *Ibid.*, p. 374.
129. *Ibid.*, p. 375.
130. Again emphasis on this point is strong and repetitive. Critics should not lightly cast aside this emphasis. It has been constant in Brownson's work (*ibid.*, pp. 384–395).
131. *Ibid.*, p. 395.

8

Afterword

... Dich stört nicht im Innern
Zu lebendiger Zeit
Unnützes Erinnern
Und vergeblicher Streit.
—GOETHE, "Den Vereinigten Staaten"

THE SOLUTIONS which Orestes Brownson found in his prolonged examination of the American Idea may have no attraction for the modern reader. The institutional nineteenth-century Catholic Church, for example, can hardly be seen now as the catalyst for either the American Experiment or Mission; for added instance, the physical sciences are today so central to our thought and action that we can be appalled at his apparently easy dismissal of them. Yet if distance may indeed lend disenchantment, it may also provide perspective— the inscrutable, to approximate Mark Twain, remains to be unscrewed. The questions Brownson raised perdure, and the importunity their simple presence provides demands again another clear and present look. Carbon forms to surfaces deceptively brilliant and alluring and hard; beyond the dreams of avarice, as Samuel Johnson once put it, there is still the search for the elemental. Certainly for this man, whose efforts have not wholly died, the American Idea was pivotal to the development of his mind; it was Brownson's attempt to investigate the bases of the optimism underlying the Idea, to get at the roots of this complex of thought, which took up so much of the *Review*s he wrote from 1838 to the Civil War. For it was in constant dialectic, with only occasional lapses into crystal form, that his mind grew.[1] The rigidly logical cast of that mind forced a style, free from rhetorical panache, to explore the meanings of a democracy and a republic, the need of government in the social order, the argument over progress, the feasibility and truth of a "universal history"[2] or of a philosophy of history, the place of Provi-

215

dence in an historical scheme, the viability of Christianity, the nature of man and of human society, the propriety of physical science as a rational probe of *mystère cosmique,* and a score of other questions raised by both adherents and opponents of that optimistic view that America was the New Eden, and the American, the new Adam. He had accepted the Idea early in his career, found himself forced to probe its bases, had rejected it, and then, later, came to reaccept much of it not without considerable reservation, even dubiety. The conditions of the Civil War were bound to affect his views on something like the American Idea, to force his thinking into narrow and topical channels which may unfairly reflect what under more normal circumstances might have been a more generous perspective. In 1865, Brownson was in many respects a broken man. By the time he resumed his *Review* in 1873 his position had hardened to an extent that it may be entirely unrepresentative. For that reason, that period is excluded from this study.

It should be re-emphasized here, however, that Brownson's "conservative" cast of thought seems to have had an earlier beginning than has been generally presumed. That being so, it may be prudent to question more carefully than has yet been done the precise confluence of his "conservative" trend and of his conversion to Catholicism. To assume that these occurred more or less as a nexus may be to miss a tendency of Brownson's vision which was apparent from his own words long before his conversion, and, indeed, before the most radical of his works—the "Laboring Classes" essays. To refer to Brownson as a "pre-Marxian Marx," and to intend it as a literal description, may go further than present evidence allows.

Again, it is difficult to doubt that what Brownson called "Jacobinism" in the 'forties and 'fifties was prompted by fear of violent and precipitate revolution. But this conclusion seems true only as he viewed the European scene. As far as America was concerned, "Jacobinism" was involved not so much with such overt violence as with a subtle undercutting of the principles of the common law, which itself was so vital a part of the American Experiment. Since the effect of either violence or slow subversion of law might ultimately be the same, Brownson feared that Americans might ridicule the possibility of violent revolution here, and overlook the similarly effective but more hidden threat of the gradual erosion of personal or, indeed, civil liberties. The distinction must be understood if Brownson's fulminations on the subject are not to be dismissed as wild-eyed or laughable. The distinction helps further to clarify the fact that Brownson always insisted on a proper balance between liberty and order, and not on one to the exclusion of the other. The necessary point of equipoise was the law, and the law buttressed by natural-law concepts.

Finally, Brownson's attitude toward the physical sciences prior to his studied comments on Darwin in 1863 must be carefully re-examined. Schlesinger's statement that "in 1863 [Brownson] first inquired into the pretensions of science"[3] is not strictly true. As early as 1851 Brownson had indicated that he had little respect for Newton and even less for Francis Bacon whom he had more particularly studied. Yet, Brownson's attitude is perhaps reflected best in his acceptance of the heliocentric theory as an hypothesis rather than as ontological (or cosmological) fact. How he had ever accepted the theory of progress in his early days without a like intellectual commitment to the advance of physical science, Brownson never made clear. In any case, Brownson's animadversions on this subject, startling as they are to a modern mind, might be more understandable to the pre-Darwin nineteenth century. However, certainly Emerson for one clearly surpassed him in his respect for the potentialities of the physical sciences.

Certain other matters seem to demand attention at this point. It appears, first, that the American Idea studied as a three-phase complex may be more purposeful than the assumption that the Dream, the Experiment, and the Mission are separate phenomena, and are most rewardingly scrutinized as such. General reference to "the American Dream" allows confusion between what was definite historical fact, and what was the natural outcome of the Dream, and the Experiment—itself a separate historical fact. The two are not the same. And like distinctions should be made between the Experiment and the Mission. The varied influences upon each one, and then upon the three as a whole, are of imposing complexity, and, perhaps, cannot be understood if confusion is allowed to exist concerning their separate identities, however much the three form a whole. The recognition of this principle might be very helpful for those, for instance, who are so anxious today to find America's "purpose" in her history, or those who, like George Kennan, have deplored the "moral" strand in the fabric of American foreign policy which he has traced back at least to the nineteenth century.[4]

One is compelled to suggest that an interesting juxtaposition of Brownson's views might be made with those of Henry Adams.[5] The two men present some interesting comparisons. To point out some simple ones: both were journalists and New Englanders, and, while their social and educational backgrounds differ widely, yet both came out of the Calvinistic tradition which had found optimism a bit fatuous, and a sense of sin endemic to the human condition. Brownson's tirades against corruption in American life before the Civil War, and Adams' sardonic etching of post-Civil War peculations are not completely immaterial to an understanding of modern American life. Adams' problem—his fundamental problem, it seems, in the whole dark area of being—was his search for unity in multiplicity. Brownson believed that that was the inevitable difficulty toward which Protestantism was moving. Adams got to Chartres, and wrote his moving non-believer's poem to the Virgin (a "pagan" Virgin to some); Brownson also made his pilgrimage to the Catholic Church, and felt that he had found there that unity was possible for the nineteenth century, too. There are differences, of course, and significant ones: for example, Brownson's virtual ignorance and rejection prior to 1860 of the physical sciences contrasts sharply with the later phases of Henry Adams' education. Again, Adams' theory of cosmic entropy is in some opposition to Brownson's view of Providence and of "communion." Yet these two men are to be met at as many intellectual crossroads as any other Americans of the nineteenth century. Here is Robert Spiller on Adams: "Like the age in which he lived, [Adams] offered a new paradox at every turn. He spoke its contradictions and its dilemmas, its thoughts and its feelings; he arranged neat and balanced equations to expound its insoluble riddles; he set up contrary images that could nod to each other across the chaos." These judgments seem to apply equally to Orestes Brownson.[6]

Randall Stewart's study *American Literature and Christian Doctrine* examines our literature in the light of the doctrine of Original Sin, and finds the optimisms of Whitman and Emerson opposed to the "vein of iron" which continued from Jonathan Edwards to Eliot, Tate, and Faulkner. Now, as R. W. B. Lewis has pointed out, "The fullest portrayal of the . . . American Adam was given by Walt Whitman in *Leaves of Grass*,"[7] and Whitman's "Adam" was precisely what Brownson was rejecting. Here is Stewart's summation:

For man is an imperfect, non-perfectible being. He cannot be improved by technology. He is not a machine, but a very fallible human. Poor wayward creature, he appears even now to be plotting, with all ingenuity and speed, his own destruction. But his state, unless by his own perverse wilfulness, is not beyond the reach of God's redeeming grace. This is the essence of the human condition, and the Christian hope. And this is the meaning of the dramatizations of human experience by the greatest American writers.[8]

What "the greatest American writers"—Hawthorne,[9] Melville, James—were "dramatizing," Orestes Brownson was putting into some of the most forcible, logical essays written in the nineteenth century in America. And he could be the more forcible and hard-hitting because he knew the other side so well. He had put *that* case in logical, hard-hitting forceful prose, too. The nineteenth-century argument about the nature of man, the problem Stewart finds so central to American literature, was articulated with extraordinary fullness not only in Brownson's writing, but in Brownson's intellectual life.

A fifth conclusion recommends itself, first to those historians concerned with a history of ideas, and secondly to thinkers who are Catholic, and who are interested, as are Walter Ong and Jean Daniélou, in the concept of a linear movement of history. Such men, following roughly the lead of Teilhard de Chardin, see the possibility of human history's moving providentially through an evolutionary process, and, perhaps, converging eventually in Christ. One finds here and there in Brownson quite prior to Darwin what seem to be far-off echoes of that idea. And this is strange given the cyclic sense of history which dominated his thinking from 1845 to 1855, and his rejection of the Idea of Progress, his cavalier treatment of Newman's theory of Development, and so on. Yet in the period prior to 1845—in his non-Catholic period, but at a time when he was slowly working his way toward the Church—and in the period from 1855 through 1858 there appear to be hints which may reward examination. Certainly, as we have seen, Schlesinger has praise for Brownson's handling of Darwin. And while it cannot be even remotely suggested that Brownson is in any sense a forerunner of modern thought here, yet if the evidence is read aright, at least we may have of him less the picture of the intransigent *ursus major* of American Catholic apologetics, pulling Protestant beards as he stood, eyes closed, with his feet anchored in the sixteenth century, and his back turned to the future.

And this point leads to a final comment. Both Hollis and Lewis, with varying degrees of explicitness, have concluded that Brownson belonged fully neither to the Party of Memory nor to the Party of Hope. To Lewis, Brownson belonged to a third party in American life, the "Party of Irony," for whom "in all its forms, the preoccupation of the ironic mentality was communion with the common experience and common reality of the human race. Hopefulness and nostalgia had conspired to cut the American spirit off from those crucial resources, with pathetic and potentially tragic consequences."[10] The objective of this third party was, according to Professor Lewis, "both to undermine and to bolster the image of the American as the new Adam. . . . Their irony, in short, was in the great tradition: inclusive and charitable, never restrictive. Their aim was to enlarge. The shared purpose of the party of Irony was not to destroy the hopes of the hopeful [i.e., the American Idea] but to perfect them."[11]

To C. Carroll Hollis, Brownson belonged to a "third movement" between the "rationalism that had become respectful (under its Unitarian robes) in Capitalistic Boston" and the thinking of Emerson and others "who returned to the mystical tradition of the Puritans while rebuffing Puritanism itself."[12]

The purpose here is not to comment upon the acceptability of either view, particularly when one notes that Lewis is commenting upon a somewhat later period in Brownson's life than is Hollis. What is suggested is, first, that terms like "liberal" and "conservative," "Party of Hope" and "Party of Memory," "Movement party" and "Stationary party"[13] tend to polarize and thus oversimplify any discussion of the movement of thought in the American nineteenth century; second, that when a possible "third party" is suggested as existing in either the 'thirties or the 'forties, the name of Orestes Brownson is at least prominent, if it does not, like Abu Ben Adhem's, lead all the rest. That he was at times confused, vague, and even churlish, careless in his optimisms, severe in his darker views, overly impatient of the intuitive, overly confident in the discursive, may mean quite simply that he rode in the midst of the storm, and that if he did not always see clearly, what he saw he saw well. Or as O. F. Morshead once wrote of Samuel Pepys, "he needed not to refrain from sowing on account of the birds."

As for the importance of the American Idea at which so often Brownson probed, against which he so often railed, and in support of which he so often stood, we may again remember with profit Professor Lewis' call for an intelligent review of its history in the nineteenth century. Thus, as Lewis has suggested, it may again become a "stimulus" to American thought and to American literature. Perhaps it may; indeed, the debate seems to be again under way. And it can only be hoped that, in the renewed discussion, there will somewhere be a mind as comprehensive and a tongue as trenchant as were those of Orestes Brownson.

NOTES

1. These remarks are not meant to apply in the area outside the time covered by this book; they especially do not apply to the years after 1859. Further, it may be suggested that Cousin's "syncretism" had etched a deep character; where the original substance had been rejected, the mode apparently remained.
2. One must notice that Brownson was always vague in his use of terms such as "the world" or "universal." As Voltaire said of Bossuet, he never seems to have gone beyond Europe (and America) in his use of the terms. He lived his entire life in America, and seems to have been completely untouched by any Oriental interest or influence, except in his castigation of the Neoplatonists. This fact, while it narrowed Brownson's vision, hardly made him especially exceptional in nineteenth-century America. There were, however, writers who were more aware: Emerson, Thoreau, and Whitman, for examples.
3. Schlesinger, *Brownson*, p. 262.
4. George Kennan, *American Diplomacy, 1900–1950* (New York, 1952), pp. 9–25; 49–50; 62–63; and *passim*. For another view, see Dean Acheson, *Present at the Creation* (New York, 1969), pp. 111–112.
5. See, for example, an interesting study by Melvin Lyon, *Symbol and Idea in Henry Adams* (Lincoln, Nebraska, 1970), pp. 61–64; 68–69; 147–148; 225–226; and *passim*.
6. *Literary History of the United States* (New York, 1955), rev. ed., p. 1080.
7. *The American Adam*, p. 28.
8. *American Literature and Christian Doctrine*, p. 149. A new and important study could be read together with Stewart's. See Quentin Anderson, *The Imperial Self* (New York, 1971).
9. "If Brownson had been a novelist he might at this moment have composed fiction not unlike the fiction of Hawthorne . . ." (Lewis, *The American Adam*, p. 188).
10. *Ibid.*, p. 192. Other members of the Party of Irony: Hawthorne, Holmes, the elder James, Melville, and Parkman.
11. *Idem.*
12. Hollis, "Literary Criticism," p. 118.
13. These latter, of course, are Brownson's own terms.

Selected Bibliography

Acheson, Dean G. *Present at the Creation.* New York: Norton, 1969.

Adams, Henry. *The Education of Henry Adams.* New York: Modern Library, 1931.

American Classics Reconsidered: A Christian Appraisal. Ed. Harold C. Gardiner. New York: Scribners, 1958.

Anderson, Quentin. *The Imperial Self: An Essay in American Literary and Cultural History.* New York: Knopf, 1971.

Beard, Charles A. *A Century of Progress.* New York, Harper, 1933.

Becker, Carl L. *The Heavenly City of the Eighteenth Century Philosophers.* New Haven: Yale University Press, 1932.

————. *Progress and Power.* Palo Alto: Stanford University Press, 1936.

Billington, Ray Allen. *The Protestant Crusade, 1800–1860: A Study of the Origins of American Nativism.* New York: Macmillan, 1938.

Boorstin, Daniel J. "We the People in Quest of Ourselves." *The New York Times Magazine,* 26 April 1959, pp. 32–34.

Brown, E. K. "The National Idea in American Criticism." *Dalhousie Review,* 14 (1934), 133–147.

Brownson, Henry F. *Life of Orestes Brownson.* 3 vols. Detroit: Brownson, 1898–1901.

Brownson, Orestes A. *Boston Quarterly Review.* 5 vols. Boston: Greene, 1838–1842.

————. *Brownson's Quarterly Review.* 16 vols. Boston: Greene, 1844–1855; New York: Dunigan, 1856–1859.

————. *The Works of Orestes Brownson.* Ed. Henry F. Brownson. 20 vols. Detroit: Nourse, 1882–1907.

Bury, John B. *The Idea of Progress: An Inquiry Into Its Origin and Growth.* New York: Macmillan, 1932.

Calvinism and the Political Order. Ed. George L. Hunt. Philadelphia: Westminster Press, 1965.

Cameron, Kenneth W. "Thoreau and Orestes Brownson." *Emerson Society Quarterly,* 51 No. 2 (1968), 53–74.

Carpenter, Frederick I. *Emerson and Asia.* Cambridge: Harvard University Press, 1930.

————. " 'The American Myth': Paradise (To Be) Regained." *PMLA,* 74 (1959), 599–606.

223

Chinard, Gilbert. "The American Dream." *Literary History of the United States*. Edd. Robert Spiller *et al*. Rev. ed. New York: Macmillan, 1955, Pp. 192–215.

Coit, Margaret C. *John C. Calhoun: American Portrait*. Boston: Houghton Mifflin, 1950.

Curti, Merle. *The Growth of American Thought*. New York: Harper, 1953.

Daniélou, Jean. *The Lord of History: Reflections on the Inner Meaning of History*. Tr. Nigel Abercrombie. Chicago: Regnery, 1958.

D'Arcy, Martin. *The Meaning and Matter of History: A Christian View*. New York: Farrar, Straus and Cudahy, 1959.

Ekirch, Arthur. *The Idea of Progress in America, 1815–1860*. New York: Peter Smith, 1951.

Fitzsimmons, Matthew. "Brownson's Search for the Kingdom of God: The Social Thought of an American Radical." *Review of Politics*, 16 (1954), 22–36.

Gabriel, Ralph Henry. *The Course of American Democratic Thought*. 2nd ed. New York: Ronald Press, 1956.

Gasquet, Francis A., O.S.B. *Lord Action and His Circle*. London: Burns & Oates, 1906.

Gibbens, V. E. "Tom Paine and the Idea of Progress." *Pensylvania Magazine of History and Biography*, 66 (1942), 191–204.

Gohdes, Clarence. *The Periodicals of American Transcendentalism*. Durham: Duke University Press, 1931.

Guardini, Romano. *The End of the Modern World: A Search for Orientation*. New York: Sheed and Ward, 1956.

Guttmann, Alan. *The Conservative Tradition in America*. New York: Oxford University Press, 1967.

Harson, M. J. "Orestes Brownson, LL.D." *Catholic World*, 79 (1904), 1–21.

Holden, Vincent F. *The Yankee Paul: Isaac Thomas Hecker*. Milwaukee: Bruce, 1958.

Hollis, C. Carroll. "The Literary Criticism of Orestes Brownson." University of Michigan Ph.D. dissertation, 1954.

Howe, Daniel Walker. *The Unitarian Conscience: Harvard Moral Philosophy, 1805–1861*. Cambridge: Harvard University Press, 1970.

Inge, William Ralph. *The Idea of Progress*. New York: Oxford University Press, 1920.

Kennan, George. *American Diplomacy, 1900–1950*. Chicago: University of Chicago Press, 1951.

Kirk, Russell. "Catholic Yankee: Resuscitating Orestes Brownson." *Triumph*, April, 1969, pp. 24–26.

——. *The Conservative Mind: From Burke to Santayana*. Chicago: Regnery, 1953.

——. "Two Facets of the New England Mind: Emerson and Brownson." *The Month*, 8 No. 4. N.S. (October 1952), 208–217.

Krummel, Carl. "Catholicism, Americanism, Democracy, and Orestes Brownson." *American Quarterly*, 6 (1954), 19–31.

Laski, Harold. *The American Democracy: A Commentary and an Interpretation*. New York: Viking, 1948.

Lewis, R. W. B. *The American Adam: Innocence, Tragedy, and Tradition in the Nineteenth Century*. Chicago: University of Chicago Press, 1955.

Löwith, Karl. *Meaning in History*. Chicago: University of Chicago Press, 1958.

Lyon, Melvin, *Symbol and Idea in Henry Adams*. Lincoln: University of Nebraska Press, 1970.

MacDougall, Hugh. *The Acton–Newman Relations*. New York: Fordham University Press, 1962.

McCarthy, Eugene. *Frontiers in American Democracy*. Cleveland: World, 1960.

McCarthy, Leonard. "Rhetoric in the Works of Orestes Brownson." Fordham University Ph.D. dissertation, 1960.

McDowell, Tremaine. "The Great Experiment." *Literary History of the United States*. Edd. Robert Spiller *et al*. Rev. ed. New York: Macmillan, 1955. Pp. 219–227.

McNeill, John T. *The History and Character of Calvinism*. New York: Oxford University Press, 1967.

Malone, George. *The True Church: A Study in the Apologetics of Orestes Augustus Brownson*. Mundelein, Ill.: Saint Mary of the Lake Seminary Press, 1957.

Martin, Kingsley. *French Liberal Thought in the Eighteenth Century*. Ed. J. P. Mayer. New York: New York University Press, 1954.

Maynard, Theodore. *Orestes Brownson: Yankee, Radical, Catholic*. New York: Macmillan, 1943.

Menczer, Béla. *Catholic Political Thought, 1789–1848*. Westminster, Md.: Newman, 1952.

Mims, Helen S. "Early Democratic Theory and Orestes Brownson." *Science and Society*, 3 (1939), 166–198.

Mott, Frank Luther. *A History of American Magazines*. 5 vols. Cambridge: Harvard University Press, 1938–1968.

Ong, Walter J. *Frontiers in American Catholicism: Essays in Ideology and Culture*. New York: Macmillan, 1957.

Raemers, Sidney. *America's Foremost Philosopher*. Washington, D.C.: Benedictine Press, 1931.

Ripley, George. "Brownson's Writings." *The Dial*, 1 (1840), 27–28.

Roemer, Lawrence. *Brownson on Democracy and the Trend Towards Socialism*. New York: Philosophical Library, 1953.

Ryan, Thomas R. "Orestes A. Brownson and Historiography." *The Irish Ecclesiastical Record*, 85 (1956), 10–17, 122–130.

——. *The Sailor's Snug Harbor*. Westminster, Md.: Newman, 1952.

Schapiro, Jacob S. *Condorcet and the Rise of Liberalism*. New York: Harcourt, Brace, 1934.

Schlesinger, Arthur M., Jr. *The Age of Jackson*. Boston: Little, Brown, 1945.

——. *Orestes A. Brownson: A Pilgrim's Progress*. Boston: Little, Brown,

1939; rpt. as *A Pilgrim's Progress: Orestes A. Brownson.* Boston: Little, Brown, 1966.
——. "Orestes Brownson, An American Marxist before Marx." *Sewanee Review,* 47 (1939), 317–323.
Seton-Watson, Hugh. "Neither War Nor Peace—A Survey of Our Times." *U.S. News and World Report,* 29 August 1960, pp. 67–71.
Stewart, Randall. *American Literature and Christian Doctrine.* Baton Rouge: Louisiana State University Press, 1958.
Transitions in American Literary History. Ed. Harry Hayden Clark. Durham: Duke University Press, 1953.
Thompson, William Irwin. *At the Edge of History: Speculations on the Transformation of Culture.* New York: Harper and Row, 1971.
Turner, Frederick Jackson. *The Frontier in American Life and History.* New York: Holt, 1921.
Wellek, René, "The Minor Transcendentalists and German Philosophy." *New England Quarterly,* 15 (1942), 652–680.
Williams, T. Harry. *Huey Long.* New York: Knopf, 1969.
Wood, James Playsted. *Magazines in the United States.* 2nd ed. New York: Ronald Press, 1956.

Index

227